THE **NEW VEGAN** COOKBOOK

INNOVATIVE **VEGETARIAN** RECIPES
FREE OF DAIRY, EGGS, AND **CHOLESTEROL**

BY **LORNA SASS**

PHOTOGRAPHS BY **JONELLE WEAVER**

CHRONICLE BOOKS
SAN FRANCISCO

THIS COLLECTION OF RECIPES IS DEDICATED TO COOKS WHO AGREE THAT "THE DISCOVERY OF A NEW DISH DOES MORE FOR THE HAPPINESS OF MANKIND THAN THE DISCOVERY OF A STAR."

(BRILLAT-SAVARIN, 1755–1826)

Text copyright © 2001 by Lorna Sass.
Photographs copyright © 2001 by Jonelle Weaver.

Library of Congress Cataloging-in-Publication Data available.

ISBN 0-8118-2760-7

Printed in Hong Kong

Food styling by Victoria Granoff and Melanie Harvin
Prop styling by Loren Simons and Paige Hicks
Designed by Sara Schneider
Typesetting by Jaime Robles

Tupperware ® is a registered trademark of Tupperware World

The photographer wishes to thank Victoria Granoff and Melanie Harvin for their beautiful food, Loren Simons for her gorgeous props, Paige Hicks for her production/styling assistance, Jordan Hollender, and Sara Schneider at Chronicle Books for the opportunity to work on such a great project.

Distributed in Canada by Raincoast Books
9050 Shaughnessy Street
Vancouver, BC V6P 6E5

10 9 8 7 6 5 4 3 2 1

Chronicle Books LLC
85 Second Street
San Francisco, California 94105
www.chroniclebooks.com

ACKNOWLEDGMENTS

Attempts to tame a dish by caging it into a recipe are always daunting because the transformation of raw into cooked rarely happens the same way twice. Nevertheless, with the help of my dear recipe-testing "elves," I have done my best to accommodate the vagaries of ingredients and taste.

First and foremost, I offer heartfelt thanks to super-elves Cathy Roberts and Marcia Kindlmann. Cathy has encouraged me with unfailing generosity through many books, kindly pointing out potential trouble spots, conversing with me through her detailed notes, and decorating the pages with a coveted star when she and Neil enjoyed their dinner. Marcia graciously transformed the solitary nature of recipe development into a collaborative effort through her discerning e-mail reflections on creativity, clarity, and preferred brands and her cheerful reports on husband Pete's response to last night's vegan dinner. I am very grateful to Tristan Roberts and Glen Kindlmann for inspiring their moms to be such dedicated vegan cooks!

Many others contributed their time and energy to this project. My devoted group of elves includes Judy Bloom, Nancy Brin, Heather and Gerhard Bock, Banoo and Jeevak Parpia, and Rosemary Serviss. Sally O'Brien helped me launch the project and, when she brought over some slow-roasted tomatoes, prompted me to keep the oven turned on. Michele Lunt assisted me during most of the recipe-testing sessions, bringing her good cheer and years of vegan cooking experience to the task. Elizabeth Schneider, produce specialist and dear friend, generously shared her vast understanding of vegetables and how they best like to be selected, stored, and cooked. Splendid vegan dessert classes taught by Fran Costigan and Myra Kornfeld at the Natural Gourmet Cooking School were inspirational. Colleague and coffee-mate Dorie Greenspan cast her keen editorial eye over the introductory section.

Consulting and recipe development for Eden Foods, Inc. have provided an ongoing opportunity to work with superb organic soymilks, canned beans, tomatoes, pasta, and other high-quality vegan products. Jean Richardson of Gold Mine Natural Food Co. kept me posted on the ingredients she's most excited about and provided a generous supply of samples.

Thanks to Bill LeBlond for inviting me to take on this challenging project and for celebrating the bounty in living color. Gracias and besos to Richard Isaacson, who understood when I postponed our trip to Spain and who continues to be my loving and devoted companion on the bigger journey.

TABLE OF CONTENTS

INTRODUCTION

Are you trying to figure out what on earth to cook for a vegan child or friend? Or perhaps you'd like to experience an occasional vegan meal yourself?

Grains, vegetables, and fruits fill the abundant vegan pantry, but you won't find any meat, fish, eggs, cheese, or milk in sight. Since plants contain no cholesterol, vegan meals are 100 percent cholesterol free.

Understandably, many people are attracted to vegan cooking for health reasons. Others have philosophical or ecological concerns. And kosher cooks find vegan recipes appealing because they can be slipped into any type of menu. Whatever the impulse, it's clear that a growing number of Americans are choosing broccoli over beef.

Impelled by the word "new" in this book's title, I've made it my goal to create innovative dishes that everyone will eat with pleasure. The source of my inspiration has been the global kitchen, but I have made no attempt at authenticity. Rather, I offer you dishes of my own invention that celebrate the fresh and flavor-packed bounty of our good earth.

I hope that a glance at the table of contents will make you hungry and eager to join me in savoring the harvest.

HAPPY COOKING!

—LORNA SASS

1

STOCKING THE **VEGAN PANTRY**

Like a painter working from a large palette of colors, a cook takes inspiration from a pantry full of high-quality ingredients. Fortunately, most of the building blocks of vegan cooking are good keepers, and it's easy to have them on hand.

In this chapter, I've organized the ingredients into major categories and presented these categories in alphabetical order, offering relevant tips on purchasing, preparation, and storage. Once you have stocked the staples, you'll be able to cook most of the recipes. Then, little by little, you can branch out and purchase specialized ingredients for a particular dish. (Items called for only once are described in recipe headnotes rather than here.)

Although you may need to visit a health-food or gourmet shop for some of the ingredients, supermarkets are continually expanding the shelf space given to natural foods, organic produce, and specialty fare. Making requests of the grocery manager is a good way to keep this trend in motion and eventually create one-stop shopping. Mail order is also a convenient way to purchase what you can't easily find locally. For a list of my favorite mail-order sources, see page 113.

BEANS

Dried beans last indefinitely but lose flavor and moisture as they age, so shop for them in stores that have a high turnover. Look for unbroken beans with intact, brightly colored skins. Store them in airtight containers in a cool, dark place, and aim to use them within six months.

It's practical to prepare beans in quantity and freeze extra for later use. See page 19 for details and to learn about an exciting way to cook beans.

Recipes that call for cooked beans use $1^3/_4$ cups,
giving you the option of using home-cooked or canned. (A 15-ounce can holds $1^1/_2$ to $1^3/_4$ cups of drained beans.) Now that canned organic beans are so readily available, they provide a convenient preservative-free (and often salt-free) alternative to standard supermarket brands. There's no need to rinse organic beans, and you can use the canning liquid in cooking.

> **SUGGESTED STAPLES:** black turtle beans, navy beans, chickpeas, split peas.

> **BRANCHING OUT:** red lentils, black soybeans, cannellini beans, French Le Puy green lentils, Spanish pardina lentils, black beluga lentils, "boutique" or heirloom beans such as Christmas limas, scarlet runners, and black valentines.

BROTHS

INSTANT VEGETABLE BROTH It's convenient to have a substitute when homemade broth is not available. One reasonable option is Frontier brand vegetable broth powder, sold in bulk bins at some health-food stores and also available directly from the company (www.frontiercoop.com; 800-669-3275). The company also sells a reduced-sodium version.

Using broth instead of water is a wise choice in recipes whose success depends upon depth of flavor. Homemade broth tastes better than commercial preparations, which are usually dreadfully salty and loaded with MSG. I've included two simple recipes for homemade broths on the following pages, and you'll find a third one on page 19.

In this version, I speed up preparation by beginning to brown the onions as I chop and toss in the carrots and celery. Tomato paste gives the broth an earthy color, and a bit of salt draws out the vegetables' flavors.

Tip: A wide 2-quart Pyrex measuring cup with spout comes in very handy for collecting the broth as you pass it through a large colander or strainer.

BASIC **VEGETABLE** BROTH

MAKES **6 TO 8** CUPS

1 1/2 **TABLESPOONS OLIVE OIL**

3 **MEDIUM ONIONS, DICED**

3 **LARGE CARROTS**

2 **LARGE CELERY RIBS**

1 **TABLESPOON TOMATO PASTE**

1/2 **CUP DRY WHITE WINE OR VERMOUTH**

10 **CUPS WATER**

3 **LARGE CLOVES GARLIC, CRUSHED (PEELING IS NOT NECESSARY)**

STEMS FROM 1 BUNCH PARSLEY, CHOPPED

1/4 **OUNCE (1/4 CUP LOOSELY PACKED) DRIED MUSHROOMS (YOU CAN USE AN INEXPENSIVE SUPERMARKET BRAND)**

1/4 **CUP RED LENTILS**

1/4 **TEASPOON DRIED THYME LEAVES**

1/4 **TEASPOON SALT**

1/4 **TEASPOON WHOLE BLACK PEPPERCORNS**

01 In a 6-quart (or larger) heavy-bottomed pot, heat the oil. Add the onions and begin browning them over medium-high heat as you chop and toss in the carrots and celery. Continue cooking, stirring frequently, until the onions are nicely browned, 10 to 15 minutes. Lower the heat if the vegetables begin to burn or stick.

02 Stir in the tomato paste and cook about 30 seconds. Add the wine, stir to release any browned bits sticking to the bottom of the pot, and cook over high heat until most of the wine has evaporated, a minute or two. Add the water and remaining ingredients and bring to a boil.

03 Set the lid off-center to create a 1/4-inch steam vent. Lower the heat and simmer until the broth develops a good flavor, 1 to 1 1/2 hours. Cool, then strain through a colander set over a large bowl, pressing down the vegetables to extract as much broth as possible. Refrigerate for up to 4 days, or freeze in convenient quantities for up to 3 months.

OTHER IDEAS

Include a few leek greens and scrubbed potato peels.

Use 1/4 pound chopped fresh mushrooms (or leftover portobello stems) instead of dried.

See Bonus Bean Broth, page 19.

6 CUPS WATER OR GRAIN OR BEAN COOKING LIQUID (OR A COMBINATION)

FISTFUL OF LEEK GREENS (FROM 3 MEDIUM LEEKS), TRIMMED AND COARSELY CHOPPED

STEMS FROM 1 BUNCH PARSLEY

$\frac{1}{2}$ OUNCE ($\frac{1}{2}$ CUP LOOSELY PACKED) DRIED MUSHROOMS (USE A SUPERMARKET VARIETY, NOT YOUR BEST PORCINI OR MORELS)

1 BAY LEAF

$\frac{1}{4}$ TEASPOON SALT (OPTIONAL)

$\frac{1}{8}$ TEASPOON BLACK PEPPERCORNS

Here's a quick and dandy way to make good use of leek greens, which give up their mild and pleasing flavor with great dispatch. The broth's taste is predominantly leek, with a subtle mushroom backdrop. Use it in any recipe that calls for vegetable broth.

BUSY COOK'S **LEEK** BROTH

01 Combine the ingredients in a large pot and bring to a simmer. Set the cover slightly off-center to create a $\frac{1}{4}$-inch steam vent, and simmer over low heat until the broth develops a good flavor and color, 20 to 30 minutes.

02 Cool, then strain through a colander set over a large bowl, pressing down the vegetables to extract all of the liquid. Refrigerate in a tightly sealed container for up to 3 days, or freeze in convenient quantities for up to 3 months.

OTHER IDEAS

Instead of dried mushrooms, substitute a cup or two of chopped fresh mushrooms or leftover portobello stems.

Toss in a few chopped celery or fennel stalks, if you have them on hand.

NUTS AND NUT BUTTERS

With their luxurious richness and intense flavor, nuts and nut butters make a valuable contribution to vegan sauces and desserts—and a superb spread for bread. Although nuts are high in fat, most of that fat is the heart-healthy kind.

To avoid rancidity, store nut butters in the refrigerator and nuts in the freezer. Try to use them within three months.

SUGGESTED STAPLES: almonds, walnuts, pecans, almond or cashew butter, peanut butter.

BRANCHING OUT: pine nuts, hazelnuts, pistachios, hazelnut butter, sesame tahini.

TOASTING NUTS AND SEEDS Toast nuts on a baking pan in a toaster oven (most convenient) or standard oven set to 375°F until fragrant and lightly browned, 2 to 5 minutes. Stir once halfway through. Seeds can also be toasted in a skillet set over medium-high heat; stir them frequently. Nuts and seeds burn easily, so watch them closely.

OILS

For the variety and elegant finish they offer, high-quality, aromatic oils can't be beat. Although expensive, a tablespoon goes a long way. Store them in the refrigerator or in a dark, cool place, and your oils will last the better part of a year.

Unfortunately, even expensive oils vary in quality and freshness, so your best bet is to purchase them from a gourmet shop that prides itself on carrying the best. Zingerman's is a good mail-order source.

SUGGESTED STAPLES: pure olive oil for cooking and a fine extra-virgin olive oil for salads; a neutral (bland-tasting) vegetable oil such as grapeseed, corn, peanut, safflower, or canola for cooking.

BRANCHING OUT: rosemary- or basil-infused olive oil (Consorzio brand is reliably good); hazelnut oil; walnut oil (French and Italian imports tend to be superior); toasted (Asian) sesame oil; roasted peanut oil (Loriva is a good brand); organic, unrefined coconut oil (available by mail from Gold Mine Natural Food Co.) for cooking and baking.

SOYFOODS

It's hard to open a newspaper nowadays without reading about the health benefits of soy. Because I focused on these "miracle" foods in *The New Soy Cookbook,* I have featured them only occasionally in this recipe collection.

TOFU is certainly the best-known soyfood. Also called bean curd, it is prepared by coagulating soymilk in a process that resembles cheese-making. Tofu is labeled firm or soft, depending upon its water content. For stir-fries and other dishes that require the tofu to hold its shape, opt for the firm or extra-firm variety.

Soft tofu is often a better choice for sauces and dressings, since it creates a smoother purée and contains sufficient liquid to result in a pourable consistency. Most soft tofu is labeled "silken," referring to a Japanese preparation technique that results in a custardlike texture. You can use either the shelf-stable, aseptic-packed silken-soft tofu or the fresh, refrigerated variety. In either case, note the expiration date marked on the package.

Once you've opened the container, cover any leftovers with water and refrigerate in a sealed container. Change the water every other day and the tofu will remain fresh for about five days.

TEMPEH is a dense soybean cake whose taste is often described as "mushroomy" or "yeasty." In recipes, it comes across as heartier than tofu. Because tempeh is a fermented product, many people who experience difficulty digesting other soyfoods have an easy time with it.

Tempeh is typically sold in 8-ounce slabs, and you'll find it in the refrigerator or frozen-food section of your market. Tempeh made entirely of soybeans has a stronger taste than tempeh made with a mixture of soybeans and grains. You can use either type in the recipes. Cook tempeh before the expiration date, or freeze it for up to three months (assuming it hasn't already been frozen).

SOYMILK is made by simmering ground soybeans in water and then pressing out the liquid. Most soymilk is sold in shelf-stable aseptic "bricks." Since manufacturers add a variety of ingredients to enhance taste, the nutrient profile varies considerably among brands. Compare labels and sample widely before settling on a favorite. I use Eden Foods soymilk, as it is made from organic soybeans (never genetically modified) and is among the highest in protein. Once you've opened a container, soymilk remains fresh under refrigeration for at least five days.

(The soyfoods miso and soy sauce are discussed later in the Other Good Things section, page 15.)

> **SUGGESTED STAPLES:** soymilk, 12-ounce aseptic-packed silken-soft tofu.
>
> **BRANCHING OUT:** tempeh.

VEGETABLES

There's nothing like the color and promise of fresh vegetables to infuse the kitchen with a sense of vitality and well-being. I particularly love hearty greens and members of the onion family. For details on handling these and other vegetables, check the Veggie Prep section below.

> **SUGGESTED STAPLES:** onions, scallions (green onions), garlic, ginger, carrots, celery, salad greens.
>
> **BRANCHING OUT:** leeks, shallots, fennel, kale, collard greens.

VEGGIE PREP

When it comes to efficiently preparing vegetables for the pot, there's no better kitchen helper than a sharp knife. I recommend a 10-inch blade, which does a lot more of the work for you than the commonly recommended 8-inch chef's knife.

My other best prep-buddy is the Sharpery, a small, inexpensive, and cleverly designed honing device that makes your knives razor sharp in ten quick swipes. You can mail order the Sharpery from Zabar's (see page 113) or call Chantry at 800-242-6879 to locate a local source.

Following is a description of techniques needed to prepare the vegetables used in the recipes, organized into alphabetical order by ingredient.

ROASTING GARLIC Remove any loose, papery skins from a whole head of garlic. Set the whole head in a shallow baking dish in a toaster oven or standard oven and roast at 375°F until soft, 20 to 30 minutes. Use immediately or refrigerate in a sealed container for up to 10 days. Squeeze the soft flesh out of each clove as needed.

GRATING GINGER To grate ginger, use a porcelain grater, available in Asian groceries, or the side of a box grater with rice-sized holes. Better yet, use the terrific rasp sold for grating cheese, available from Cooking by the Book, Inc. (212-966-9799). It's not necessary to peel ginger before grating it, but do peel before mincing.

SELECTING AND PREPARING HEARTY GREENS When purchasing kale, collards, escarole, and other leafy greens, look for bunches with sprightly greens that are neither browned nor wilted. Chop first, then rinse or dunk to remove any sand. Although many recipes advise discarding stems and thick mid-ribs, this is not necessary: when thinly sliced, they cook up just fine.

KEEPING SALAD GREENS CRISP Wash and spin-dry the greens. Place a paper towel on the bottom of a Tupperware-style plastic container large enough to hold the greens without crushing them. Cover the container and set it in the bottom third of the refrigerator. Greens will remain crisp for 5 to 7 days. (Really!)

"WHITTLING" HERBS AND WATERCRESS To quickly cut the leaves from parsley, cilantro, dill, or watercress, try this dandy technique: Hold the bunch of herbs by the stems at a slight angle so that some of the leaves are resting on a clean, flat surface. Place a very sharp chef's knife at a 45-degree angle at the point where the leaves meet the stems. Then glide the knife toward the top of the bunch with a swift stroke. When you've removed the leaves from one section, turn the bunch and continue whittling. Some leaves will inevitably still be attached to their slender stems; pinch them off one by one only if a recipe demands such perfection. This technique doesn't work with basil, mint, and other herbs that have woody stems.

SLICING AND CLEANING LEEKS Slice off the root ends, and then slice the white and light green part, removing any bruised or tough outer layers. Rinse well, separating the rings, and release all sand hidden between the layers. Drain thoroughly. Reserve dark green leaf-tops for stock.

ZESTING LEMONS OR ORANGES Use organic fruit when available. The best tool for zesting is the rasp available from Cooking by the Book, Inc. (212-966-9799). You can also use a standard zester or the finest side of a box grater.

STORING AND CLEANING FRESH MUSHROOMS Refrigerate mushrooms in an open paper bag, and use them as soon as possible. Before use, gently brush off any dirt with a damp paper towel.

ROASTING RED PEPPERS Set peppers over a high gas flame. Rotate with tongs until thoroughly charred. (If using an electric oven, cut the peppers in half, remove the seeds, and core. Press firmly to flatten. Set cut side down under the broiler, as close to the broiling element as possible.) Wrap each pepper in a wet paper towel and enclose in a plastic bag. When cool, use the paper towels to rub off the skins. (It's okay if a few charred bits remain intact.) Core and seed the peppers. If not using immediately, toss the peppers in olive oil and refrigerate them in a tightly sealed container.

WHOLE GRAINS

I enjoy the go-down-easiness of white rice, and basmati usually comes to mind when I'm serving Indian food, but for providing a sense of satiety, there is nothing quite like chewy whole grains. I encourage you to try the easy, foolproof technique for cooking and storing them described on pages 20–22.

To avoid rancidity, freeze raw whole grains in well-sealed containers. (I use zipper-topped plastic freezer bags, which can easily be tucked into nooks and crannies.) Although frozen grains will last a year or more, I try to use them within six months.

SUGGESTED STAPLES: short-grain brown rice, basmati rice, pearl barley, wheat berries.

BRANCHING OUT: wild rice, Colusari red rice, kamut, hulled barley, black buffalo barley, quinoa.

OTHER GOOD THINGS

BREWER'S YEAST Don't let its unappealing name get in your way; this fine-tasting, nutritious powder adds savory depth and a hint of Parmesan cheese flavor to vegan dishes. The best-tasting brewer's yeast I've found is made by Lewis Laboratories. Look for it in the supplements section of health-food stores, or call 800-243-6020. Opt for the powder rather than buds or flakes, and don't substitute another brand unless you like the way it tastes.

CHOCOLATE AND COCOA POWDER Many brands of unsweetened cocoa powder and dark chocolate are vegan (check the labels), and numerous organic brands are available in health-food stores. Tropical Source produces tasty espresso and chocolate chips. Scharffen Berger makes particularly fine cocoa powder and baking chocolate (www.scharffen-berger.com).

HERBS AND SPICES Some lucky folks live near health-food stores that sell dried herbs and spices in bulk bins, making it possible to purchase small quantities. This is ideal, since dried herbs in particular lose their vitality after about six months. (You can mail order small quantities from Penzeys, page 113.)

You can purchase mixtures of Italian or Provençal herbs in bottles, but it's fun and more economical to make your own. Be sure to use dried herb leaves, not ground.

TWO **HERB** BLENDS

MAKES ABOUT ¼ CUP EACH

ITALIAN HERB BLEND

1 TABLESPOON DRIED OREGANO

1 TABLESPOON DRIED BASIL

2 TEASPOONS DRIED THYME

2 TEASPOONS DRIED ROSEMARY

1 ½ TEASPOONS FENNEL SEEDS

1 TEASPOON CRUSHED RED PEPPER FLAKES (OPTIONAL)

HERBES DE PROVENCE

1 TABLESPOON DRIED BASIL

2 TEASPOONS DRIED TARRAGON

2 TEASPOONS DRIED SAVORY

2 TEASPOONS DRIED ROSEMARY

2 TEASPOONS DRIED MARJORAM

2 TEASPOONS DRIED CHERVIL (OPTIONAL)

Combine the herbs for either blend in a small, wide-mouthed jar. Shake well. Store in a dark, cool place for up to 6 months.

Store dried herbs and spices away from heat and light. For optimum flavor, buy whole spices and grind them just before use in a coffee grinder set aside for this purpose or with a mortar and pestle.

My favorite store-bought curry blend is Merwanjee Poonjiajee & Sons Madras Curry Powder, sold in small tins in many gourmet shops and Indian groceries (and available by mail from Zabar's). It is a mild blend that you can punch up, if you wish, by adding cayenne. I used this brand in all recipe testing and, since it contains salt, you may need to make adjustments if using another curry blend.

MAPLE SYRUP Opt for pure maple syrup, and avoid any products that contain corn syrup and artificial coloring. Grade A Dark Amber has the most flavor.

MISO Miso is a thick paste made by fermenting soybeans or a combination of soybeans and grains. In general, dark misos are saltier and have a more intense, "beefy" flavor than light misos. Dissolve miso in liquid before adding it to your dish. Look for miso in the refrigerated section of health-food stores and Asian markets (or order by mail from Gold Mine Natural Food Co., page 113). Miso Master is a good brand. Refrigerate miso in a tightly sealed container, and it will last for years.

SALT I favor sea salt because I like its taste and the fact that it has trace minerals. Sea salt from the Atlantic coast of Brittany is excellent. (Supermarket salt contains additives that are not health-promoting, so I avoid it.) Measurements assume that you are using finely ground salt.

SOY SAUCE Much of the soy sauce sold in this country is made with artificial ingredients and is of very poor quality. I recommend traditionally brewed, imported Japanese soy sauces—either tamari or shoyu—which have more complex flavor and are less assertively salty than Chinese soy sauces. Eden Foods and Ohsawa, both sold in health-food stores, are good brands. Eden has a reduced-sodium version. Refrigerate opened bottles or store them in a cool place, and they will last for at least a year.

SUGAR Those who prefer organic and strictly vegan products (charcoal made from animal bone is used in some sugar refinement processes) can now find various brands of dehydrated cane juice in health-food stores. Any of these products can be used instead of standard sugar.

VINEGARS AND CITRUS JUICES When I need an acid to sharpen the flavor of a dish or to prepare a salad dressing, I usually opt for the vibrant freshness of lemon or lime juice. There are times, however, when a good vinegar is the better choice.

A touch of aged, mellow balsamic vinegar added after cooking melds the tastes of individual ingredients and adds a subtle layer of sweetness, resulting in a dish that is more satisfying. My favorite balsamic is Cavalli, available in gourmet shops and by mail order from Zabar's and Zingerman's (see page 113). An excellent substitute is balsamic syrup, which you can easily make at home from an inexpensive brand. (See Balsamic Syrup recipe on page 16.)

SUGGESTED STAPLES: lemons, limes, good-quality balsamic vinegar.

BRANCHING OUT: raspberry vinegar, sherry vinegar, Balsamic Syrup.

A teaspoon or two of balsamic syrup can magically transform a ho-hum dish into something that you want to savor slowly. Fortunately, it is easy to make. However, be sure to open all of the kitchen windows and turn on the exhaust before you begin: the process creates potent fumes.

BALSAMIC SYRUP

MAKES ⅓ CUP

1 CUP BALSAMIC VINEGAR (SUPERMARKET QUALITY IS FINE)

Pour the vinegar into a small, heavy, nonreactive saucepan, preferably one with a pouring spout. Bring to a boil over high heat. Reduce the heat and cook at a moderate boil until thickened and reduced to about ⅓ cup, about 12 minutes. Cool in the pot, and then pour into a small glass jar and store at room temperature. Lasts indefinitely.

2

NEW WAYS WITH BEANS AND GRAINS

**1 POUND (ABOUT 2 ½ CUPS) DRIED
BEANS, PICKED OVER AND RINSED**

**1 TEASPOON SALT, PREFERABLY
SEA SALT**

**BOILING WATER TO COVER BEANS BY
2 INCHES**

Over the past decade, I've experimented with various ways to cook beans and grains. Assuming that you can find standard approaches in any basic cookbook, I'm using this space to describe two less common techniques that I'm excited about.

For beans that hold their shape perfectly and have an intensely creamy texture, try slow-baking them in the oven, and you will be amazed. Although the process may take as long as three hours, almost no work is involved. Since slow-baked beans hold their flavor and shape very nicely when frozen, it's practical to make a large quantity for later use.

I was convinced to try slow-baking beans while reading and cooking from Sylvia Thompson's The Kitchen Garden Cookbook, *a fresh and fetching collection of recipes I heartily recommend. Thompson credits Russ Parsons of the* Los Angeles Times *for introducing her to this fine technique. I thank them both, and you will too.*

By eliminating presoaking and adding salt right from the start, the cooked beans develop maximum flavor, maintain good color, and end up with their glossy skins intact. Especially when seasoned with the ingredients for a Bonus Bean Broth (see opposite), they are tasty enough to serve as a simple side dish, tossed lightly with olive oil or garnished with fresh herbs.

For a special treat, try this technique with some of the unusual boutique beans now on the market—or slow-bake large limas, which end up looking like suitable fare for Gargantua. For advice on purchasing and storing dried beans, see page 8.

SLOW-BAKED BEANS

01 Place a rack in the center of the oven and preheat to 250°F.

02 Set the beans in a large Dutch oven or lidded casserole. Sprinkle with salt. Pour enough boiling water over them to cover by 2 inches. Cover and bake until the beans are tender, 1 to 4 hours, depending on size and condition. (Most beans take 2 to 3 hours, but an occasional batch can surprise you.) Add boiling water, if needed, to keep the beans covered.

03 If you like the way the cooking liquid tastes, reserve it when you drain the beans. Refrigerate the beans for up to 3 days, or freeze until needed (see Freezing Cooked Beans opposite).

OTHER IDEAS

FREEZING COOKED BEANS

After the beans have cooled, freeze them in heavy, zipper-topped plastic bags. It's convenient to store them in $1^3/_4$-cup quantities, the approximate amount contained in a 15-ounce can, and the amount I call for in recipes. Defrost frozen beans either at room temperature or in a microwave.

BONUS BEAN BROTH

Cook the beans with 1 chunked carrot, 2 sliced celery ribs, 1 large bay leaf, 1 halved shallot or small onion, 1 or 2 crushed cloves of garlic (optional), and $1/_8$ teaspoon peppercorns. Remove and discard the vegetables after draining the beans. Use the broth for soups and stews.

Make a tasty side dish or a spread for baguette by mashing the cooked beans coarsely with roasted garlic and olive oil. Season well with salt and pepper.

Garnish the beans with Gremolata (page 63).

See the recipe for Slow-Baked Cannellini with Olives, Escarole, and Gremolata (page 63) for another approach to this technique.

MAKES ABOUT *6 CUPS* COOKED
GRAINS (BARLEY YIELDS
7 TO 8 CUPS)

3 QUARTS WATER

1 TEASPOON SALT (OPTIONAL)

**1 POUND (ABOUT 2 ½ CUPS) WHOLE
GRAINS**

FEARLESS WHOLE-GRAIN COOKERY

Cook whole grains like pasta in an abundance of boiling water. When they are tender, drain the grains and steam them in the hot, covered pot for a few minutes. You'll end up with perfectly cooked morsels every time.

I first read about this method in The Cook's Bible *by Christopher Kimball and have been happily experimenting with it ever since. The approach successfully deals with the reality that no two batches of grains absorb exactly the same amount of liquid. Because the pot is open during cooking, you can easily taste for doneness along the way—a great boon since timing can vary widely depending upon harvesting conditions and freshness.*

No more scorched pots! As if that weren't enough, this technique often cuts down cooking time by 5 or 10 minutes. Are you sold?

Use this recipe for pearl, hulled, and black buffalo barley; wheat or rye berries; wild rice; kamut; quinoa; millet; Colusari red rice; and short-grain brown rice. It's not necessary to rinse grains before cooking except in the case of quinoa. See Grain Cooking Times (opposite) for timing and comments specific to individual grains.

Since cooked grains freeze so well, this recipe calls for preparing 1 pound of dried grains at a time, with the idea of storing leftovers for later use (see Freezing Cooked Grain, page 22).

BASIC GRAINS

01 In a 6-quart (or larger) pot, bring the water, salt (if using), and grains to a boil. Cook uncovered at a moderate boil, stirring occasionally to prevent any grains from sticking to the bottom of the pot. Add more boiling water, if necessary, to keep the grains covered.

02 When the grains are tender (see Grain Cooking Times for approximate cooking times), drain thoroughly. (Taste the cooking liquid before draining and, if you like it, set the strainer over a bowl to reserve the liquid for future use.) Bounce the strainer up and down to shake as much water off the grains as you can. Immediately transfer the grains back to the hot pot. Cover the pot and set aside off heat to steam and dry out the grains, 8 to 10 minutes. (If the grains are quite tender and you are fearful of overcooking them, skip this step.)

03 Fluff up the grains before serving. Refrigerate any reserved cooking liquid and use within 24 hours, or freeze for up to 3 months.

GRAIN COOKING TIMES

Cook grains just a tad short of tender, since they will steam for a few more minutes after you drain them. Keep in mind that some whole grains, such as short-grain brown rice, kamut, and wheat berries, remain chewy even when thoroughly cooked.

BARLEY (BLACK BUFFALO OR HULLED)	35 to 45 minutes	Black buffalo is a large, dark grain; striking in a medley
BARLEY (PEARL)	25 to 35 minutes	Accommodates well to cooking with other grains
BROWN RICE (SHORT-GRAIN)	35 to 40 minutes	Texture and taste far superior to long-grain varieties
COLUSARI RED RICE	20 to 25 minutes	Holds color nicely; a good alternative to wild rice
KAMUT	45 minutes	A large, buttery grain; highly recommended
MILLET	12 to 15 minutes	Dry-toast (see Other Ideas, page 22) before boiling; turns to mush if over-cooked
QUINOA	12 to 14 minutes	Before cooking, swish in several changes of water to remove natural bitter coating
WHEAT BERRIES (HARD WHEAT)	50 to 60 minutes	A small, dense, and chewy grain best used in medleys
WILD RICE (PRESOAKED)	35 to 45 minutes	Presoaking for a few hours or overnight results in more even cooking but is not essential when cooking in a medley

OTHER IDEAS

DRY-TOASTING GRAINS Dry-toasting gives grains a hint of nuttiness and usually shaves a few minutes off the boiling time. I consider dry-toasting optional except in the case of millet, whose taste and texture are considerably improved by taking this extra step.

To dry-toast grains, place the uncooked grains in a large, nonstick skillet set over medium heat. Once the skillet is hot, stir or shake the grains almost constantly until they emit a strong, toasted fragrance, turn a shade darker, or begin to pop (whichever happens first), 2 to 5 minutes. If the grains begin to scorch, immediately transfer them out of the skillet. Allow the toasted grains to cool before further cooking.

FREEZING COOKED GRAINS When the grains are cool, transfer them to storage containers or freezer-weight reclosable bags in convenient quantities, such as 1- or 2-cup portions. If you need less than the amount of frozen grains in any bag, simply bang the bag gently against the kitchen counter to release the amount you need.

REHYDRATING AND REHEATING REFRIGERATED OR FROZEN GRAINS
Leftover grains become dry and brittle after an overnight sojourn in the refrigerator. The microwave does an impressive job of revitalizing them. Simply place the refrigerated or frozen cooked grains in a strainer and rinse under hot water. Transfer to a bowl, cover lightly with a paper towel or waxed paper, and microwave until piping hot. (You'll probably have to stir once or twice to reheat the grains evenly.)

If you don't own a microwave, steam the grains over hot water.

GRAIN MEDLEYS For textural and visual variety, try boiling a few different grains together. Start by selecting grains that have approximately the same cooking times. Short-grain brown rice and barley are excellent together in a ratio of 3 to 1. A small handful of wild rice, Colusari red rice, or black barley adds nice color to the mix.

If you are a risk-taker, you can give longer-cooking grains a head start in the pot and then add shorter-cooking grains at appropriate intervals. For example, start with wheat berries and then add short-grain brown rice 15 minutes later. Alternatively, if you soak the wheat berries overnight, you can cook them with the brown rice right from the start.

Whole grains are more forgiving than white rice or pasta, and most offer a 10-minute window of chewiness before tasting waterlogged and over-cooked. But use this approach only if you have tolerance for occasional imperfection. (Avoid combos with quinoa and millet, as these grains quickly turn to mush if overcooked.) A safer way to create grain medleys is to cook and freeze each type of grain separately. Combine and heat them as the spirit moves you.

SEASONING GRAINS Coat grains very lightly with your finest olive, nut, or herb-infused oil (or a combination).

Toss grains with finely chopped fresh herbs and/or toasted seeds or chopped nuts.

See the recipe for Savory Grains on page 84.

3

DESIGNING **VEGAN MENUS**

With this book in hand, planning dinner couldn't be easier: most of the recipes in the Main Course chapter can be served on their own, and everyone will walk away from the table feeling satisfied. To design a more complex meal, first select the main course. Then follow the suggestions for accompaniments offered in the recipe's introduction. Alternatively, skim through the book and select a companion dish that suits your mood.

Two good ways to expand a meal are to serve grains with a vegetable entrée or beans with a grain-based main dish. See pages 18 to 22 for ways to keep cooked grains and beans on hand and ideas for dressing them up at the last minute.

Keep in mind that when dishes contain no animal protein, portions tend to be about 20 percent larger. I've taken this into account when estimating servings and have erred on the side of providing too much rather than too little.

Here are some themed menu possibilities and a few quick-reference lists. An item in parentheses indicates that I've provided no specific recipe and am leaving the creative details to you.

MEDITERRANEAN FEAST

Hiziki Tapenade

Slow-Baked Cannellini with Olives, Escarole, and Gremolata

Slow-Roasted Tomatoes and Fennel

Pine Nut–Anise Crescents

PASSAGE TO INDIA

Skillet Grain Medley with Curried Tempeh or Tomato-Chickpea Curry in Eggplant Shells

Cucumber-Mint "Raita"

Carrot Slaw with Mango Chutney Dressing

Mango-Coconut Tapioca

COMPANY IS COMING

Mediterranean Red Lentil Pâté

Stuffed Collard Rolls with Roasted Red Pepper Sauce

(Radicchio and Endive Salad) with Creamy Herb Dressing

Rustic Apple Tart

ASIAN MEDLEY

Split-Pea Soup with Shiitake and Star Anise

Brussels Sprouts and Udon Noodles in Miso Sauce

(Napa Cabbage Slaw) with Sesame-Watercress Dressing

(Pineapple Chunks Tossed with Canned Lichees)

SIMPLE SOUP MEAL

Roasted Sweet Potato and Corn Chowder

(Wholegrain Bread or Crackers with Almond, Cashew, or Hazelnut Butter)

(Tossed Green Salad) with Creamy Herb Dressing

FAST LUNCH OR SUPPER IDEAS

As-You-Please Grain and Bean Salad

Portobello "Steaks" with (Baked Potatoes) or (Tossed Green Salad) with Creamy Herb Dressing

Thai-Inspired Broccoli in Coconut-Cilantro Sauce

Crisp Tortilla Stacks with Roasted Corn and Black Beans

Black Soybean and Vegetable "Sushi"

LUNCHBOX FARE

Black Soybean and Vegetable "Sushi"

Mediterranean Red Lentil Pâté in Pita

Portobello "Steak" Sandwich

As-You-Please Grain and Bean Salad

Baked Beet and Brown Rice Salad

BREAKFAST AND BRUNCH IDEAS

Wholegrain Waffles

Sweet Polenta with Maple-Glazed Walnuts

Phyllo Triangles filled with Kale, Pine Nuts, and Currants

Rustic Apple Tart

QUICK DESSERT OPTIONS

Chocolate Rice Pudding

Sweet Polenta with Maple-Glazed Walnuts

(Dairy-free Ice Cream or Sorbet)

CHAPTER FOUR

STARTERS, SOUPS, AND LITTLE MEALS

1 OUNCE HIZIKI (ALSO SPELLED HIJIKI)

1 SMALL CLOVE GARLIC, PEELED

½ CUP PITTED, OIL-CURED BLACK OLIVES (SAVE TIME BY BUYING THEM ALREADY PITTED)

3 TABLESPOONS DRAINED CAPERS (PACKED IN BRINE)

2 TABLESPOONS OLIVE OIL, PLUS MORE IF NEEDED

1 TO 2 TABLESPOONS FRESHLY SQUEEZED LEMON JUICE

SALT (OPTIONAL)

FRESH THYME LEAVES, FOR GARNISH

Tapenade is a heady Provençal blend of olives, capers, and anchovies. In this version, I've used the mildly briny, jet-black sea vegetable called hiziki instead of anchovies. The result is a bold and rustic dip for raw vegetables or chips and a memorable spread for bread or wafer-thin rice crackers.

It's wise to purchase the hiziki in a health-food store, where the quality is likely to be better than you'll find in an Asian market. During processing, hiziki's large leaves are shredded and dried in such a tangle that it's impossible to give you a dry-cup measurement. If you don't have a kitchen scale, just "guesstimate" for now. Then please go out and buy one.

HIZIKI TAPENADE

01 Place the hiziki in a large bowl and pour enough boiling water on top to cover it by 2 inches. Let sit until tender and pliable, 10 to 20 minutes, stirring once or twice. Drain thoroughly.

02 With the motor of the food processor running, pop the garlic into the feed tube and chop. Add the hiziki, olives, capers, and oil. Process to create a coarse paste, scraping down the sides of the bowl as needed.

03 Add enough lemon juice and salt, if needed, to give the tapenade an assertive flavor. (The amount you'll need will depend upon the saltiness and flavor of the olives and capers; I've added as much as 1 teaspoon of salt and 2 tablespoons of lemon juice.)

04 If serving as a dip, thin the mixture slightly with olive oil, if necessary. Transfer to a bowl and garnish with thyme.

OTHER IDEAS

For a pleasing appetizer, set small mounds of tapenade in the center of plates and surround them with Slow-Roasted Tomatoes and Fennel (page 80). Serve with sliced, toasted baguette.

Use a tablespoon or two of tapenade as a flavor booster in soups and stews.

Thin the tapenade with olive oil and/or a tablespoon or two of pasta cooking-water, and toss with hot pasta. Add chopped fresh thyme, parsley, or basil, if you wish.

2 TABLESPOONS OLIVE OIL, PLUS MORE FOR OILING RAMEKINS OR LOAF PANS

3 TABLESPOONS TOASTED SUN-FLOWER SEEDS OR CHOPPED PISTACHIOS

1 ½ CUPS FINELY DICED ONIONS

1 CUP FINELY DICED SHALLOTS

1 TEASPOON FENNEL SEEDS, GENTLY CRUSHED IN A MORTAR OR UNDER A CHEF'S KNIFE

½ TEASPOON DRIED THYME LEAVES

1 LARGE CLOVE GARLIC, MINCED

1 TABLESPOON TOMATO PASTE

¼ CUP DRY WHITE WINE OR VERMOUTH

3 CUPS WATER

1 ½ CUPS RED LENTILS, PICKED OVER AND RINSED

1 BAY LEAF

1 TEASPOON SALT

FRESHLY GROUND BLACK PEPPER

ACCOMPANIMENTS: OLIVES, SLOW-ROASTED TOMATOES AND FENNEL (PAGE 80), CORNICHONS, PICKLED ONIONS, MARINATED ARTICHOKE HEARTS, OR MUSHROOMS

A FEW PARSLEY LEAVES, FOR GARNISH

Red lentils seasoned with Mediterranean herbs quickly melt down into a savory purée. (Some people have been observed spreading a hot spoonful of it onto bread.) When chilled, the mixture firms up into an elegant pâté. Like most pâtés, this one ages and keeps well, so you can count on enjoying it for a week or more.

Use either two 2-cup mini-loaf pans or 8 individual ½-cup ramekins for chilling the pâté. If using loaf pans, unmold the pâté and serve it whole on a buffet platter, or set slices on individual plates. Either unmold the ramekins or serve individual portions right in them.

For an appetizer or light lunch, serve the pâté with a small salad of mixed greens and a variety of the intensely flavored accompaniments suggested below. And, of course, a sliced baguette.

You'll find red lentils in health-food stores, most supermarkets, and in Indian groceries, where they are called masoor dal. Be forewarned that heat turns these lovely red lentils yellowish tan, a reminder that cooking is chemistry—or should I say alchemy?

MEDITERRANEAN **RED LENTIL** PÂTÉ

01 Brush oil on the bottom and sides of the loaf pans or ramekins. Sprinkle sunflower seeds on the bottom. Set aside.

02 In a large, heavy, nonreactive pot, heat the oil. Cook the onions and shallots over medium-high heat, stirring frequently, until golden brown, 6 to 8 minutes. Stir in the fennel, thyme, garlic, and tomato paste and cook, stirring constantly, for about 30 seconds. Add the wine and scrape up any browned bits sticking to the bottom of the pot. Cook until most of the wine evaporates, about 30 seconds.

03 Add the water, lentils, and bay leaf and bring to a boil. Cover and simmer, stirring occasionally, for 20 minutes. Add the salt and pepper and continue cooking until the lentils have melted into a coarse purée, 10 to 20 minutes longer. Remove the bay leaf and adjust the seasonings. (Be sure there's enough salt.)

04 Stir well, smashing any whole lentils onto the sides of the pot to create a fairly smooth, thick mixture, with a texture similar to oatmeal. If the purée is loose and soupy, boil it uncovered, stirring frequently, until it thickens.

05 Ladle the purée immediately into the oiled loaf pans or ramekins. Smooth the top with a spatula. Cool to room temperature. Cover and chill for at least 2 hours.

06 If you want to unmold the pâté, first run a knife along the edges. Then set a plate on top, turn both loaf pan and plate over, and pray. (Actually I've never had a problem.) Bring the pâté to room temperature. Arrange on a platter or individual plates with accompaniments. Press a few parsley leaves into the seed-strewn top.

OTHER IDEAS

Stuff pâté into a pita or use it to make a focaccia sandwich. Add some shredded radicchio or arugula leaves.

Thin leftovers into a soup by stirring in tomato juice. Adjust seasonings and garnish with parsley.

Serve the pâté freshly cooked and still warm and runny, in small bowls as a starchy vegetable side dish akin to a dal.

Make these unconventional sushi by spreading a flavor-packed black soybean paste on tortillas. Top with a sheet of nori, the sea vegetable commonly used to wrap traditional sushi. Then pile on strips of carrot, cucumber, and red bell pepper, and roll the tortillas up. Slice them on an angle to expose pretty pinwheels with bright splashes of color. They make good finger food or a pleasing appetizer or light lunch. (See Other Ideas.)

Organic black soybeans have much better flavor and texture than the beige variety and are available in cans. Look for Eden brand in health-food stores, where you'll also find the other ingredients. (Or try an Asian market for the nori and condiments.) The soybean spread can be prepared a few days in advance, but the "sushi" taste best when freshly assembled.

BLACK SOYBEAN AND VEGETABLE "SUSHI"

MAKES **20 TO 24** PIECES OF "SUSHI"

BLACK SOYBEAN SPREAD

ONE 15-OUNCE CAN ORGANIC BLACK SOYBEANS, DRAINED (RESERVE LIQUID)

1 TABLESPOON TOASTED (ASIAN) SESAME OIL

1 TABLESPOON JAPANESE SOY SAUCE (SHOYU OR TAMARI), PLUS MORE IF NEEDED

2 TABLESPOONS PICKLED GINGER, PLUS MORE IF NEEDED

CHILI OIL TO TASTE (OPTIONAL)

"SUSHI"

4 SHEETS NORI (SOMETIMES LABELED SUSHI NORI)

4 TORTILLAS, 8 TO 9 INCHES IN DIAMETER (WHOLE WHEAT ARE NICE)

1 CUP FINELY SHREDDED RED CABBAGE

8 STRIPS RED BELL PEPPER, ABOUT $1/4$ INCH WIDE

8 CARROT STICKS, ABOUT $1/8$ INCH IN DIAMETER AND 5 INCHES LONG

1 KIRBY (PICKLING) CUCUMBER, HALVED LENGTHWISE, SEEDED, AND CUT INTO 8 STICKS ABOUT $1/4$ INCH IN DIAMETER

SPRIGS OF WATERCRESS, FOR GARNISH

01 To make the Black Soybean Spread: In a food processor, combine the ingredients for the spread. Blend in enough of the reserved bean liquid (usually 1 to 2 tablespoons) to create a thick but spreadable paste. Add more soy sauce and/or pickled ginger, if needed, to give the spread an assertive taste. Season with chili oil, if you wish.

02 To assemble the "Sushi": Stack the nori and use kitchen scissors to trim the sheets into circles about $1/2$ inch smaller than the tortillas.

03 Spread 2 tablespoons of the soybean mixture onto one of the tortillas, leaving a 1-inch border all around. Distribute $1/4$ cup of the shredded cabbage over the bean spread. Gently press a piece of nori on top. Spread another 2 tablespoons of the soybean mixture on the nori. Set 2 red pepper strips horizontally about 1 inch from the bottom of the tortilla. Arrange 2 carrot and 2 cucumber sticks in a cluster on top.

04 Wrap the bottom edge of the tortilla over the vegetables and roll up tightly. If necessary, moisten the top edge of the tortilla lightly with soybean paste or water to seal. Gently press the roll to shape it into an even log. Proceed to fill and roll the remaining tortillas.

05 To slice the "Sushi": Set each roll on a cutting board seam side down, and use a very sharp knife to trim off the edges. Holding the

CONTINUED

roll firmly with one hand, use a gentle sawing motion of the knife to cut the roll into 5 or 6 pieces, making every other cut on the diagonal. Arrange the pieces flat side down on a platter. Garnish with watercress sprigs.

OTHER IDEAS

Instead of tortillas, use a rectangular flatbread, such as Garden of Eatin's Thin Thin Wraps, available in natural-food stores.

For a light luncheon entrée, cut each roll in half on the diagonal and lean one piece against the other in a criss-cross on a plate. Accompany with a green salad tossed with Sesame-Watercress Dressing (page 94).

Don't cut the roll, and serve it as a wrap.

Thin the spread with a few more tablespoons of bean liquid and use it as a dip for raw vegetables.

Use a pickle instead of the cucumber.

Serve the spread on wafer-thin rice crackers.

Tear the trimmed-off nori into tiny bits and use as a garnish for grains, soups, or salads.

This recipe is simplicity itself. When you have homemade vegetable broth on hand, use it to prepare this simple and restorative soup, made by infusing the broth with the earthy scent of porcini.

In The Italian Country Table, Lynne Rossetto Kasper reports that a simple broth like this is known in that country of knowledgeable eaters as an apristomaco, or tummy opener. I can also attest that the bouillon will warm you up quickly on a bone-chilling day.

The bouillon looks especially pretty when served in shallow, white soup bowls, garnished with a few snippets of chive.

PORCINI BOUILLON

SERVES 2

1 ½ CUPS BOILING WATER

½ OUNCE (GENEROUS ½ CUP, LOOSELY PACKED) DRIED PORCINI

¼ TEASPOON SALT, PLUS MORE IF NEEDED

2 CUPS HOMEMADE VEGETABLE OR LEEK BROTH (PAGES 9 TO 10)

SNIPPED CHIVES, FOR GARNISH (OPTIONAL)

01 Pour the boiling water into a glass liquid measuring cup and press the dried porcini into the water. Cover and let steep until the porcini are soft enough to chop, usually about 10 minutes.

02 Lift the porcini out of the water with a slotted spoon, and coarsely chop any large pieces. (Set the soaking liquid aside.) Heat a large nonstick skillet. Add the porcini and immediately sprinkle them with salt. Cook over medium-high heat, stirring constantly, until the porcini turn a shade darker and develop more intense flavor, 30 to 60 seconds. Pour in the soaking liquid, taking care to leave behind any grit that has settled on the bottom of the cup. Boil vigorously over high heat until the liquid is reduced by about half, 2 to 3 minutes.

03 Pour the vegetable broth into a saucepan and heat. Add the porcini mixture and heat thoroughly. Add salt to taste. Simmer until the broth is infused with porcini flavor, about 3 minutes. Ladle the broth through a fine sieve into bowls or cups, pressing the porcini to release all liquid. Garnish with chives, if you wish.

OTHER IDEAS

Toss the leftover soaked porcini into your next batch of rice or Savory Grains. They have little or no flavor, but their texture is pleasant, so why throw them away?

Cook grains in the bouillon. Use it as a base for soup or stew.

*¾ OUNCE DRIED SHIITAKE (ABOUT
10 SMALL)*

2 WHOLE STAR ANISE "FLOWERS"

*2 CUPS BOILING WATER, PLUS
4 CUPS ADDITIONAL WATER*

*1 TABLESPOON PEANUT OIL (LORIVA
BRAND ROASTED IS ESPECIALLY
GOOD)*

*5 SCALLIONS, THINLY SLICED (KEEP
WHITE AND GREEN PARTS
SEPARATE)*

1 CUP FINELY DICED ONION

2 TEASPOONS MINCED GARLIC

¼ CUP DRY SHERRY

*1 ½ CUPS SPLIT PEAS, PICKED OVER
AND RINSED*

½ TEASPOON SALT

*5-INCH CHUNK FRESH GINGER
(ABOUT 4 OUNCES)*

*2 TO 3 CUPS LOOSELY PACKED
WATERCRESS LEAVES (FROM
1 AVERAGE BUNCH)*

*1 TO 3 TABLESPOONS JAPANESE SOY
SAUCE (SHOYU OR TAMARI)*

*1 ½ TO 3 TEASPOONS ASIAN
(TOASTED) SESAME OIL (OPTIONAL)*

*1 TABLESPOON TOASTED BLACK
SESAME SEEDS, FOR GARNISH
(OPTIONAL)*

Dried shiitake mushrooms provide depth of flavor and star anise lends its unique tangle of licorice, resin, and smokiness to this Asian-inspired split-pea soup. Ginger juice and watercress leaves offer bright finishes of taste and color to the soothing, familiar backdrop of split peas.

The generous supply of meaty shiitake makes this soup substantial enough to serve as the main course. Opt for small shiitake—with dried caps no more than 1 inch across—if you can find them, as they rehydrate quickly. (About 10 of this size weigh ¾ ounce). If using larger ones, you may need to soak them longer; chop them into bite-sized morsels. You'll find dried shiitake and star anise in Asian groceries and in some health-food stores.

If you own a pressure cooker, by all means use it to make this soup. Twelve minutes under pressure melts the split peas down into a purée.

SPLIT-PEA SOUP WITH SHIITAKE AND STAR ANIS

01 Place the shiitake and star anise in a large glass measuring cup and pour the 2 cups boiling water over them. Cover and set aside until the mushrooms are tender enough to cut, usually about 10 minutes. Lift out mushrooms and star anise with a slotted spoon. Slice the caps thinly, discarding any stems (they are too woody to eat) as you go. Set the shiitake, star anise, and soaking liquid aside.

02 Heat the oil in a large soup pot. Add the white part of the sliced scallions, the onion, and the garlic, and cook over medium-high heat, stirring frequently, until they soften slightly, about 2 minutes. Add the sherry and cook over high heat, stirring constantly, until the sherry evaporates, about 30 seconds. Add the 4 cups of water, split peas, sliced shiitake, star anise (discard any broken pieces), and salt. Pour in the shiitake soaking liquid, taking care to leave behind any grit on the bottom of the cup.

03 Cover and bring to a boil. Cook at a gentle boil, stirring from time to time, until most of the peas have lost their shape, 50 to 60 minutes (or longer if the split peas are old and dried out). Taste the soup from time to time and remove the star anise if you feel it has given off sufficient flavor.

04 While the soup is cooking, prepare the ginger juice: Trim and grate the ginger (see page 13). Once you have about a tablespoon, press

the wad firmly between your fingertips and thumbs and collect the juice in a small bowl. Discard the ginger pulp. Continue grating ginger and expressing juice until you have 1 tablespoon of ginger juice. (The juice will look cloudy; some chunks of ginger are juicier than others, so you may have some ginger left over.) Set aside.

05 When the soup is done, remove the star anise "flowers." Stir well to dissolve the peas in the liquid and thicken the soup. For a creamier texture, purée part of the soup with a standard or immersion blender.

06 Just before serving, stir in the watercress and scallion greens. Add ginger juice, soy sauce, and toasted sesame oil (if using) to taste. Cook just until the watercress is wilted and tender, usually a matter of seconds. To serve, divide among 3 or 4 bowls and sprinkle with sesame seeds, if you wish.

OTHER IDEAS

Consider making the Sesame-Watercress Dressing (page 94) with the watercress stems. Toss the dressing with a slaw of shredded Chinese cabbage, carrots, and scallions for a side salad.

Replace the watercress with mesclun or chopped spinach leaves.

Instead of stirring the ginger juice into the soup, serve it in a small bowl and invite each person to add it according to personal taste.

2 MEDIUM SWEET POTATOES (ABOUT 1 POUND), PEELED AND CUT INTO ½-INCH DICE

2 TABLESPOONS CORN OIL (SPECTRUM NATURAL HAS A GOOD CORN TASTE)

SALT AND FRESHLY GROUND PEPPER

1 POUND FROZEN (RINSED AND DEFROSTED) OR FRESH CORN KERNELS (ABOUT 4 CUPS)

1 CUP WATER

1 ½ CUPS FINELY DICED CELERY

1 CUP DICED RED ONION

¼ CUP DICED SHALLOTS

1 TABLESPOON TOMATO PASTE

½ TEASPOON DRIED THYME LEAVES

3 CUPS VEGETABLE BROTH

1 BAY LEAF

1 RUSSET (BAKING) POTATO (ABOUT 8 OUNCES)

2 TABLESPOONS MINCED PARSLEY

½ TO 1 CUP UNFLAVORED SOYMILK (OPTIONAL)

This cheery chowder has a satisfying, long-cooked taste. Roasting the sweet potatoes intensifies their flavor, and puréeing most of the corn kernels instantly creates a creamy broth. I've had excellent results using frozen organic corn. Cascadian Farms and Tree of Life are two good brands.

To streamline cooking, begin preparing the soup while the sweet potatoes are roasting. If the chowder becomes too thick, stir in soymilk to thin it while adding richness and flavor.

ROASTED **SWEET POTATO** AND **CORN** CHOWDER

01 Set the oven rack in the center and preheat the oven to 425°F. Oil a large roasting pan.

02 Scatter the sweet potatoes in one layer in the roasting pan and drizzle with 1 tablespoon of the oil. Season well with salt and pepper. Roast until tender, tossing once or twice, 15 to 20 minutes. If you'd like to brown the sweet potatoes more deeply, set them about 5 inches below the broiling element for a minute or two. Set aside.

03 Reserve 1 cup of corn kernels. In a blender, purée the remaining corn with the water until very smooth, about 2 minutes. (If the corn kernel skins refuse to break down, and they look unsightly to you, pass the mixture through a sieve.) Set aside.

04 In a heavy soup pot, heat the remaining tablespoon of oil. Cook the celery, onion, and shallots over medium-high heat, stirring frequently, until the onions are slightly softened, about 3 minutes. Add the tomato paste and thyme and cook another minute, stirring frequently. Add the broth, puréed corn, bay leaf, 1 teaspoon salt, and pepper to taste.

05 While bringing the chowder to a boil, peel the potato, cut it into ½-inch dice, and add it to the pot. Cover the pot and simmer until the potato is tender, 25 to 35 minutes.

06 Remove the bay leaf. Add the reserved corn kernels, roasted sweet potatoes, and parsley. Thin with soymilk, if necessary. Adjust seasonings. Cook (but do not boil after adding soymilk) until heated throughout.

CHAPTER FIVE

THE **MAIN COURSE**

SERVES **4**

Layer tortillas with a colorful roasted corn and black bean salad to create a stack. Top it with a dollop of rich Silken Cilantro Sauce for a very pretty dish—good for a festive lunch or supper.

Since the tortillas are crisped in the oven, they crack rather than slice. Encourage your guests to use their hands to lift a chip of tortilla with some of the topping when a fork isn't practical.

CRISP TORTILLA STACKS WITH ROASTED
CORN AND BLACK BEANS

01 Set the broiler rack about 5 inches from the element and preheat the broiler. Spread out the corn, jalapeños, and green bell pepper on a large, nonstick roasting or baking pan. Drizzle with 1 table-spoon of the olive oil, and sprinkle with salt and pepper. Broil for 3 minutes, stir, and then continue broiling until some of the corn kernels are speckled with brown spots, 3 to 5 minutes longer. Transfer the vegetables to a large bowl.

02 Spread out the tomatoes and red onion on the same pan. Drizzle with the remaining tablespoon of oil. Season well with salt and pep-per. Broil for 4 minutes, toss, and then continue to broil until the onions or tomatoes begin to be tinged around the edges, 3 to 5 minutes longer. Add to the bowl along with the black beans and cilantro. Add enough salt, pepper, and lime juice to give the mixture lots of flavor.

03 Turn off the broiler. Set a shelf in the middle of the oven and set the temperature to 400°F. Just before you are ready to serve, set the tortillas directly on the oven rack and toast until crisp, 3 to 4 minutes. (Or, if you prefer, heat the tortillas just until they are warm, but still pliable.)

04 To assemble each stack, set a tortilla on a large dinner plate and mound about $3/4$ cup of roasted corn salad on top. Cover with a second tortilla and another $3/4$ cup of corn salad. Spoon a heaping tablespoon of Silken Cilantro Sauce on top. Place 2 lime wedges on either side of the plate. Serve warm or at room temperature. Pass the extra Cilantro Sauce in a bowl.

3 CUPS FRESH OR FROZEN CORN KERNELS

1 OR 2 JALAPEÑOS, SEEDED AND FINELY DICED

1 LARGE GREEN BELL PEPPER, SEEDED AND DICED

2 TABLESPOONS OLIVE OIL

SALT AND FRESHLY GROUND PEPPER

1 POUND PLUM TOMATOES, COARSELY CHOPPED

2 CUPS DICED RED ONION

ABOUT 1 $3/4$ CUPS COOKED BLACK BEANS OR ONE 15-OUNCE CAN, DRAINED AND RINSED

$1/2$ CUP CHOPPED CILANTRO

4 TO 5 TABLESPOONS FRESHLY SQUEEZED LIME JUICE

8 CORN TORTILLAS (ABOUT 6 INCHES IN DIAMETER)

SILKEN CILANTRO SAUCE (PAGE 93)

2 LIMES, CUT INTO WEDGES

2 TO 3 TABLESPOONS OLIVE OIL

12 OUNCES CREMINI OR BUTTON MUSHROOMS, TRIMMED AND SLICED

SALT

1 ½ CUPS THINLY SLICED LEEKS

2 TEASPOONS MINCED GARLIC

2 TEASPOONS DRIED HERBES DE PROVENCE (PAGE 14) OR ½ TEA-SPOON EACH DRIED TARRAGON, THYME OR MARJORAM, BASIL, AND ROSEMARY (BREAK INTO TINY PIECES)

1 TEASPOON FENNEL SEEDS

½ CUP DRY WHITE WINE OR VERMOUTH

4 CUPS VEGETABLE BROTH

1 CUP FRENCH GREEN LENTILS

2 CUPS DICED FENNEL OR CELERY

TWO 9-OUNCE PACKAGES FROZEN ARTICHOKE HEARTS

½ CUP PICHOLINE OR NIÇOISE OLIVES OR OTHER SMALL MEDITERRANEAN BRINE-CURED OLIVES (OR A COMBINATION)

2 TEASPOONS GRATED LEMON ZEST

2 TO 3 TEASPOONS BALSAMIC SYRUP (PAGE 16)

PARSLEY AIOLI (RECIPE OPPOSITE)

CHOPPED FENNEL FRONDS, FOR GARNISH (OPTIONAL)

The small, speckled green legumes known as Le Puy lentils have a fine taste and can be counted on to hold their shape. Usually labeled French lentils, they are sold in gourmet shops and some health-food stores.

In this soupy stew, I've used the lentils as a backdrop for ingredients common to the south of France: artichoke hearts, mushrooms, black niçoise and green picholine olives, and the garlicky mayonnaise known as aioli. Warn your guests to be on the lookout for olive pits, which are tedious to remove.

The Parsley Aioli gives this wintry dish a bright finish. The aioli also makes a nice spread for slices of baguette—an ideal accompaniment to the stew, as is an arugula and endive salad. For an even heartier meal, set a wedge of Potato Cake (page 85) alongside each portion.

PROVENÇAL GREEN LENTILS WITH ARTICHOKES MUSHROOMS, AND PARSLEY AIOLI

01 Heat 1 tablespoon of the oil in a heavy 5- to 6-quart, nonreactive pot. Add the mushrooms and immediately sprinkle them with ½ teaspoon salt. Cook over medium-high heat, stirring almost constantly, until the mushrooms are nicely browned, 4 to 5 minutes. Add more oil during this time if the mushrooms begin to stick.

02 Add another tablespoon of oil, the leeks, garlic, herbs, and fennel seeds. Cook over medium-high heat, stirring frequently, until the leeks soften slightly, 2 to 3 minutes. Add the wine and cook until most of it evaporates, about 1 minute.

03 Add the broth, lentils, and fennel and bring to a boil. Cover and cook at a gentle boil until the lentils are tender, 40 to 50 minutes. About halfway through, taste the stew and add more herbs if you think they're needed.

04 Set the artichoke hearts in a colander and run them under hot water to break up the blocks and wash away any ice crystals. Stir the artichoke hearts and olives into the lentils. Cover and cook until the artichoke hearts are tender, 3 to 4 minutes.

05 Add salt to taste, lemon zest, and enough Balsamic Syrup to round out the flavors. Serve in shallow soup bowls, topped with Parsley Aioli. Garnish with fennel fronds, if available, and pass any extra aioli in a bowl.

PARSLEY AIOLI

01 Put the lemon juice and oil in a blender jar, and then add the remaining ingredients. Process until very smooth, about 2 minutes, scraping down the sides of the jar once or twice. Add more lemon juice and salt, if needed, to balance the flavors.

02 Use immediately or refrigerate in a tightly sealed container for up to 3 days. (The color is likely to turn olive, but the flavor will be fine.) Thin leftovers, if necessary, with a little water.

OTHER IDEAS

Use mixed wild mushrooms instead of cremini.

Omit the Parsley Aioli and stir in fresh thyme leaves just before serving.

Leftover aioli makes a good topping for baked potato or a dip for raw vegetables. It also makes a fine mayonnaise-like sandwich spread.

MAKES ¾ CUP

2 TABLESPOONS LEMON JUICE, PLUS MORE IF NEEDED

2 TABLESPOONS OLIVE OIL

2 CUPS TIGHTLY PACKED PARSLEY LEAVES AND TENDER STEMS

4 OUNCES (½ CUP) SILKEN SOFT OR FIRM TOFU

10 LARGE CLOVES ROASTED GARLIC (PAGE 12), PEELED

½ TEASPOON DIJON MUSTARD

½ TEASPOON SALT, PLUS MORE IF NEEDED

1 POUND OR TWO 10-OUNCE PINTS BRUSSELS SPROUTS

2 TEASPOONS OLIVE OIL

1 TABLESPOON PEELED, MINCED GINGER

1/2 TEASPOON MINCED GARLIC

6 SCALLIONS, THINLY SLICED (KEEP WHITE AND GREEN PARTS SEPARATE)

1/2 CUP FINELY DICED RED BELL PEPPERS

1/2 CUP FINELY DICED YELLOW OR PURPLE BELL PEPPERS, OR ADDITIONAL RED PEPPERS

1/4 TO 1/2 TEASPOON CRUSHED RED PEPPER FLAKES

3/4 CUP WATER

8 OUNCES UDON NOODLES (EDEN FOODS MAKES A NICE BROWN RICE UDON)

2 1/2 TABLESPOONS DARK MISO

1 TABLESPOON ROSEMARY-INFUSED OLIVE OIL (OR 1 TABLESPOON OLIVE OIL AND 1 TO 2 TEASPOONS CHOPPED FRESH ROSEMARY), PLUS MORE IF NEEDED

1 TO 2 TABLESPOONS JAPANESE SOY SAUCE (SHOYU OR TAMARI)

1/2 CUP TOASTED PECANS

If you've never sliced Brussels sprouts before tossing them into the pot, you're about to discover the ideal way to prepare this underappreciated vegetable. Since the slices cook evenly and maintain their sprightly green odor and crunch, you will feel like you are being introduced to a new vegetable.

In this dish, you'll be tossing the sliced Brussels sprouts with Japanese udon noodles, bell peppers, and pecans. An East-West sauce is quickly made by blending the fermented soybean paste called miso with rosemary-infused olive oil and a little of the noodle cooking-water. This recipe calls for dark miso (page 15), which is generally saltier and aged longer than light miso, so avoid any temptation to make a substitution. You'll find udon noodles and miso in Asian groceries and health-food stores. Leftovers are likely to need perking up with soy sauce or lemon juice.

BRUSSELS SPROUTS AND UDON NOODLES IN MISO SAUCE

01 Trim off the root end of the Brussels sprouts, and discard any browned or damaged outer leaves. Cut the Brussels sprouts lengthwise into 1/4-inch slices. Set aside. Begin bringing a large pot of water to the boil for the udon.

02 In a large skillet, heat the oil. Add the ginger and garlic, and cook over medium-high heat, stirring constantly, for about 20 seconds. Add the sliced white part of the scallions, bell peppers, and red pepper flakes and cook, stirring frequently, for 1 minute.

03 Turn off the heat. Standing back to avoid spattering oil, add the water. Add the Brussels sprouts, cover, and cook over medium-high heat until the sprouts are tender-crisp and still bright green, 2 to 4 minutes. (Add a few tablespoons additional water during this time if the mixture becomes dry.) Set the skillet aside, uncovered.

04 Break the udon in half and add them to the boiling water. In a small bowl, dissolve the miso in 1/2 cup of the noodle cooking-water. Stir in the rosemary-infused oil and 1 tablespoon of soy sauce.

05 When the noodles are just short of done, drain them. Set them in the skillet with the Brussels sprouts, and stir in the miso sauce and reserved scallion greens. Add more soy sauce and rosemary oil, if needed. Cook over medium heat, stirring constantly, just until the mixture is good and hot. Toss in the pecans and serve immediately.

CURRIED TEMPEH

8 OUNCES TEMPEH (SOY OR THREE-GRAIN)

2 TABLESPOONS MILD CURRY POWDER, SUCH AS THE ONE MADE BY MERWANJEE POONJIANJEE & SONS

1/2 TEASPOON GROUND TURMERIC

PINCH OF SALT

1 1/2 TABLESPOONS GRATED FRESH GINGER (SEE PAGE 13)

2 TABLESPOONS PEANUT OIL

1/3 CUP WATER

SKILLET GRAIN MEDLEY

1 CUP WATER, PLUS MORE IF NEEDED

1/2 CUP GRATED, DRIED, UNSWEETENED COCONUT (AVAILABLE IN HEALTH-FOOD STORES)

1 TEASPOON FENNEL SEEDS

1 TEASPOON CUMIN SEEDS

1/4 TEASPOON SALT, PLUS MORE IF NEEDED

1/4 TEASPOON GROUND CINNAMON

1/8 TEASPOON CAYENNE (OPTIONAL)

3 CUPS COOKED GRAINS (SEE PAGE 21; IF FROZEN, POUR BOILING WATER OVER THEM TO PARTIALLY DEFROST)

1/2 CUP FROZEN GREEN PEAS

CUCUMBER-MINT "RAITA" (PAGE 92)

Season tempeh cubes with a curry marinade, and then mound these exotic "croutons" on top of Indian-spiced grains. You can use whatever cooked grains you have on hand, but the texture is more interesting when you use two or three different types.

Make this dish only if you have time to prepare the Cucumber-Mint "Raita" as well, since a soupy accompaniment is needed to moisten the grains and offer a smooth contrast to their chewiness. A side dish of Carrot Slaw with Mango Chutney Dressing (page 90) adds a welcome crunch. Offer a bowl of Patak's Brinjal Eggplant Relish (this is really good!) for those who would enjoy a hit of intense flavor. (You can find Patak's products in Indian groceries and many supermarkets.)

Microwave any leftovers in a bowl lightly covered with a paper towel or waxed paper. If the grains are quite dried out, sprinkle them with a little water before reheating.

SKILLET **GRAIN** MEDLEY WITH CURRIED **TEMPEH**

01 Set the rack in the middle of the oven and preheat the oven to 425°F.

02 To prepare the curried tempeh: Use a fork to prick both sides of the tempeh deeply about 20 times. Cut the slab into 1/2-inch cubes and set aside.

03 In a sealable storage container, combine the curry powder, turmeric, salt, grated ginger, oil, and water. Add the tempeh cubes, close the container, and shake gently to coat the cubes evenly. (Most of the marinade will be absorbed instantly.) Set aside for 5 minutes.

04 Arrange the tempeh in one layer in a nonstick baking pan or shallow roasting pan. (Set aside the storage container and any unabsorbed marinade.) Bake the tempeh for 5 minutes. Toss, and then continue to bake until the cubes feel crisp and dry to the touch, 5 to 7 minutes longer. (Do not bake longer than 12 minutes, as the tempeh will dry out; it may not brown significantly.) Set aside in a warm place.

05 To prepare the grain medley: Pour the water into the container you used for the tempeh marinade, and blend in any unabsorbed marinade. Heat a large, nonstick skillet and add the coconut, fennel seeds, and cumin seeds. Stir almost constantly until the coconut becomes fragrant and about half of the batch turns golden, 1 to 2 minutes. (Take care as the coconut can burn quickly.)

06 Immediately pour the marinade water into the pan and stir. Add the salt, cinnamon, and cayenne (if using). Boil gently for 2 minutes. Stir in the grains, peas, and more salt, if needed. Cover and cook over medium-low heat until good and hot, stirring occasionally to prevent the grains from sticking, 2 to 3 minutes. Stir in a few table-spoons more water during this time if the mixture becomes dry.

07 To serve: Mound the grains in the center of large lipped plates or shallow soup bowls. Surround with "moats" of Cucumber-Mint "Raita," and top with the Curried Tempeh.

OTHER IDEAS

Prepare the Curried Tempeh on its own and stuff cubes into pita with shredded lettuce or chopped, steamed vegetables. Use the "Raita" as a dressing.

Crumble any leftover Curried Tempeh on top of a green salad or steamed vegetables.

Jade-green broccoli vies with red and yellow bell peppers for center stage in this exotic Asian stew. For relatively little effort, this recipe rewards you with a sophisticated sauce reminiscent of Thai restaurant fare.

The only ingredient you may not recognize here is seitan, a dense, high-protein meat substitute made of wheat gluten. Seitan plays a big role in the Buddhist vegetarian kitchen and is traditionally seasoned with soy sauce (and sometimes ginger); its flavor contributes nicely to the sauce.

You'll find seitan in the refrigerated section of health-food stores. Don't be discouraged when you open the plastic tub and discover large, strange-looking chunks. Once chopped finely, the seitan adds real substance and a delightfully chewy texture.

Lime juice is needed to balance the sauce, but it quickly dulls the sprightly color, so serve wedges of lime on the side and let everyone squeeze to taste. I like to serve this dish in large, shallow soup bowls over Thai jasmine or basmati rice.

THAI-INSPIRED **BROCCOLI** IN **COCONUT-CILANTRO** SAUCE

01 Cut the broccoli florets from the stalks, and separate them into small pieces. Trim the stalks, and use a paring knife or peeler to remove the fibrous outer layers. Cut the stalks into 1/2-inch chunks. Set the florets and stalks aside.

02 With the motor of the food processor running, pop the garlic and then the ginger, shallot, and jalapeño(s) into the feed tube, and chop finely. Reserve 1/2 cup tightly packed cilantro leaves. Chop the remaining cilantro a few times, add to the processor, and chop finely. Add the coconut milk, sugar, and salt, and process to blend thoroughly.

03 Transfer the coconut milk mixture to a 4- or 5-quart pot, and bring to a boil. Boil gently, uncovered, stirring occasionally, for 3 minutes.

04 Meanwhile, remove the seitan from its tub. Reserve any marinating liquid if you like its taste, and add enough water to equal a total of 1 cup liquid. Stir this liquid (or 1 cup plain water) into the coconut milk mixture. Chop the seitan finely in the processor, and add it to the pot along with the reserved broccoli.

CONTINUED

2 POUNDS BROCCOLI (3 LARGE STALKS)

1 LARGE CLOVE GARLIC

1-INCH CHUNK GINGER, TRIMMED AND CUT INTO EIGHTHS (PEELING IS NOT NECESSARY)

1 MEDIUM SHALLOT (ABOUT 2 OUNCES), PEELED AND QUARTERED

1 OR 2 JALAPEÑOS (DEPENDING UPON DESIRED HEAT), HALVED AND SEEDED

1 GOOD-SIZED BUNCH CILANTRO (ABOUT 4 OUNCES; INCLUDE STEMS AND ROOTS, IF AVAILABLE, BUT RINSE THOROUGHLY TO REMOVE ALL SAND)

ONE 13.5-OUNCE CAN COCONUT MILK (NOT LIGHT)

1 1/2 TEASPOONS SUGAR

1/2 TEASPOON SALT

8 TO 12 OUNCES SEITAN (WHEAT GLUTEN)

1 LARGE RED BELL PEPPER, SEEDED AND CUT INTO 1/4-INCH STRIPS

1 LARGE YELLOW BELL PEPPER, SEEDED AND CUT INTO 1/4-INCH STRIPS

1 TO 3 TABLESPOONS JAPANESE SOY SAUCE (TAMARI OR SHOYU)

A FEW BASIL LEAVES, SHREDDED, FOR GARNISH (OPTIONAL)

2 LIMES, CUT INTO WEDGES

05 Cover and cook at a moderate boil for 2 minutes. Add the bell peppers, cover, and continue cooking, stirring once or twice, until the broccoli is tender but still bright green, 3 to 4 minutes longer. Add more water during this time if the mixture becomes dry.

06 Just before serving, coarsely chop the reserved cilantro leaves and stir them in. Add enough soy sauce to create a good balance of flavors. Ladle into soup bowls, and garnish with basil, if you wish. Accompany each portion with a few lime wedges.

OTHER IDEAS

Toss with cooked rice noodles. Season with additional soy sauce and garnish with chopped roasted peanuts and bean sprouts.

Substitute Smart Ground for the seitan. Smart Ground, crumbles made of soy protein concentrate and wheat gluten, is available in health-food stores and some supermarkets.

Here's the game plan for preparing this wintry casserole. While cooking brown rice in a rich, herb-scented porcini broth on top of the stove, you'll be roasting root vegetables in the oven. Scatter the vegetables over the moist grains and season with a drizzle of sweet-puckery balsamic syrup, which brings this dish over the top. It's a colorful medley, full of contrasting tastes and textures.

I love the chewiness of short-grain brown rice—it's so much more interesting than the long-grain variety. Toss in some black buffalo barley or Colusari red rice to add visual interest. You don't have to worry about exact quantities of vegetables for roasting: a little more or less doesn't matter.

This casserole may seem a bit soupy at first, but any extra liquid will disappear quickly as the thirsty grains drink it up.

PORCINI BROWN RICE WITH ROASTED ROOT VEGETABLES AND BALSAMIC SYRUP

SERVES **4 TO 6**

1 OUNCE PORCINI OR OTHER DRIED MUSHROOMS (ABOUT $^3/_4$ CUP LOOSELY PACKED)

4 CUPS BOILING WATER

1 POUND RED-SKINNED POTATOES, TRIMMED AND CUT INTO 1-INCH CHUNKS

$^1/_2$ POUND BABY-CUT CARROTS

$^1/_2$ POUND PARSNIPS, PEELED AND CUT INTO $^1/_2$-INCH CHUNKS

3 MEDIUM RED ONIONS (ABOUT 1 POUND), PEELED AND QUARTERED

3 TABLESPOONS OLIVE OIL, DIVIDED

1 TO 2 TEASPOONS DRIED ROSEMARY (BROKEN INTO BITS), THYME, OR MARJORAM

SALT AND FRESHLY GROUND PEPPER

2 CUPS CHOPPED LEEKS OR ONIONS

1 CUP DICED FENNEL OR CELERY

2 TEASPOONS ITALIAN HERB BLEND (PAGE 14 OR STORE-BOUGHT)

1 CUP SHORT-GRAIN BROWN RICE

$^1/_2$ CUP BLACK BUFFALO BARLEY, COLUSARI RED RICE, OR ADDITIONAL BROWN RICE

1 BAY LEAF

3 TABLESPOONS MINCED PARSLEY, FOR GARNISH (OPTIONAL)

BALSAMIC SYRUP (PAGE 16)

01 Set the porcini in a bowl and pour the boiling water on top. Cover and set aside for 10 minutes or longer.

02 Arrange the potatoes, carrots, parsnips, and red onions in one layer in one or two roasting pans. Drizzle with 2 tablespoons of the olive oil. Sprinkle with the rosemary, and season well with salt and pepper. Set two racks in the middle portion of the oven, and start preheating the oven to 450°F. Set the vegetables aside while you turn your attention to the rice.

03 Lift the porcini from the soaking liquid with a slotted spoon, and coarsely chop any large pieces. Set the porcini and soaking liquid aside.

04 Heat a tablespoon of oil in a heavy 3-quart pot over medium-high heat. Cook the leeks and fennel for 3 minutes, stirring frequently. Stir in the Italian herbs and cook for another few seconds. Pour in the reserved porcini liquid, taking care to leave any grit behind. Add the porcini, grains, bay leaf, and 1$^1/_4$ teaspoons salt. Bring to a boil, reduce the heat, cover, and cook over low heat until the grains are tender, about 40 minutes. (Some broth may not be absorbed.)

CONTINUED

05 While the grains are cooking, roast the vegetables, tossing every 10 or 15 minutes, until tender and easily pierced with the tip of a paring knife, 30 to 40 minutes in all. (A few tips: Rotate the roasting pan(s) if the vegetables are browning unevenly. The onions are done when lightly singed around the edges; they'll remain slightly crunchy. Remove any vegetables that begin to burn or dry out before the others are done.)

06 When the grains are ready (they will remain slightly chewy, even when fully cooked), remove the bay leaf and add more salt, if needed. Cover and let sit off the heat for 5 minutes, or until the roasted vegetables are ready.

07 To serve, reheat the roasted vegetables, if necessary. Mound the grains on individual plates. Spoon any unabsorbed porcini broth over the grains. Distribute the vegetables on top or alongside. Sprinkle with parsley, if you wish, and drizzle 1 to 2 teaspoons of Balsamic Syrup over each portion.

OTHER IDEAS

KAMUT AND WILD RICE VARIATION

Substitute kamut for the brown rice and wild rice for the black buffalo barley. Soak the kamut and wild rice overnight, then drain and proceed as directed. The grains may need as long as 50 minutes to cook, and the mixture will be somewhat soupy.

Instead of rice and barley, use a colorful grain mix, such as the one sold under the Lundberg label.

Substitute fresh herbs for the dried, using double the amount.

In my version of this zesty Cuban lunch-counter favorite, finely chopped wheat gluten (usually sold under its Japanese name, seitan; see page 51) makes an admirable substitute for the traditional ground beef. Sweet raisins, salty olives, and pickled capers infuse the tomato sauce and seitan with irresistible flavor. For optimum taste, prepare the picadillo a few hours before serving, or even the day before.

Opt for chicken-style seitan if you can find it, as the taste is more appropriate to this dish. Traditionally seasoned seitan, typically flavored with soy sauce and ginger, can be used successfully in the picadillo if you rinse away most of the seasoning, as directed in the recipe. Serve the picadillo over quinoa or rice tossed with toasted pumpkin seeds or with Savory Grains (page 84).

A CUBAN PICADILLO

SERVES 4

12 TO 16 OUNCES SEITAN (WHEAT GLUTEN), PREFERABLY CHICKEN STYLE, DRAINED

1 TABLESPOON OLIVE OIL

1 TABLESPOON CHOPPED GARLIC

1 CUP CHOPPED ONION

2 MEDIUM GREEN PEPPERS, SEEDED AND DICED

1 TEASPOON DRIED OREGANO LEAVES

¼ TEASPOON GROUND CUMIN

2 CUPS UNSEASONED TOMATO JUICE

ONE 15-OUNCE CAN DICED TOMATOES WITH GREEN CHILES, WITH LIQUID

⅓ CUP PIMENTO-STUFFED GREEN OLIVES, CUT INTO THIRDS CROSS-WISE

¼ CUP RAISINS

2 TABLESPOONS DRAINED CAPERS

½ TEASPOON SALT

FRESHLY GROUND BLACK PEPPER

01 Place the seitan in the bowl of a food processor and pulse until it is chopped to a texture resembling ground meat. (Or chop finely by hand.) If using the traditionally seasoned variety, soak the chopped seitan in water to cover for 10 minutes. Drain. Taste and repeat with fresh water, if necessary, until the seitan tastes fairly bland. Drain thoroughly and set aside.

02 Heat the oil in a large saucepan over medium-high heat. Add the garlic and cook, stirring frequently, until it is lightly browned, about 30 seconds. Immediately stir in the onion and green peppers and cook over medium heat, stirring occasionally, until the vegetables have softened somewhat, 4 to 5 minutes. Stir in the oregano and cumin and cook for about 30 seconds. Then add the reserved chopped seitan and the remaining ingredients.

03 Bring to a boil over high heat, reduce the heat, and cook uncovered at a gentle boil, stirring occasionally, until the mixture has thickened slightly and the seitan has picked up the flavor of the sauce, 30 to 45 minutes. Adjust seasonings before serving.

OTHER IDEAS

Substitute Smart Ground for the seitan. Smart Ground, crumbles made of soy protein concentrate and wheat gluten, is available in health-food stores and some supermarkets.

There's something delightful and festive about stuffed vegetables. In this case, each diner gets an impressive eggplant "barge" bearing a cargo of curried chickpeas. Unlike most stuffed vegetable dishes, this one is quick and easy to prepare.

You'll start by roasting halved eggplants, then scooping out the flesh and cooking it with chickpeas, tomatoes, dried coconut, and toasted mustard seeds. You can make this filling as hot as you like by adding cayenne. Since cayenne is potent stuff, start with a pinch and add more gradually. To speed things up, begin preparing the ingredients for the filling while the eggplant is in the oven.

Carrot Slaw with Mango Chutney Dressing (page 90) makes a nice accompaniment. The stuffed eggplant is quite filling, so most people will do just fine without rice.

TOMATO-CHICKPEA CURRY IN EGGPLANT SHELLS

SERVES 4

2 MEDIUM EGGPLANTS (1 TO 1 $\frac{1}{4}$ POUNDS EACH)

2 TO 3 TABLESPOONS VEGETABLE OIL, DIVIDED

SALT TO TASTE, PLUS $\frac{1}{4}$ TEASPOON FRESHLY GROUND PEPPER

2 TABLESPOONS BROWN MUSTARD SEEDS (THEY'RE ACTUALLY REDDISH BROWN)

2 CUPS COARSELY CHOPPED ONIONS

1 $\frac{1}{2}$ TABLESPOONS MILD CURRY POWDER, SUCH AS MERWANJEE POONJIANJEE & SONS, PLUS MORE IF NEEDED

ONE 15-OUNCE CAN DICED TOMATOES, WITH LIQUID

1 $\frac{1}{2}$ CUPS COOKED CHICKPEAS OR ONE 15-OUNCE CAN, DRAINED

$\frac{1}{2}$ CUP DRIED, UNSWEETENED, GRATED COCONUT (AVAILABLE IN HEALTH-FOOD STORES)

CAYENNE

CHOPPED CILANTRO, FOR GARNISH (OPTIONAL)

01 Set the rack in the middle of the oven and preheat to 450°F. Lightly oil one or two roasting pans large enough to hold the eggplant halves in one layer. Add $\frac{1}{8}$ inch of water.

02 Leaving the stem intact, halve the eggplants lengthwise. Use the tip of a paring knife to score the flesh side deeply in a crisscross pattern. Brush the cut side with oil, season with salt and pepper, and set flesh side down in the roasting pans. Brush the skins with oil.

03 Roast until the eggplants are tender and easily pierced with the tip of a paring knife, 18 to 25 minutes. (Check after 10 minutes and add more water, if needed.) When the eggplants are cool enough to handle, use a paring or grapefruit knife to create a $\frac{1}{2}$-inch "wall" all around, and then scoop out the flesh. Coarsely chop the flesh (including seeds) and set aside. Lightly season the eggplant shells with salt and pepper, and reserve them in a warm place.

04 To prepare the filling, first toast the mustard seeds: Heat 1 tablespoon of oil in a large, heavy saucepan over high heat. Stir in the mustard seeds, cover the pot, and leave the heat turned to high. Listen carefully: as soon as you hear the mustard seeds begin to pop against the lid, turn off the heat (remove to a cool burner if using an electric stove), and wait for the popping to subside. Most of the seeds should now be gray.

CONTINUED

05 Stir the onions into the mustard seeds and cook over medium-high heat, stirring frequently, until the onions start to brown, 4 to 5 minutes. Add a bit more oil during this time if the onions are sticking. Stir in the curry powder and cook for 10 seconds. Then add the tomatoes, chickpeas, coconut, reserved eggplant flesh, salt, and cayenne to taste. Cover and simmer over medium heat, stirring occasionally, until the chickpeas develop a curried flavor, about 15 minutes. During this time, add more curry and salt, if needed, and stir in a few tablespoons of water if the mixture becomes dry.

06 Mound the filling into the eggplant shells. (If you have a little extra filling, enjoy a snack.) Garnish with a sprinkling of cilantro, if you wish, and serve immediately.

OTHER IDEAS

If you're not fond of coconut, feel free to leave it out. (You may need less salt.)

Substitute diced tomatoes with green chiles for the plain tomatoes.

This combination was inspired by the popular street food of Trinidad and Jamaica. In my version, chunks of tempeh are quickly marinated with typical jerk spices and then baked. The dense, zesty cubes are dotted on top of meltingly soft, curried calabaza—a large West Indian pumpkin that is sold in wedges in many Hispanic markets. (You can substitute butternut squash.) The combination is quite filling, so you probably won't need a grain accompaniment.

I've organized the recipe for maximum efficiency, so you'll be preparing the curried pumpkin while the tempeh is marinating. If it's more convenient, you can marinate the tempeh overnight.

WEST INDIAN **PUMPKIN** WITH JERK-SPICED **TEMPEH**

01 With a fork, deeply prick the tempeh about 20 times on each side. Cut into $^1/_2$-inch dice. Set aside.

02 In a blender, combine the soy sauce, oil, brown sugar, garlic, ginger, thyme, allspice, pepper, salt, and onion. Purée until very smooth, about 1 minute. Add hot sauce to taste. Reserve $^1/_4$ cup of the marinade.

03 Pour half of the remaining marinade into a storage container. Add the diced tempeh. Pour the rest of the marinade on top. Cover, then shake gently to coat the tempeh evenly. Set aside for 15 minutes (or refrigerate overnight).

04 While the tempeh is marinating, prepare the curried pumpkin: Heat the oil in a large, heavy saucepan. Cook the onion and green pepper over medium heat, stirring frequently, until softened, 4 to 5 minutes. Stir in the tomatoes, $^1/_2$ cup tomato juice, 3 tablespoons of the reserved tempeh marinade, and the smaller amounts of curry, cinnamon, cloves, and salt. Stir in the pumpkin. Cover and simmer, stirring occasionally, until the pumpkin is tender, 20 to 25 minutes. During this time, adjust the seasoning by adding more marinade and spices if you wish. Add more tomato juice or water if the sauce becomes too thick.

05 While the pumpkin is cooking, preheat the oven to 425°F. Brush a large nonstick baking sheet or roasting pan with oil (if not nonstick,

CONTINUED

SERVES **6**

JERK-SPICED TEMPEH

8 OUNCES TEMPEH (SOY OR THREE-GRAIN)

3 TABLESPOONS JAPANESE SOY SAUCE (SHOYU OR TAMARI)

2 TABLESPOONS VEGETABLE OIL, PLUS OIL FOR PREPARING THE PAN

$^1/_4$ CUP DARK BROWN SUGAR

2 LARGE CLOVES GARLIC, PEELED AND QUARTERED

1 TEASPOON GROUND GINGER

$^3/_4$ TO 1 TEASPOON DRIED THYME LEAVES

$^1/_2$ TEASPOON GROUND ALLSPICE

$^1/_4$ TEASPOON FRESHLY GROUND BLACK PEPPER

$^1/_4$ TEASPOON SALT

1 MEDIUM VIDALIA, WALLA WALLA, OR OTHER SWEET ONION (ABOUT 6 OUNCES), PEELED AND CUT INTO EIGHTHS

PICKAPEPPA, TABASCO, OR OTHER HOT SAUCE

WEST INDIAN PUMPKIN

1 TABLESPOON VEGETABLE OIL

1 CUP CHOPPED ONION

1 LARGE GREEN BELL PEPPER, SEEDED AND DICED

**ONE 15-OUNCE CAN DICED TOMATOES
(WITH LIQUID)**

**¹/₂ TO 1 CUP UNSEASONED TOMATO
JUICE OR WATER**

**3 TO 4 TABLESPOONS MARINADE
(RESERVED FROM JERK-SPICED
TEMPEH)**

1 TO 2 TEASPOONS CURRY POWDER

¹/₄ TEASPOON GROUND CINNAMON

¹/₈ TO ¹/₄ TEASPOON GROUND CLOVES

¹/₂ TEASPOON SALT

**2 ¹/₂ POUNDS CARIBBEAN PUMPKIN
(CALABAZA) OR BUTTERNUT
SQUASH, PEELED AND CUT INTO
³/₄-INCH CUBES**

line with oiled foil). Spread the marinated tempeh in the pan in one layer. (It's okay if some of the unabsorbed marinade ends up in the pan.) Bake until the color deepens and the top of each piece feels fairly dry and is no longer sticky to the touch, 10 to 12 minutes. (Do not cook the tempeh longer than 12 minutes, as it will dry out.)

06 To serve, spoon the curried pumpkin onto dinner plates and set the jerk-spiced tempeh on top.

OTHER IDEAS

Instead of using hot sauce, flavor the tempeh marinade with ¹/₄ to 1 teaspoon chipotle in adobo, a condiment made of smoked jalapeños in a seasoned tomato sauce (available in Hispanic groceries and gourmet shops).

WEST INDIAN "ROTI" WRAPS

Place chunks of pumpkin and tempeh just below the center of a large flour tortilla. Fold the bottom of the tortilla over the filling. Fold over the sides and then the top to create a packet. Reheat in the microwave if necessary. It's best to serve these on plates with knives and forks, as they're messy to eat.

WEST INDIAN "PIZZA"

Place a warm flour tortilla on each plate and spoon the pumpkin and tempeh on top.

This nourishing winter casserole takes only a few minutes to assemble but a few hours to bake. The recipe is based on the principle of slow-cooking unsoaked beans for a few hours in a 250°F oven (see page 18). The beans develop a creamy texture, and the mountain of escarole melts into the olive-infused broth, creating a voluptuous environment. For optimum flavor, try to locate cannellini, which are available in Italian markets and gourmet shops; they have better flavor and texture than Great Northern beans.

To give this mellow dish a bright finish, dot the top with a sprinkling of vibrant gremolata, the classic Italian condiment made of finely chopped parsley, lemon peel, and garlic.

While the casserole is in the oven, consider making Slow-Roasted Tomatoes and Fennel (page 80) on the rack below. Serve them on the side.

SLOW-BAKED **CANNELLINI** WITH **OLIVES, ESCAROLE,** AND **GREMOLATA**

SERVES **4**

2 TABLESPOONS OLIVE OIL

8 OUNCES CREMINI OR BUTTON MUSHROOMS, TRIMMED AND SLICED

$1/2$ TEASPOON SALT

2 CUPS THINLY SLICED LEEKS

2 LARGE CLOVES GARLIC, THINLY SLICED

1 $1/2$ TEASPOONS DRIED ROSEMARY (CRUMBLED INTO BITS) OR ITALIAN HERB BLEND (PAGE 14)

4 CUPS VEGETABLE BROTH (USE HALF WATER IF BROTH IS SALTED)

$1/2$ CUP OIL-CURED BLACK OLIVES (PITTING OPTIONAL)

1 $1/2$ TO 2 POUNDS ESCAROLE, COARSELY CHOPPED

1 CUP DRIED CANNELLINI OR GREAT NORTHERN BEANS, PICKED OVER AND RINSED

FRESHLY GROUND PEPPER

BALSAMIC SYRUP (PAGE 16) OR GOOD-QUALITY BALSAMIC VINEGAR TO TASTE

GREMOLATA

1 MEDIUM LEMON

1 CUP TIGHTLY PACKED PARSLEY LEAVES

1 CLOVE GARLIC (SMALL OR LARGE, DEPENDING ON HOW MUCH YOU LOVE IT), THINLY SLICED

01 Set the rack in the middle of the oven. (If slow-roasting fennel and tomatoes, set the second rack a few inches below.) Preheat the oven to 250°F.

02 Heat the oil in a heavy, 6-quart stove-to-oven casserole or Dutch oven. Cook the mushrooms over medium-high heat, stirring frequently, for 1 minute. Sprinkle with the salt (this will force the mushrooms to give up some liquid), and continue cooking and stirring until the mushrooms are browned and tender, 3 to 4 minutes longer.

03 Toss in the leeks, garlic, and rosemary, and cook over medium-high heat, stirring frequently, until the leeks have wilted, about 3 minutes. Add the broth and olives and bring to a boil. Add half of the escarole, cover, and cook until it wilts, about 1 minute. Stir well. Add the remaining escarole and repeat.

04 Turn off the heat. Push the vegetables aside and add the beans, taking care that they are buried under the escarole and covered with liquid. Cover, transfer the casserole to the oven, and bake until the beans are tender, $1/2$ to 3 hours. Toward the end of cooking,

CONTINUED

add salt if needed and pepper to taste. (The stew may seem soupy at first, but will quickly thicken as it stands.)

05 Just before serving, prepare the gremolata: Use a standard swivel vegetable peeler with very gentle pressure to remove the lemon zest (the yellow part only) in strips. (I find this works best when I move the peeler back and forth as I'm moving it down.) Place the strips on a chopping board with the parsley and garlic and finely chop them together. Cut 4 thin slices of the lemon to use as garnish.

06 To serve, stir in enough Balsamic Syrup to sharpen the flavors. Ladle the stew into large, shallow soup bowls. (Pasta bowls work well.) Float the lemon slices in the middle, and sprinkle a generous amount of gremolata on top.

OTHER IDEAS

Add finely chopped fennel stalks when you add the beans. Include chopped fennel fronds in the gremolata.

Substitute large lima beans for the cannellini. They will expand to the size of small potatoes.

Here's my favorite way to prepare roasted portobello caps: Brush them with a mixture of olive oil, soy sauce, and balsamic vinegar and pop them into the oven. Although you won't taste the soy sauce, it turns the caps a deep burnished brown and enhances the mushrooms' flavor.

Serve the portobellos whole, or cut each on a sharp angle and fan out the slices. I particularly like to lean the mushrooms against mounds of Carrot, Bean, and Caramelized Shallot Purée (page 87) for a satisfying vegan version of steak and potatoes.

PORTOBELLO "STEAKS"

SERVES **4**

2 TABLESPOONS OLIVE OIL, PLUS OIL FOR PREPARING THE PAN

4 LARGE PORTOBELLO MUSHROOM CAPS (5 TO 6 INCHES IN DIAMETER)

1 TABLESPOON JAPANESE SOY SAUCE (SHOYU OR TAMARI)

2 TEASPOONS BALSAMIC VINEGAR

SALT AND FRESHLY GROUND PEPPER

01 Place the rack in the center of the oven and preheat to 450°F. Oil one or two shallow roasting pans large enough to hold the caps in one layer.

02 Lightly wipe the portobello caps with a damp kitchen towel. Remove any stems that prevent the caps from sitting flat in the pan. With the gill sides down, tap the mushrooms gently on the kitchen counter to dislodge any dirt caught in the crevices. Arrange on the roasting pan with gill sides down.

03 In a small bowl, use a fork to combine and emulsify the oil, soy sauce, and vinegar. Liberally brush the mixture onto the tops and sides of the caps. Season with salt and pepper.

04 Roast until the color of the tops and edges deepens, 5 to 6 minutes. Flip over. Give the oil mixture a good stir, and then brush the bottoms. Roast until cooked through and tender (they will look slightly collapsed and yield to the touch), 3 to 5 minutes more. Serve immediately, whole or sliced.

OTHER IDEAS

Sprinkle the portobellos with fresh or dried thyme when seasoning with salt and pepper.

Make roasted portobello sandwiches on split focaccia smeared with Creamy Herb Dressing (page 95) or Parsley Aioli (page 45).

Using collards as wrappers for a savory grain filling provides a welcome opportunity to appreciate their forest green color and artistic veining. When set on a pool of Roasted Red Pepper Sauce, the verdant rolls are fresh and inviting. If your prior encounters with collards have been limited to olive drab puddles drowning in the stewpot, this recipe will introduce you to a new and elegant aspect of this fine vegetable.

Collard bunches inevitably come with leaves of varying sizes. Rather than fight nature, just stuff and roll whatever comes your way until you run out of either leaves or filling. To divide the labor-intensive aspect of this dish, have cooked grains on hand (page 20), and make the Roasted Red Pepper Sauce in advance.

STUFFED **COLLARD** ROLLS WITH ROASTED **RED PEPPER** SAUCE

01 Prepare the Roasted Red Pepper Sauce, and set aside.

02 Cut off the collard stems, and trim any leaves that measure longer than 10 inches from top to stem end. Thinly slice 1 cup of the stems and set aside. (Save the remaining stems for another use.)

03 Select a pot wide and deep enough to contain the collard leaves without bending them too much. Fill it about halfway with water. Add ¹/₂ teaspoon of the salt. Bring to a boil.

04 Press the collard leaves into the boiling water. (If necessary, cook in two batches.) Cover and boil until just tender, 5 to 10 minutes. (To test for doneness, use scissors to snip off a small piece of leaf near the stem end; err on the side of undercooking, as the leaves tear more easily if overcooked.)

05 Drain the collard leaves in a colander set over a bowl, reserving the cooking broth. Set the collards under cold running water, gently turning them once or twice, until they are thoroughly cooled. Set aside to drain.

06 Heat the oil in the same pot. Add the leeks and cook over medium-high heat, stirring often, until they wilt, about 3 minutes. Meanwhile crush the fennel seeds using a mortar and pestle, or coarsely chop them with a chef's knife. Add the fennel seeds, celery, carrot,

ROASTED RED PEPPER SAUCE (RECIPE FOLLOWS)

1 ¹/₂ TO 2 POUNDS COLLARD GREENS (HAVE AT LEAST 25 LEAVES)

1 TEASPOON SALT, PLUS MORE IF NEEDED

1 TABLESPOON VEGETABLE OIL

2 CUPS FINELY CHOPPED LEEKS

2 TEASPOONS FENNEL SEEDS

³/₄ CUP FINELY DICED CELERY

³/₄ CUP FINELY DICED CARROT

FRESHLY GROUND BLACK PEPPER

3 CUPS COOKED PEARL BARLEY

2 CUPS COOKED SHORT-GRAIN BROWN RICE OR ADDITIONAL BARLEY

²/₃ CUP HAZELNUTS, TOASTED AND COARSELY CHOPPED

¹/₂ TABLESPOON HAZELNUT OIL, PLUS MORE IF NEEDED

¹/₃ CUP LOOSELY PACKED CHOPPED FRESH DILL

2 TO 3 TABLESPOONS FRESHLY SQUEEZED LEMON JUICE

CONTINUED

reserved collard stems, $1/2$ cup reserved collard broth, the remaining $1/2$ teaspoon salt, and pepper to taste. Cover and cook over medium-high heat until the vegetables are tender but still firm, 8 to 10 minutes. Add more collard broth if the mixture becomes dry.

07 Using a blender or food processor, blend $1/2$ cup of collard broth with 1 cup of barley to create a coarse purée. Add the purée, remaining grains, hazelnuts, hazelnut oil, and dill to the leek mixture. Season to taste with salt and pepper and additional hazelnut oil, if needed. Stir in enough lemon juice to give a distinct lemony edge.

08 To assemble the rolls: Set a collard leaf on a flat surface with the smoother side up and the mid-rib running from left to right (i.e., horizontally). Patch any tears with pieces of another leaf.

09 Mound $1/4$ to $3/4$ cup of the stuffing (depending upon the size of the leaf) just below and along the full length of the mid-rib. Flip the leaf edge closest to you over the filling and roll the leaf up so that the mid-rib runs along its length. (You may also fold in the sides of the leaf to create a packet, as shown on page 66.) Set the roll seam-side down on a microwavable or ovenproof platter. Continue to assemble rolls until you have used up all of the filling or leaves.

10 Just before serving, reheat the rolls in a microwave or in the oven, loosely covered with foil. To serve, ladle Roasted Red Pepper Sauce onto dinner plates, and arrange the rolls on top.

OTHER IDEAS

COLLARD "SPAGHETTI"

Stack any extra cooked collard greens in a pile and roll them tightly into a cigar. Slice thin. Brown slivered garlic in olive oil, add the sliced collards, and cook, tossing frequently, until heated.

Use leftover collard broth as a base for soup. It also makes a soothing hot drink, perhaps seasoned with a drop of soy sauce.

ROASTED **RED PEPPER** SAUCE

01 In a blender or food processor, purée the peppers with the oil, ³/₄ cup of the beans, and the salt.

02 Transfer the purée to a saucepan and stir in the remaining beans. Add more salt if needed and enough Balsamic Syrup to enhance the taste.

03 If the sauce is thin or lacks a finished flavor, bring it to a boil and simmer, stirring frequently, until it has a good consistency and the flavors are integrated. Set aside until needed; reheat when ready to serve.

MAKES ABOUT 3 ¹/₂ CUPS

3 LARGE RED BELL PEPPERS (ABOUT 1 ³/₄ POUNDS), ROASTED (PAGE 13) AND CUT INTO CHUNKS

2 TABLESPOONS OLIVE OIL

1 ³/₄ CUPS COOKED NAVY BEANS OR ONE 15-OUNCE CAN, DRAINED

¹/₂ TEASPOON SALT, PLUS MORE IF NEEDED

¹/₂ TO 1 TEASPOON BALSAMIC SYRUP (PAGE 16) OR BALSAMIC VINEGAR

THE BASICS

3 CUPS COOKED GRAINS (AT ROOM TEMPERATURE)

1 CUP COOKED BEANS

FOR CRUNCH

1 CUP DICED CARROT, CELERY, BELL PEPPER, SEEDED CUCUMBER, OR FENNEL

1/4 TO 1/2 CUP TOASTED NUTS (CHOPPING OPTIONAL)

1/4 CUP TOASTED SUNFLOWER OR PUMPKIN SEEDS

1 TO 2 TABLESPOONS FLAX SEEDS OR TOASTED SESAME SEEDS

FOR AN HERBAL ACCENT

1/4 TO 1/2 CUP FINELY CHOPPED FRESH PARSLEY, DILL, BASIL, CILANTRO, OR MINT

FOR A POP OF INTENSE FLAVOR

2 TABLESPOONS DRAINED CAPERS

1/4 CUP CHOPPED PITTED OLIVES, PICKLES, OR SUN-DRIED TOMATOES (OIL-PACKED)

1/2 CUP THINLY SLICED SCALLION GREENS OR DICED RED ONION

1/2 CUP CHOPPED MARINATED ARTICHOKE HEARTS

1 TO 2 TABLESPOONS CHOPPED, SEEDED JALAPEÑOS

I always turn to this mix-and-match recipe when I need to create an attractive and hearty grain and bean salad from ingredients on hand. If you store cooked grains in the freezer (see page 22) and have a can of beans in the pantry, this salad makes a dandy impromptu lunch or dinner, perhaps accompanied by a green salad.

I usually start my creative plan with whatever fresh herb is available. If it's basil or parsley, for example, I'll make a Mediterranean-inspired salad using brown rice or wheat berries, chickpeas, celery, roasted red pepper, capers, and scallions with a dressing based on olive oil and lemon juice. If I'm starting with cilantro, I'll go the Southwest or Latin route, using quinoa, black beans, toasted pumpkin seeds, pimento-stuffed olives, corn, and red onion, with lime juice in the dressing. Or I'll make an Asian salad with black soybeans, brown rice, red bell pepper, snow peas, scallion greens, toasted sesame seeds, and a dressing of toasted sesame oil, lemon juice, and soy sauce.

Quantities suggested below are approximate and intended as rough guidelines. The idea is to have fun and taste as you go until you arrive at a combination that pleases you. For a pretty salad with varied tastes and textures, plan to toss the grains and beans with at least one ingredient from the categories labeled Crunch, Herbal Accent, and Pop of Intense Flavor. (Leftovers will need perking up with extra acid.)

AS-YOU-PLEASE **GRAIN** AND **BEAN** SALAD

01 Toss the grains, beans, and your choice of additional salad ingredients together in a large bowl or storage container.

02 Thoroughly blend your choice of oil, acid, and seasonings in a small jar or bowl.

03 Toss the dressing into the salad. Add more acid or salt, if needed, to create a good balance of flavors. (I like my salads to have an assertive acid component.) Serve at room temperature.

OTHER IDEAS

The oil drained from marinated sun-dried tomatoes is very tasty.

Serve the salad on a bed of greens or shredded cabbage. Red cabbage is especially striking.

Accompany with slices of avocado or tomato seasoned with salt.

If you've used dense whole grains such as wheat berries or kamut, toss in some shredded Romaine to lighten the mixture.

FOR COLOR CONTRAST AND VARIETY (OPTIONAL)

2 TO 4 TABLESPOONS RAISINS, DRIED CURRANTS, OR DRIED CRANBERRIES

$1/2$ CUP DICED ROASTED RED PEPPER

1 CUP COOKED CORN OR GREEN PEAS

1 CUP BLANCHED SNOW PEAS, CUT ON THE DIAGONAL

1 CUP CHERRY TOMATOES, HALVED OR QUARTERED

SIMPLE VINAIGRETTE DRESSING

OIL:

2 TABLESPOONS OLIVE OIL, OR 1 TABLESPOON NUT OIL PLUS 1 TABLESPOON NEUTRAL OIL SUCH AS CORN OR PEANUT, OR 1 TABLESPOON TOASTED SESAME OIL

ACID:

2 TO 4 TABLESPOONS FRESHLY SQUEEZED LEMON OR LIME JUICE, OR 1 TO 2 TABLESPOONS WINE VINEGAR

SEASONINGS TO TASTE:

SALT OR JAPANESE SOY SAUCE (SHOYU OR TAMARI)

FRESHLY GROUND PEPPER

DIJON MUSTARD

The spices of the Moroccan kitchen tantalize me time and again. After years of experimenting, I've discovered that they happily marry the ingredients of far-off shores.

A case in point is this brightly colored vegetable stew featuring the sweet, dense, orange-fleshed Japanese pumpkin known as kabocha. Kabocha is a roundish, striped, green-orange squash whose appearance closely resembles a buttercup squash (which can be used as a substitute). Kabochas are almost always available in health-food stores that carry organic produce. Look for one that feels firm and heavy for its size, and chances are you'll be in for a real treat. Kabocha's rind becomes as tender as its flesh, making peeling unnecessary. What more could you ask of a squash?

This stew makes fine company fare. The fragrance of far-away places will welcome guests to your home, and the bright splashes of squash orange and spinach green will bring good cheer. The dish is substantial enough to serve on its own, but couscous makes a natural companion. It's fun to press individual portions of couscous into ramekins or flat-bottomed coffee cups and unmold them on one end of the plate.

KABOCHA **SQUASH** AND **SPINACH** WITH MOROCCAN SPICES

½ TEASPOON SAFFRON THREADS

1 TABLESPOON WATER

1 ½ TABLESPOONS CORIANDER SEEDS

1 ½ TEASPOONS CUMIN SEEDS

¼ TEASPOON GROUND CINNAMON

PINCH OF CAYENNE (DEPENDING UPON DESIRED HEAT)

2 TABLESPOONS OLIVE OIL

1 LARGE RED ONION (ABOUT 8 OUNCES), THINLY SLICED INTO RINGS

1 LARGE YELLOW ONION (ABOUT 8 OUNCES), THINLY SLICED INTO RINGS

1 ½ TABLESPOONS PEELED, MINCED FRESH GINGER

2 ½ CUPS CHICKPEA COOKING-LIQUID (IF IT TASTES GOOD), VEGETABLE BROTH, OR WATER, PLUS MORE IF NEEDED

1 TEASPOON SALT

FRESHLY GROUND PEPPER

10 DRIED APRICOTS (CUT SOME IN QUARTERS AND OTHERS IN HALF)

1 ½ CUPS COOKED CHICKPEAS OR ONE 15-OUNCE CAN, DRAINED

2 POUNDS KABOCHA SQUASH, TRIMMED, SEEDED, AND CUT INTO 1-INCH CHUNKS (OR SUBSTITUTE PEELED BUTTERNUT, BUTTERCUP, OR OTHER WINTER SQUASH)

01 Crumble the saffron into a small bowl and pour the water on top. Set aside.

02 Place the coriander and cumin seeds in a small, heavy skillet and set over high heat. Toast, stirring frequently, until the spices emit a fragrance, pop, or begin to darken, 1 to 2 minutes. (Take care not to burn them.) Immediately transfer the seeds to a coffee grinder reserved for this purpose (or use a mortar and pestle). Cool for a minute or two, then grind into a fairly fine powder. Blend in the cinnamon and cayenne. Set aside.

03 In a heavy 5-quart pot, heat the oil. Stir in the red and yellow onion rings and cook over medium-high heat, stirring frequently, until they begin to brown, 4 to 5 minutes. Stir in the ginger and reserved ground spices and cook for 20 seconds. Add the chickpea cooking-liquid, reserved saffron and its soaking water, salt, and a few twists of pepper. Bring to a boil.

04 Stir in the apricots, chickpeas, and squash. Cover and cook over medium heat, stirring occasionally, until the squash is tender but

CONTINUED

10 OUNCES SPINACH, TRIMMED OF THICK STEMS AND TORN INTO BITS

1 TEASPOON GRATED LEMON ZEST

1 TO 2 TABLESPOONS FRESHLY SQUEEZED LEMON JUICE

1/3 CUP SLIVERED TOASTED ALMONDS, FOR GARNISH (OPTIONAL)

still firm, 20 to 35 minutes. (Peeled butternut or buttercup will probably take less time than unpeeled kabocha.) Stir in a bit of broth or water during this time if the mixture becomes dry.

05 Stir in the spinach and lemon zest. Cover and cook just until the spinach is tender, a minute or two. Adjust the seasonings. Just before serving, stir in enough lemon juice to balance the sweetness.

06 The stew will thicken as it stands, but if you wish to thicken the sauce immediately, mash a few pieces of squash against the sides of the pot with a fork, and stir well to blend. Garnish individual portions with slivered almonds, if you wish.

OTHER IDEAS

Substitute pitted prunes for the apricots.

Omit the spinach and cook the squash with 1 pound of Swiss chard, stems thinly sliced and leaves coarsely chopped. Ruby chard is especially pretty.

These flaky phyllo packets get rave reviews, the requisite payoff for a labor-intensive dish. For the unusual filling, cooked kale is combined with allspice-scented leeks, toasted pine nuts, and chewy grains. I also include brewer's yeast (page 14), which lends a savory note to both the filling and the phyllo crust. With a colorful tossed salad, the triangles make a substantial entrée.

Shaping phyllo triangles is much like folding the flag. If using frozen phyllo (available in 1-pound packages at most supermarkets), defrost it according to package directions. You probably won't need the full pound, but it's good to have extra on hand in case of tears. Just lay torn pieces beside each other, as if you were working a jigsaw puzzle. The triangles will still look and taste fine.

Any leftover phyllo can be sandwiched in plastic wrap, loosely rolled up, and then put in a zipper-topped plastic bag. Refrigerate or refreeze. Or consider making the Rustic Apple Tart (page 104), which requires only four sheets of phyllo.

PHYLLO TRIANGLES FILLED WITH **KALE, PINE NUTS,** AND **CURRANTS**

MAKES **8 TRIANGLES**

1/4 CUP DRIED CURRANTS

2 TABLESPOONS BOILING WATER

1 TABLESPOON DRY SHERRY

1 TEASPOON SALT, PLUS MORE TO TASTE

1 POUND KALE

7 TABLESPOONS OLIVE OIL, DIVIDED

1 CUP CHOPPED LEEKS OR ONION

1/2 TEASPOON GROUND ALLSPICE

1 1/2 CUPS COOKED CHEWY GRAINS, SUCH AS WHEAT BERRIES OR SHORT-GRAIN BROWN RICE

1/3 CUP (ABOUT 2 OUNCES) PINE NUTS, TOASTED

2 TABLESPOONS FRESHLY SQUEEZED LEMON JUICE

6 TABLESPOONS LEWIS LABORATORIES BREWER'S YEAST, DIVIDED

FRESHLY GROUND PEPPER

1 POUND PHYLLO (ALSO SPELLED FILO)

01 Place the currants in a small bowl and add the boiling water and sherry. Cover and set aside.

02 Fill a 6-quart pot about three-fourths full of water and add the salt. Bring to a boil. Holding the kale in a bunch, trim off and discard about an inch at the bottom of the stems. Thinly slice the remaining stems and leaves.

03 Add the kale to the boiling water in several batches, submerging each batch under the water with a large, long-handled spoon. Cover and cook over high heat until the kale is tender, 5 to 8 minutes. Pour the kale into a colander to drain, reserving the cooking liquid if you wish. Set the kale under cold running water to stop the cooking process. Set aside to continue draining.

04 In a nonstick skillet, heat 1 tablespoon of the oil. Stir in the leeks, allspice, and a generous pinch of salt. Cover and cook over medium-low heat until the leeks are tender, about 10 minutes. Add the currants and any unabsorbed soaking liquid and cook uncovered over high heat, stirring constantly, until all of the liquid has evaporated, another minute or two. Set aside.

CONTINUED

05 Squeeze small amounts of the cooked kale between your palms to extract as much liquid as possible. Place the squeezed kale in the bowl of a food processor as you go. Process the kale until finely chopped. Transfer the kale to a bowl and stir in the reserved leeks, grains, pine nuts, lemon juice, and 2 tablespoons of the brewer's yeast. Season well with salt and pepper. (You can refrigerate the filling until needed, but bring it back to room temperature before assembling the packets.)

06 Place 2 racks in the lower half of the oven, and preheat the oven to 425°F. Line 2 baking sheets with parchment paper and set aside. Wet a lightweight kitchen towel and thoroughly wring out the excess water. Place the remaining 6 tablespoons of olive oil and remaining brewer's yeast in separate small bowls, and have them nearby.

07 To assemble the triangles: Unwrap the phyllo and unroll it onto a clean flat surface. Immediately cover the pile of phyllo completely with the damp kitchen towel to prevent it from drying out and becoming brittle.

08 Gently peel off 1 sheet of phyllo and set it on a flat surface. Replace the damp towel over the remaining phyllo. Working rapidly, use a pastry brush to lightly coat the phyllo with olive oil. Sprinkle with a scant teaspoon of brewer's yeast. Lay a second sheet on top and brush with more oil and sprinkle with yeast. Fold the 2 sheets in half lengthwise to create a rectangle.

09 Have the longer side of the rectangle running horizontally. Set ¹/₂ cup of filling about an inch from the left edge. Fold the bottom left corner of the phyllo up over the filling to encase the filling in a triangular shape. Press the edges of the triangle to seal the filling inside. Brush the top surface with oil and sprinkle with brewer's yeast.

10 Gently lift the triangle and fold it over to the right to maintain the triangular shape. Continue folding, brushing, and sprinkling until you reach the end, usually 4 folds in all. Trim off any excess phyllo and brush the top with oil. Continue with the remaining phyllo and filling, placing triangles in a single layer on the parchment paper as you go.

11 Bake until the edges are crisp and golden brown, 8 to 10 minutes. If you'd like the tops browner, set the triangles about 4 inches from the broiling element for a minute or two. Watch very carefully, as the phyllo burns easily. Serve hot.

OLIVE OIL FOR PREPARING PANS AND DRIZZLING OVER FENNEL

2 POUNDS PLUM TOMATOES, QUARTERED LENGTHWISE

SALT

2 MEDIUM FENNEL BULBS OR 1 LARGE BULB (ABOUT 1 ½ POUNDS WEIGHED WITH STALKS)

1 TO 2 TABLESPOONS EXTRA-VIRGIN OLIVE OIL

1 TO 2 TEASPOONS BALSAMIC SYRUP (PAGE 16), FOR GARNISH (OPTIONAL)

To prepare this simple side-dish salad, you roast plum tomatoes and fennel in a 250°F oven, and then arrange them attractively on small plates. Season them simply, with just a drizzle of salt and your best extra-virgin olive oil.

The dish requires only a few minutes of preparation but two to three hours of cooking. I developed it specifically to be made with and served alongside the Slow-Baked Cannellini with Olives, Escarole, and Gremolata (page 63).

Two pounds of plum tomatoes yields about 2 cups roasted, enough to serve 4 to 6 as part of this side dish. Why not double the amount to have some on hand for garnishes (great on sandwiches) or to serve with the Hiziki Tapenade (page 28)? Refrigerated in a well-sealed container, they last about 10 days.

SLOW-ROASTED **TOMATOES** AND **FENNEL**

01 Preheat the oven to 250°F. Select one or two baking sheets large enough to arrange the tomatoes in one layer and brush with oil. Arrange the tomatoes on the sheets cut side up and sprinkle them lightly with salt. Set aside.

02 Select a heavy roasting pan or large gratin dish for the fennel (it does not have to fit in a single layer), and brush the bottom with oil. Remove any fennel fronds and set aside for garnish. Cut the top stalks from the fennel and reserve for stock. Trim the base, and quarter each bulb, top to base. Discard any tough or bruised outer layers. Slice the quartered bulbs ¼ inch thick, leaving the core as intact as possible to hold the layers together. (This won't be possible with all of the slices.) Set in the roasting pan, seasoning lightly with salt and drizzling with olive oil as you go. Cover the pan tightly with foil.

03 Bake the tomatoes until collapsed and shriveled, 2 to 2 ½ hours. (For the first hour or so, it will look like nothing is happening.) At the same time, bake the fennel until tender and easily pierced with the tip of a paring knife, 1½ to 2 hours. (Once the fennel is tender, you can roast it uncovered to brown it and achieve a more intense flavor.)

04 To serve, arrange the fennel and tomatoes decoratively on small plates and drizzle with extra-virgin olive oil. Finely chop the reserved fennel fronds and use them as a garnish. If you wish, dot a few drops of Balsamic Syrup decoratively around the plate.

The next time you spot a large cauliflower and a healthy bunch of fresh basil, try this festive dish. Steam the cauliflower whole and drape it decoratively with basil pesto and a crown of sun-dried tomato pesto. Cut the wedges as you would a cake so everyone gets a taste of both sauces.

The pestos will adhere to the cauliflower only if it has cooled down completely, so plan to serve this dish at room temperature. It's important to spin-dry the basil leaves thoroughly to avoid having a pesto that is too watery to give the cauliflower a nice, thick coating.

RED, WHITE, AND GREEN CAULIFLOWER

01 Slice off the base and large leaves of the cauliflower. Use a paring knife to cut away the smaller leaves and expose the base of the florets. Even off the bottom so that the cauliflower will sit upright.

02 Pour an inch of water into a pot tall enough to hold the cauliflower upright. Bring the water to a boil. Set the cauliflower in the water, cover, and steam over high heat until you can easily slip a paring knife 2 inches deep into the florets, 8 to 10 minutes. (The cauliflower should be tender but still firm.)

03 Transfer the cauliflower to a colander and run cold water over it to hasten cooling. Set aside to cool further, or refrigerate overnight.

04 To make the pestos, pop the garlic through the feed tube of a food processor with the motor running. Add the walnuts, oil, lemon juice, salt, and brewer's yeast (if using). Process to create a coarse paste.

05 Transfer 3 tablespoons of this paste to a small bowl and set aside. Add the basil leaves to the processor bowl and process to make the basil pesto, adjusting seasonings and scraping the bowl as needed. Transfer to a small bowl. Scrape down the processor bowl thoroughly or wipe it clean. Blend the sun-dried tomatoes with the remaining 3 tablespoons of walnut paste.

06 Set the cauliflower on a serving platter. Blot it completely dry with a towel. Using a rubber spatula and your fingers (this will remind you of finger painting), spread a circle of sun-dried tomato pesto on the top of the cauliflower. Coat the remainder of the cauliflower with the basil pesto. To serve, halve the cauliflower, then cut into thick wedges.

SERVES **6 TO 8**

1 LARGE HEAD CAULIFLOWER (2 $\frac{1}{2}$ TO 3 POUNDS BEFORE TRIMMING)

2 LARGE CLOVES ROASTED GARLIC OR 1 SMALL CLOVE RAW GARLIC

1 CUP WALNUTS, LIGHTLY TOASTED

2 TABLESPOONS OLIVE OIL

2 TABLESPOONS FRESHLY SQUEEZED LEMON JUICE

1 TEASPOON SALT

1 TABLESPOON LEWIS LABORATORIES BREWER'S YEAST (PAGE 14; OPTIONAL BUT HIGHLY RECOMMENDED)

2 CUPS VERY TIGHTLY PACKED BASIL LEAVES, RINSED AND SPUN DRY

$\frac{1}{4}$ CUP SUN-DRIED TOMATOES (OIL-PACKED)

1 TO 2 TABLESPOONS VEGETABLE OIL (OLIVE, HERB-INFUSED, ROASTED PEANUT, TOASTED SESAME, CORN)

2 CUPS COARSELY CHOPPED YELLOW OR RED ONIONS, LEEKS, SHALLOTS, OR SCALLION BULBS

1/2 TO 1 CUP DICED CELERY (OPTIONAL)

1 TO 2 CLOVES GARLIC, MINCED (OPTIONAL)

1/4 TO 1 TEASPOON DRIED HERBS

1/2 TO 1 1/2 CUPS WATER OR VEGETABLE BROTH

3 CUPS COOKED GRAINS (ONE TYPE OR A MEDLEY; SEE PAGE 22)

SALT AND FRESHLY GROUND PEPPER

OPTIONAL ADD-ONS

FROZEN PEAS OR CORN

CHOPPED, COOKED VEGETABLES OR COOKED BEANS

SAUTÉED SLICED MUSHROOMS

DRIED CURRANTS, RAISINS, OR CRANBERRIES

1/4 TO 1/2 CUP CHOPPED FRESH HERBS

A FEW TABLESPOONS TOASTED NUTS

A DRIZZLE OF BALSAMIC SYRUP (PAGE 16) TO ENHANCE FLAVOR

SNIPPED FRESH CHIVES OR SCALLION GREENS, FOR GARNISH (OPTIONAL)

Use this recipe as a template for sprucing up leftover or frozen cooked grains (page 22). The main flavor provider is browned onions (or another member of the allium family), chopped coarsely so that they have a distinct presence in the finished dish.

Depending upon the seasonings and the number of add-ons you choose, you'll end up with either a side-dish grain that complements the rest of your meal or a medley substantial enough to serve as the entrée.

For example, if I were serving the grains to accompany an Italian meal, I'd use olive oil, scent the mixture with dried oregano, and add toasted, chopped hazelnuts. For a quick Southwestern supper, I'd sauté red onion with ground cumin and then add black beans, corn, toasted pumpkin seeds, and chopped fresh cilantro. For Asian grains, I'd cook the onions in 1 tablespoon of toasted sesame oil and use soy sauce instead of salt, adding cooked edamame (green soy beans) at the end.

If you are starting with frozen cooked grains, place them in a colander or strainer and pour boiling water over them to break up the blocks and partially defrost them before you proceed. For a pleasing presentation, press the savory grains into a ramekin and unmold one or two onto each plate.

SAVORY GRAINS

01 In a large, nonstick skillet, heat the oil. Add the onions, celery, and garlic (if using), and cook over medium heat, stirring frequently, until the onions are wilted and beginning to brown, 4 to 6 minutes. Crumble in the minimum amount of dried herbs and continue cooking until the onions are nicely browned, about 5 minutes more.

02 Stir in 1/2 cup of water and the grains. Season with salt, pepper, and additional herbs to taste. When the mixture starts to sizzle, turn down the heat, cover, and cook over low heat until the grains are moist and heated throughout, 2 to 3 minutes. Stir in more water during this time if the grains taste dry or begin sticking to the skillet.

03 At the last minute, stir in any frozen or cooked vegetables and beans, and continue cooking until heated throughout. Just before serving, stir in dried fruit, fresh herbs, or nuts (if using). Season with Balsamic Syrup and garnish with chives, if you wish.

Pommes Anna minus all the butter, cream, and fat? This potato cake is a tasty vegan alternative, made by baking thinly sliced Yukon Golds that have been pressed down firmly into a cake tin by the weight of a heavy, water-filled pot. The potatoes are seasoned with a savory, "cheesy" blend of brewer's yeast (page 14), salt, and pepper.

The cake is easy to assemble. Leave the potato peels intact for added flavor, and use the 1/8-inch slicing disk of the food processor to make quick work of the preparation. (Or slice the potatoes as thinly as you can by hand.) If you use a springform pan, you'll be able to unmold the potato cake before slicing it into wedges; otherwise, just serve the wedges from the pan.

POTATO CAKE

*SERVES **4 TO 6***

**OLIVE OIL FOR PREPARING THE PAN,
PLUS 1 TABLESPOON ADDITIONAL**

**1/4 CUP LEWIS LABORATORIES
BREWER'S YEAST**

1 1/4 TEASPOONS SALT

**1/4 TEASPOON FRESHLY GROUND
BLACK PEPPER**

**2 POUNDS YUKON GOLD POTATOES,
TRIMMED OF BLEMISHES (DRY
OFF AFTER RINSING)**

01 Place a rack in the lower third of the oven and preheat to 450°F. Liberally coat the bottom and sides of an 8- or 9-inch cake pan or springform pan with some of the oil. To weigh down the potato cake, locate a heavy pot or ovenproof casserole that will fit into the pan.

02 In a small bowl, combine the brewer's yeast, salt, and pepper. Set aside.

03 Using the thinnest slicing disk of your food processor, slice the potatoes. Arrange a fairly even layer of slices in the bottom of the pan. Sprinkle some of the brewer's yeast mixture on top. Repeat this process, creating a total of 6 or 7 layers and ending with a sprinkling of the brewer's yeast mixture on top. Drizzle on the remaining olive oil.

04 Lay 2 large sheets of aluminum foil on top of the pan. Set the heavy pot on top and firmly press it into the potatoes. Seal the cake pan well by pressing the overhanging foil tightly to the sides and under the bottom. If using a springform pan, set it on a foil-lined baking sheet to catch any drips.

05 Transfer to the oven and fill the pot halfway with water to make it heavier still. Bake until the center of the "cake" offers no resistance when pierced (right through the foil) with a paring knife, about 1 hour.

CONTINUED

06 Preheat the broiler. Remove the foil and set the "cake" about 5 inches beneath the broiler until the top is lightly browned and crisp, 2 to 5 minutes. Let cool for 5 minutes.

07 If you've used a springform pan, run a knife along the edges and remove the ring. Leave the "cake" on the base and transfer to a platter. If you've used a cake pan, cut the "cake" into wedges and serve directly from the pan. Serve hot.

OTHER IDEAS

Increase the ground pepper to a scant $\frac{1}{2}$ teaspoon for a distinctively peppery accent. Use a fine-quality black pepper, such as Malabar or Telicherry.

Rub the bottom and sides of the oiled baking pan with the cut side of a clove of garlic. Scatter a few whole peeled garlic cloves on top of the assembled "cake." (Minced and granulated garlic don't work well in this recipe.)

Cut 8 to 10 thin slices of red onion and break them into rings. Scatter the rings on top of the raw potato cake and drizzle with olive oil. Proceed to cover and bake as directed. Take care when browning under the broiler, as the onions burn easily.

Carrots give this comfort-food purée an attractive, pale, autumn orange color. Caramelized shallots add earthy depth and balance the carrots' sweetness, while white beans contribute their buttery smooth texture. If you have the impression that shallots are no more than "onions with an attitude," this recipe may change your mind. I like to serve this purée with Portobello "Steaks" (page 65).

CARROT, BEAN, AND CARAMELIZED SHALLOT PURÉE

SERVES **3 OR 4**

3 TABLESPOONS OLIVE OIL

1 $\frac{1}{2}$ CUPS CHOPPED SHALLOTS (8 OUNCES)

$\frac{1}{2}$ TEASPOON DRIED SAVORY LEAVES, PLUS MORE IF NEEDED

12 OUNCES CARROTS, PEELED AND CUT INTO $\frac{3}{4}$-INCH CHUNKS

1 $\frac{3}{4}$ CUPS COOKED WHITE BEANS, SUCH AS CANNELLINI OR NAVY, OR ONE 15-OUNCE CAN, DRAINED

1 CUP VEGETABLE BROTH

$\frac{1}{2}$ TEASPOON SALT

FRESHLY GROUND PEPPER TO TASTE

01 Heat the oil in a large, heavy skillet. Add the shallots and savory and cook over medium-low heat at a gentle sizzle, stirring occasionally, until the shallots turn golden brown, 20 to 25 minutes.

02 While the shallots are cooking, steam the carrots until very tender, 10 to 12 minutes. Leave the carrots in the covered pot and set aside off the heat.

03 When the shallots are golden brown, add the beans, broth, salt, and pepper. Bring to a boil. Add more savory, if you wish. Cover and simmer over medium heat until the beans taste lightly seasoned, about 10 minutes. If the mixture is soupy, boil it over high heat, stirring frequently, until most of the liquid evaporates and the mixture becomes thick and porridgelike.

04 Combine the steamed carrots and the bean-shallot mixture in a food processor or blender and purée. Adjust the seasonings. Reheat in the microwave if necessary.

OTHER IDEAS

Thin the purée with homemade vegetable broth and serve as a soup.

Substitute dried tarragon for the savory. Start with $\frac{1}{8}$ teaspoon, and add more if needed. Or add chopped fresh tarragon after cooking.

It goes without saying that beets are a gorgeous color. Baking them in individual foil packets develops a flavor intensity to match their brilliant hue and makes it easy to slip off their skins—an ingenious technique discovered by produce specialist Elizabeth Schneider.

Since diced red beets bleed like crazy, they dye the rice a striking hot pink. To avoid getting beet stains under your fingernails, wear rubber gloves when handling them. The light dressing of olive oil and lemon juice calls for just a hint of raspberry vinegar to enhance the beets' natural sweetness.

A few tips: Use your most delicate extra-virgin olive oil, one that will not distract from the beet flavor. (My favorite is the Ligurian Roi available by mail from Zingerman's.) Opt for short-grain brown rice, which has a chewier and more interesting texture than the long-grain variety.

You can turn this side salad into a light lunch entrée by serving it on a bed of Boston (butter) lettuce, with a few slices of avocado on the side.

BAKED **BEET** AND **BROWN RICE** SALAD

01 Preheat the oven to 375°F. Trim off any beet greens, leaving about a half-inch of stem intact. Rinse the beets. Wrap each beet individually in a tightly sealed aluminum foil packet. Set the beets on a foil-lined baking pan and bake until you can easily pierce them to the center with a cake tester or paring knife, 60 to 90 minutes. (You can pierce the beets right through the foil.)

02 When they are cool enough to handle, gently rub the foil of each still-sealed packet against the skin of each beet. Slip off the beet skins along with the foil. Trim off the tail and stems ends. Cut the beets into 1/4-inch dice and set them in a bowl or storage container. Add the rice and toss until the rice is "dyed" beet red.

03 In a small bowl, whisk together the oil, lemon juice, vinegar, and salt. Toss the dressing with the beets. Adjust the seasonings, adding more vinegar and/or salt, if needed, to intensify the flavors. Let the salad sit until the grains absorb some flavor, about 15 minutes. Stir in the scallion greens (if using) just before serving. Garnish with pine nuts. Serve at room temperature.

SERVES **3 OR 4**

1 POUND RED BEETS (3 MEDIUM)

2 1/2 CUPS COOKED SHORT-GRAIN BROWN RICE (PAGE 21)

2 TABLESPOONS EXTRA-VIRGIN OLIVE OIL

1 TABLESPOON FRESHLY SQUEEZED LEMON JUICE

1 TEASPOON RASPBERRY VINEGAR, PLUS MORE IF NEEDED

1/4 TEASPOON SALT, PLUS MORE IF NEEDED

2 TABLESPOONS THINLY SLICED SCALLION GREENS (OPTIONAL)

2 TABLESPOONS PINE NUTS, FOR GARNISH

MANGO CHUTNEY DRESSING

3 TABLESPOONS SWEET MANGO CHUTNEY

3 TABLESPOONS FRESHLY SQUEEZED LIME JUICE

2 TABLESPOONS PEANUT BUTTER

2 TO 3 TABLESPOONS WATER

1 TEASPOON SALT

CARROT SLAW

1 POUND CARROTS, PEELED AND SHREDDED (ABOUT 4 CUPS)

1/2 CUP CHOPPED CILANTRO

1/3 CUP THINLY SLICED SCALLION GREENS

ADDITIONAL LIME JUICE, IF NEEDED

ADDITIONAL SALT, IF NEEDED

1/4 CUP CHOPPED ROASTED, SALTED PEANUTS, FOR GARNISH (OPTIONAL)

Mango chutney gives the tart-sweet dressing for this slaw a mysterious complexity. Use your favorite chutney or try Patak's brand, which is widely available and very tasty.

Although I designed this salad to accompany either the Tomato-Chickpea Curry in Eggplant Shells (page 57) or the Skillet Grain Medley with Curried Tempeh (page 48), it is versatile enough to serve at a picnic or a potluck.

CARROT SLAW WITH **MANGO** CHUTNEY DRESSING

01 In a blender, purée the dressing ingredients, using 2 tablespoons of water, until very smooth. Blend in additional water if the dressing is too thick to coat the carrots.

02 In a large bowl, toss the carrots, cilantro, and scallions with the dressing. Add more lime juice and salt, if needed. Garnish with peanuts, if you wish.

12 OUNCES (1 ½ CUPS) SILKEN-SOFT TOFU

2 LARGE CUCUMBERS (ABOUT 12 OUNCES EACH), PEELED AND CUT INTO CHUNKS

4 TO 5 TABLESPOONS FRESHLY SQUEEZED LIME JUICE

1 TABLESPOON NEUTRAL OIL, SUCH AS CORN OR CANOLA

1 CUP TIGHTLY PACKED FRESH MINT LEAVES

½ CUP TIGHTLY PACKED CILANTRO LEAVES

½ TEASPOON DIJON MUSTARD, PLUS MORE IF NEEDED

1 ¾ TEASPOONS SALT, PLUS MORE IF NEEDED

Inspired by the yogurt-based raitas of India, I created this pale green, frothy sauce with soft tofu rather than the traditional yogurt. When my friends from Bombay gave it their thumbs up, I felt even more convinced about tofu's potential to please those who wish to include more soy in their diets or avoid dairy products.

I created this sauce to serve alongside the Skillet Grain Medley with Curried Tempeh (page 48), where it creates a refreshing counterpart to the dense texture of the grains. Prepare it at least a half hour in advance to give the flavors a chance to meld.

Be sure to use standard, watery cucumbers—not the burpless kind—and don't remove the seeds.

CUCUMBER-MINT "RAITA"

01 In a blender, purée the tofu, cucumbers, 4 tablespoons of the lime juice, oil, mint, cilantro, mustard, and salt. Adjust the seasonings to your taste by adding more mustard, lime juice, and salt.

02 Refrigerate the mixture for at least ½ hour before serving. It keeps well for up to 3 days.

OTHER IDEAS

Serve chilled as a refreshing hot-weather soup. Or thin slightly with water and serve as a drink.

Use as a salad dressing for greens or sliced tomatoes.

This zesty sauce has the texture of mayonnaise and is quite versatile. It makes a tasty topping for Crisp Tortilla Stacks with Roasted Corn and Black Beans (page 43), a good dressing for slaw, and a fine dip for corn chips. In fact, its taste and olive color are reminiscent of guacamole.

The creamy, rich base of the sauce is silken-soft tofu, but that can be the cook's secret, since the cilantro and garlic dominate, with the sun-dried tomatoes contributing an additional layer of flavor. One small clove of garlic creates the right balance for me, but serious garlic lovers will want more.

Although it lasts a few days, the sauce tastes best when freshly made.

SILKEN **CILANTRO** SAUCE

MAKES *1 ¾ CUPS*

1 ½ TABLESPOONS OLIVE OIL OR OIL FROM SUN-DRIED TOMATOES

1 SMALL SHALLOT, CHOPPED

1 OR 2 SMALL CLOVES GARLIC, CHOPPED

1 TO 1 ¼ TEASPOONS SALT

12 OUNCES (1 ½ CUPS) SILKEN-SOFT TOFU

2 CUPS TIGHTLY PACKED CILANTRO LEAVES AND TENDER STEMS (1 GOOD-SIZED BUNCH)

¼ CUP CHOPPED SUN-DRIED TOMA-TOES (OIL-PACKED)

1 TO 2 TABLESPOONS FRESHLY SQUEEZED LIME JUICE

01 Place the ingredients in a blender in the order listed, using the smaller amounts of salt and lime juice. Purée until very smooth, about 1 minute. Add more salt and lime juice, if needed, to give the sauce a good balance of flavors.

02 Use immediately or refrigerate in a tightly covered container up to 3 days. Stir well before each use. Thin with lime juice or water if the sauce becomes too thick.

¾ CUP (6 OUNCES) SILKEN-SOFT TOFU

2 TABLESPOONS JAPANESE SOY SAUCE (SHOYU OR TAMARI)

2 TABLESPOONS FRESHLY SQUEEZED LEMON JUICE

1 TABLESPOON TOASTED (ASIAN) SESAME OIL

1 CUP TIGHTLY PACKED, CHOPPED WATERCRESS STEMS (LEFT OVER FROM 1 AVERAGE BUNCH)

I usually whip up this dressing when I've made the Split-Pea Soup with Shiitake and Star Anise (page 36) and have watercress stems left over. The spiciness of the watercress is nicely balanced by the toasted sesame oil, and the tofu provides a creamy base. Lemon juice and soy sauce were made for each other—it just took Western cooks a few millennia to realize it.

This dressing is quite versatile and works well with all kinds of salads: green, bean, pasta, and grain. Think of it when you need a salad to accompany Asian-inspired dishes. Double the recipe if you're serving a crowd.

SESAME-WATERCRESS DRESSING

01 In a blender or food processor, purée the ingredients until smooth and creamy, about 1 minute. Adjust seasonings.

02 Refrigerate in a tightly sealed container for up to 3 days. Stir well before each use. Thin with water or additional lemon juice if the mixture becomes too thick.

OTHER IDEAS

Serve as a topping for baked potatoes or steamed vegetables.

After tossing a salad with this dressing, garnish with toasted black or beige sesame seeds.

In this versatile recipe, lemon juice and fresh herbs mask tofu's slight beany taste. Most people will be surprised to learn that tofu is providing creaminess without the cream. Make the dressing with whatever herb matches your meal or mood.

CREAMY **HERB** DRESSING

MAKES ABOUT ¾ CUP

½ CUP (4 OUNCES) SILKEN-SOFT TOFU

3 TABLESPOONS OLIVE OIL

2 TABLESPOONS WATER

1 TO 1 ½ TABLESPOONS FRESHLY SQUEEZED LEMON JUICE

½ CUP TIGHTLY PACKED FRESH HERBS, SUCH AS BASIL, DILL, PARSLEY, OR CILANTRO

½ TEASPOON SALT, PLUS MORE IF NEEDED

01 Purée the ingredients in a blender or food processor until very smooth, using 1 tablespoon lemon juice. Add more lemon juice and salt, if needed.

02 Use immediately or refrigerate in a tightly sealed container for up to 3 days. (The vibrant color will become olive drab, but the taste will not be affected.) Stir well before each use. Thin with lemon juice or water if the dressing becomes too thick.

1 1/3 CUPS SOYMILK (NOT THE LIGHT VARIETY), PLUS MORE IF NEEDED

1 1/2 TABLESPOONS FRESHLY SQUEEZED LEMON JUICE

1 1/4 CUPS WHOLE WHEAT PASTRY (NOT BREAD!) FLOUR, PLUS MORE IF NEEDED

1/2 CUP CORNMEAL

3/4 TEASPOON SALT

1/2 TEASPOON BAKING SODA

1/2 TEASPOON BAKING POWDER

1/2 TEASPOON GROUND CINNAMON

3 TABLESPOONS NEUTRAL OIL, SUCH AS CORN OR CANOLA, PLUS ADDITIONAL OIL OR PAN SPRAY FOR GREASING THE WAFFLE IRON

2 TABLESPOONS MAPLE SYRUP

Eating homemade waffles for breakfast or brunch always feels like a special treat, and they make a delightful midafternoon snack as well. Vegan waffles are surprisingly light and crisp. Adding cornmeal to the batter gives them extra crunch.

For carefree waffle making, use a nonstick waffle iron, and oil it lightly between batches. Waffles steam and get soggy if stacked on a plate and kept waiting. If you're not eating them right away, either keep them warm in a 200°F oven or cool them completely on a rack and refrigerate or freeze them until needed. (Waffles are good keepers.) Defrost and heat the waffles in a toaster or toaster oven.

Serve the waffles with maple syrup and your choice of fresh berries, sliced bananas, or Baked Peaches and Blueberries with Crisp Pecan Topping (page 101).

WHOLEGRAIN WAFFLES

01 In a 2-cup liquid measure, combine the soymilk and lemon juice. Set aside. (The mixture will curdle.)

02 Set a large strainer or sifter over a bowl. Measure in the flour, cornmeal, salt, baking soda, baking powder, and cinnamon. Stir or sift the dry ingredients into the bowl.

03 Stir the oil and maple syrup into the soymilk. Make a well in the center of the dry ingredients and add the liquid. Stir with a fork just until blended. The batter should be medium-thick but still pourable; if it's too runny, stir in a tablespoon or two more flour. Alternatively, if the batter becomes very thick as it stands, stir in a tablespoon or two of soymilk.

04 When the waffle iron is ready, brush the top and bottom with oil or mist with pan spray. Pour a generous 1/2 cup of batter over the surface. Bake according to manufacturer's directions until crisp, usually 5 to 6 minutes. Serve immediately or transfer to a cooling rack and keep warm in the oven while you are preparing the remaining waffles.

OTHER IDEAS

Add 2 tablespoons of shelled, unsalted sunflower seeds to the batter.

3 CUPS SOYMILK

3 TABLESPOONS MAPLE SYRUP, PLUS MORE IF NEEDED

1/2 TEASPOON VANILLA EXTRACT

1/2 TEASPOON GROUND GINGER

1/2 TEASPOON GROUND CINNAMON

PINCH FRESHLY GRATED NUTMEG

1/8 TEASPOON SALT

1/2 CUP QUICK-COOKING POLENTA (THE KIND THAT COOKS IN LESS THAN 5 MINUTES)

1/4 CUP RAISINS, DRIED CRAN-BERRIES, OR DRIED BLUEBERRIES

12 TOASTED WALNUT OR PECAN HALVES TOSSED IN 1 TABLESPOON MAPLE SYRUP, FOR GARNISH

It's 4 o'clock on a cold winter Saturday, and I just had a steaming bowl of sweet polenta. It's the kind of comfort food that quickly warms a person up.

Although polenta reheats fairly well in the microwave, I enjoy it most when freshly made and still piping hot. Others disagree and like it equally well at room temperature. Fortunately, thanks to instant (quick-cooking) polenta, you can whip up a fresh batch in about five minutes. Try it for breakfast as well as dessert.

SWEET POLENTA WITH MAPLE-GLAZED WALNUTS

01 Pour the soymilk into a heavy saucepan and set over medium-high heat. Whisk in the maple syrup, vanilla, spices, salt, polenta, and raisins.

02 Bring to a boil (but take care, because soymilk easily boils over). Reduce the heat and boil gently. Adjust maple syrup and seasonings to your taste. Whisk frequently until the polenta develops a porridgelike consistency but is still runny and pourable, about 3 minutes. (Avoid overcooking, which will make the polenta stodgy.)

03 Ladle into individual ramekins or dessert bowls. Garnish with maple-glazed walnuts. Serve immediately.

OTHER IDEAS

Omit the nut garnish. While still hot, top each portion with a square or two (or three) of your favorite dark chocolate. As the chocolate melts, swirl it into the polenta.

Substitute your favorite pumpkin pie spice mix for the spices. Stir in chopped crystallized ginger or candied orange peel.

Add a tablespoon of molasses, which will darken the mix and make it reminiscent of Indian pudding.

Serve with Creamy Hazelnut Topping (page 112).

Garnish with toasted (unsalted) sunflower seeds instead of walnuts.

This homey variation of a deep-dish fruit pie offers lovely juxtapositions of tastes, colors, and textures. Pecan halves form a kind of top crust and provide crisp contrast to the soft fruit. This recipe works surprisingly well with frozen fruit, which offers the convenience of peaches that are already peeled and sliced.

Since personal taste and the sweetness of individual fruits vary, I've suggested a range of added sugar. Serve warm or chilled, on its own or with a scoop of nondairy ice cream. Alternatively, use as a topping for waffles or breakfast porridge.

BAKED **PEACHES** AND **BLUEBERRIES** WITH CRISP **PECAN** TOPPING

01 Set the rack in the middle of the oven and preheat to 400°F.

02 In a large bowl, toss together the blueberries and peaches (plus any juices they've released), tapioca, sugar, lemon juice, lemon zest, and cardamom (if using). Transfer to a 2-quart (or slightly larger) baking dish. Distribute the pecans on top. Set the pan on a foil-lined baking sheet to catch spills if the fruit bubbles over.

03 Bake until the fruit is tender and the juices are thickened and bubbly, 35 to 45 minutes. If the nuts begin to burn before the fruit is done, cover the top loosely with aluminum foil.

04 Set on a rack and cool for about 10 minutes before serving.

SERVES 8

ONE 10- OR 12-OUNCE PACKAGE FROZEN BLUEBERRIES OR 2 CUPS FRESH BERRIES, PICKED OVER AND RINSED

TWO 16- OR 20-OUNCE PACKAGES FROZEN SLICED PEACHES OR 9 CUPS (LOOSELY PACKED) PEELED, PITTED, AND SLICED RIPE FREESTONE PEACHES

1/4 CUP QUICK-COOKING TAPIOCA (GRANULATED OR INSTANT)

1/3 TO 2/3 CUP SUGAR

2 TABLESPOONS FRESHLY SQUEEZED LEMON JUICE

2 TO 3 TEASPOONS GRATED LEMON ZEST

1/2 TEASPOON GROUND CARDAMOM (OPTIONAL)

1 1/2 CUPS PECAN OR WALNUT HALVES

2 ½ CUPS WATER

⅛ TEASPOON SALT

1 CUP ARBORIO OR VALENCIA SHORT-
GRAIN WHITE RICE

2 ½ CUPS UNFLAVORED SOYMILK
(NOT THE LIGHT VARIETY)

½ TO 1 CUP UNSWEETENED COCOA
POWDER (SCHARFFEN BERGER
AND DROSTE ARE GOOD BRANDS;
ALSO SEE OTHER GOOD THINGS,
PAGE 14.)

¾ TO 1 CUP SUGAR

3 TABLESPOONS CASHEW OR
ALMOND BUTTER

2 TEASPOONS INSTANT COFFEE
POWDER (OPTIONAL, BUT
DEEPENS THE CHOCOLATE
FLAVOR)

CREAMY HAZELNUT TOPPING
(PAGE 112; OPTIONAL)

TOASTED SLIVERED ALMONDS OR
VEGAN CHOCOLATE CHIPS, FOR
GARNISH (OPTIONAL)

For chocoholics who are also fans of rice pudding, this dessert offers the best of both worlds.

To achieve the creamiest possible texture, use full-fat soymilk and a starchy, short-grain, chubby white rice like Valencia paella rice (relatively inexpensive and available in many supermarkets under the Goya label) or Arborio risotto rice.

Since cocoa powder is virtually fat-free, the pudding tastes slightly grainy unless you include some luscious nut butter in the mix (though you won't actually taste it). I've given ranges of amounts for the cocoa powder and sugar to accommodate different brands and preferences.

The pudding provides diverse experiences of pleasure when served hot, at room temperature, or chilled. Creamy Hazelnut Topping (page 112) complements it nicely.

CHOCOLATE RICE PUDDING

01 In a heavy 3-quart saucepan, bring the water and salt to a boil. Add the rice. Cover and cook over low heat until the rice is quite soft and most or all of the water has been absorbed, 25 to 30 minutes.

02 While the rice is cooking, in a blender combine the soymilk with the minimum amounts of cocoa powder and sugar, the cashew butter, and the instant coffee powder (if using). Process until all of the nut butter is completely blended in, about 1 minute. Taste and add more cocoa and/or sugar, if you wish. (Keep in mind that the flavor and sweetness will be somewhat diminished after the liquid is cooked with the rice.)

03 Stir the chocolate mixture into the cooked rice. Bring to a boil over high heat. (Take care, as soymilk easily boils over.) Then lower the heat and cook uncovered at a gentle boil, stirring frequently to prevent the rice from sticking to the bottom of the pot and to break up any skin that forms on top. Cook until the pudding thickens and some rice is visible on the surface, 10 to 12 minutes. The mixture will be fairly soupy; it will thicken as it cools.

04 Ladle into individual ramekins or dessert bowls. Serve immediately or cool and then cover and refrigerate for later use. It keeps for up to 4 days. If you wish, top with one of the optional garnishes.

SERVES *6* FOR DESSERT OR *4* AS
A BRUNCH ENTRÉE

3 TABLESPOONS DRIED CRANBERRIES

¼ CUP HOT WATER

**2 TO 2 ½ POUNDS TART, FIRM
APPLES, SUCH AS GRANNY
SMITHS OR STAYMANS**

⅓ CUP MAPLE SYRUP

**4 SHEETS PHYLLO (ALSO SPELLED
FILO)**

3 TO 4 TABLESPOONS WALNUT OIL

**½ CUP WALNUTS, TOASTED AND
FINELY CHOPPED**

This impressive pastry takes very little effort to assemble and is beautiful to behold. You create a rectangular tart without a tin by layering sheets of phyllo directly on a parchment-lined baking sheet. Then you mound maple-glazed apple slices on top and fold over a bit of phyllo to create a flaky frame.

Phyllo easy to assemble? It's true that those paper-thin sheets of dough have a way of drying out and tearing. But even if you're phyllo-phobic (as I was until recently), this recipe offers guaranteed success. There's no fancy folding, and a few rips won't affect the result. Just patch them up as you go.

You'll find phyllo in the frozen foods case in most supermarkets. Defrost it according to the package directions (usually overnight in the refrigerator).

The tart is nice for brunch as well as dessert.

RUSTIC APPLE TART

01 Put the rack in the center of the oven and preheat to 425°F. Line a large baking or cookie sheet (about 11 by 17 inches) with parchment paper and set aside.

02 Place the cranberries in a small bowl. Pour the water over them and set aside.

03 Peel and core the apples. Cut them into slices about ¼ inch thick. Scatter half of the apples in a large, nonstick skillet, and drizzle half of the maple syrup on top. Cook over medium-high heat, tossing frequently, until the apples have softened but still hold their shape, about 5 minutes. (The apples will release liquid as they cook; most of it will evaporate.) With a slotted spoon, transfer the batch to a large platter to cool. Repeat with the remaining apples and maple syrup.

04 To assemble the tart: Wet a kitchen towel and wring it well to remove as much water as possible. Unwrap the phyllo and set the stack on a flat surface. Gently remove 1 sheet of phyllo from the pile and set it on the parchment-lined baking sheet. Immediately cover the remaining phyllo with the moist towel to prevent it from drying out. Brush the sheet of phyllo with oil. Sprinkle with about a third of the walnuts, leaving about a 2-inch border around the edges. Set another sheet of phyllo on top, brush with oil, and sprinkle with walnuts. Repeat with the third sheet of phyllo. Set the fourth sheet in place and brush with oil.

05 Mound the apples haphazardly on top of the stacked phyllo in a rectangular shape, leaving about 2 inches uncovered around the edges. Gently lift the edges of the phyllo, one side at a time, and fold them over to create a "frame" about $1\frac{1}{2}$ inches wide around the apples. (Some of the slices will end up beneath the phyllo, but most will remain exposed.) Brush the phyllo "frame" with oil. Drain the cranberries and scatter them among the apples.

06 Bake until the phyllo is golden and crisp, 9 to 16 minutes. Serve warm or at room temperature. To present the tart on a platter, transfer it with the parchment in place, and then gently pull out the parchment. To serve, slice into squares.

OTHER IDEAS

Cook the apple slices with a light dusting of cinnamon.

Make apple turnovers by following the folding instructions for preparing Phyllo Triangles (page 76).

Substitute Bosc or other firm pears for the apples. Cut them into $\frac{1}{2}$-inch slices and cook only until the edges are slightly softened, 3 or 4 minutes. Season lightly with cardamom, if you wish.

An elegant cookie that celebrates the irresistible Italian combination of pine nuts and aniseeds. It comes to you compliments of Meredith McCarty, author of an award-winning vegan dessert cookbook called Sweet and Natural.

These crescents are great dunkers and have transformed numerous skeptics into anise lovers. The dough is quickly assembled, but allow a half hour to chill it for easier handling. Actually, you can leave the dough in the freezer for days or weeks (it never hardens completely), and make the cookies when you have a yen for them. The baked crescents also freeze well.

It's most economical to purchase arrowroot flour (also referred to as arrowroot powder) from an Asian grocery or the bulk bins of a health-food store. You can also mail order it from Penzeys. The small bottles sold in supermarkets for use as a thickener are quite expensive.

When you measure the flour and arrowroot, bounce the cups gently up and down. Then add a bit more, if needed, to fill them to level capacity.

PINE NUT–ANISE CRESCENTS

MAKES **16 TO 20** CRESCENTS

¾ CUP WHOLE WHEAT PASTRY (NOT BREAD!) FLOUR

¼ CUP ARROWROOT FLOUR, PLUS MORE IF NEEDED FOR SHAPING CRESCENTS

½ TEASPOON BAKING POWDER

⅛ TEASPOON SALT

¼ CUP PINE NUTS

½ TEASPOON ANISEEDS

¼ CUP MAPLE SYRUP

3 TABLESPOONS NEUTRAL OIL, SUCH AS CANOLA

½ TEASPOON VANILLA EXTRACT

01 Use a sifter or set a strainer over a bowl, and measure in the flour, arrowroot, baking powder, and salt. Sift or stir to pass the ingredients into the bowl. Set aside a tablespoon of the pine nuts, and then stir the remaining pine nuts and the aniseeds into the flour mixture.

02 Pour the maple syrup into a glass measuring cup. Blend in the oil and vanilla. With a fork, stir the wet ingredients into the flour mixture until all of the dry ingredients are absorbed and the dough holds together in a mass. (The dough will be moist and sticky.) Set the dough in a small covered storage container, or wrap it in plastic. Chill in the freezer for a half hour, or until needed.

03 Set the rack in the middle of the oven and preheat the oven to 400°F. Line a baking sheet with parchment paper.

04 Slice the chilled dough in half and return half to the freezer. Scoop off about ¹/₂ tablespoon of dough and roll it between your palms, first into a small ball and then into a log about 3 inches long. As you set the log on the parchment, curve it into a crescent shape. (If the dough feels very sticky, lightly flour your hands with arrowroot before shaping each crescent.) Continue to create crescents from

CONTINUED

all of the remaining dough, including the portion returned to the freezer. Gently press a few of the reserved pine nuts into the top of each crescent.

05 Bake until the tops feel fairly firm, yielding only slightly to gentle pressure, and the edges touching the parchment show a hint of brown, 9 to 13 minutes. (The tops will remain pale.) Slide the parchment from the baking sheet onto a cooling rack. When the crescents have cooled, peel them off the parchment. Store in an airtight container at room temperature for up to 5 days, or freeze for up to 3 months.

OTHER IDEAS

PECAN CRESCENTS

Use $1/2$ cup toasted pecans, chopped to about the size of pine nuts, instead of the pine nuts. Increase the vanilla to 1 teaspoon and add $1/4$ teaspoon ground cinnamon instead of the aniseeds.

Are you drawn to the notion of seductively soft tapioca pearls floating in a sooth-ing ocean of Caribbean flavors? This is the kind of go-down-easy dessert that I love.

The pudding comes out either soupy or thick, depending upon the whim of tapioca, an ingredient that rarely behaves the same way twice. Despite tapioca's unpredictable nature, you can count on a gorgeous golden-orange dessert with refined taste and irresistible texture—nothing like those stodgy puddings you may remember from high school cafeteria days.

Before cooking, the little white beads known as small pearl tapioca have a diam-eter of about $1/8$ inch. After soaking overnight (a necessary step), they double in size. Look for pearl tapioca in gourmet shops, health-food stores, and Asian mar-kets, or mail order it from Zabar's. Store the uncooked pearls in a well-sealed con-tainer.

Since the size and pit-to-flesh ratio varies from one variety of mango to the next, I can't tell you how many you'll need for 2 cups of puréed flesh. Buy a bountiful num-ber, and dice any left over for garnish.

Peel the mangos with a sharp paring knife, taking care to remove as little flesh as possible. Cut the flesh away from the large central pit. If the mango is fibrous, use a knife to scrape against the pit and release as much pulp and juice as you can. If tasty mangos are hard to find, don't hesitate to use the canned purée sold in Indian grocery stores (see Other Ideas).

SERVES **6** NORMAL PEOPLE OR **4** TAPIOCA LOVERS

$1/2$ CUP SMALL PEARL TAPIOCA

ONE 13.5-OUNCE CAN UNSWEETENED COCONUT MILK (NOT THE LIGHT VARIETY)

1 $1/2$ CUPS WATER

2 TABLESPOONS RUM

$1/3$ CUP SUGAR, PLUS MORE IF NEEDED

$1/8$ TEASPOON SALT

2 CUPS PURÉED FRESH MANGO

MANGO-COCONUT TAPIOCA

01 In a bowl or storage container, cover the tapioca with an ample amount of water. Cover and refrigerate for 8 hours or overnight.

02 In a 2-quart, heavy saucepan, combine the coconut milk, water, rum, sugar, and salt, and bring to a boil. Drain and rinse the tapioca and stir it in. Cook uncovered at a gentle boil, stirring frequently to prevent the tapioca pearls from sticking to the bottom, until the mixture thickens slightly and the pearls are partially or fully translu-cent, 9 to 10 minutes.

03 Stir in the mango purée. Add more sugar if you wish, keeping in mind that the sweetness will be muted if the pudding is served chilled. Continue cooking and stirring until most of the tapioca pearls look translucent and taste tender, 1 to 8 minutes longer. The mixture will be fairly thin; it will thicken and set as it cools.

CONTINUED

(A few tips: Do not cook longer than 8 additional minutes or the tapioca may become gummy. The pearls may not become uniformly translucent, and they sometimes darken after the mango purée is added, but these factors do not affect the flavor. As long as the tapioca pearls are tender, you're okay.)

04 Ladle the pudding into 1 large or 6 individual bowls. Serve warm, at room temperature, or chilled. The texture is best when the pudding is eaten within 48 hours.

OTHER IDEAS

Stirring in a scant $1/8$ teaspoon of finely ground white pepper at the end of cooking adds a haunting flavor and rounds out the fruity sweetness.

In place of fresh mangoes, substitute 2 cups of canned alphonso mango purée, sold in Indian groceries. If the purée has been sweetened, reduce the added sugar according to taste. Leftover purée can be frozen for later use or blended with soymilk and frozen banana chunks to make a tropical smoothie.

3 TABLESPOONS MAPLE SYRUP

**1 TABLESPOON PLUS 1 TEASPOON
   HAZELNUT OIL**

1 ¹⁄₂ TEASPOONS VANILLA EXTRACT

PINCH OF SALT

**4 OUNCES (¹⁄₂ CUP) EXTRA-FIRM OR
   FIRM TOFU**

This sweet topping gives an elegant finish to many of the desserts in this chapter. It is thick enough to spoon out in small dollops as you would whipped cream.

For optimum taste and texture, use the fresh, refrigerated tofu sold in sealed plastic tubs (rather than the aseptic-packed variety), and purée the topping in a blender. If you're serving 4, this recipe yields 1 heaping tablespoon per serving. You can easily double or triple it.

CREAMY HAZELNUT TOPPING

01 Place the ingredients in a blender in the order given. Blend for 30 seconds. Scrape down the sides, and continue blending until very smooth and creamy, 30 to 60 seconds more.

02 Use immediately or refrigerate in a tightly sealed container for up to 5 days. Stir well before each use.

OTHER IDEAS

Use walnut oil instead of hazelnut oil.

MAIL-ORDER SOURCES

If you have difficulty locating high-quality ingredients locally, shopping by mail is a good option. In any case, the catalogs offered by these companies are fun to read and often quite informative. Sources for a few specialized items are provided in the pantry chapter.

GOLD MINE NATURAL FOOD CO.

800-475-3663

www.goldminenaturalfood.com

Jean Richardson is devoted to selling the best organic foods she can find, including heirloom grains and beans, sea vegetables, and traditionally made soy sauces and misos. In fact, you can come close to stocking your entire vegan pantry by ordering from her educational catalog.

PENZEYS

800-741-7787

www.penzeys.com

Nine different types of peppercorns. Four grades of cinnamon. An impressive range of high-quality spices and dried herbs, available in small or large quantities.

ZABAR'S

800-697-6301

www.zabars.com

A good source of ethnic and international gourmet ingredients, including Patak's sweet mango chutney, Merwanjee Poonjiajee & Sons Madras Curry Powder, French green lentils, niçoise olives, and imported nut oils—plus a large selection of cookware at discount prices.

ZINGERMAN'S

www.zingermans.com

888-636-8162

To learn which oils, vinegars, and condiments one knowledgeable taster considers the best in the world, consult this catalog.

INDEX

TABLE OF **EQUIVALENTS**

The exact equivalents in the following tables have been rounded for convenience.

LIQUID/DRY MEASURES

U.S.	METRIC
1/4 teaspoon	1.25 milliliters
1/2 teaspoon	2.5 milliliters
1 teaspoon	5 milliliters
1 tablespoon (3 teaspoons)	15 milliliters
1 fluid ounce (2 tablespoons)	30 milliliters
1/4 cup	60 milliliters
1/3 cup	80 milliliters
1/2 cup	120 milliliters
1 cup	240 milliliters
1 pint (2 cups)	480 milliliters
1 quart (4 cups, 32 ounces)	960 milliliters
1 gallon (4 quarts)	3.84 liters
1 ounce (by weight)	28 grams
1 pound	454 grams
2.2 pounds	1 kilogram

OVEN TEMPERATURE

FAHRENHEIT	CELSIUS	GAS
250	120	1/2
275	140	1
300	150	2
325	160	3
350	180	4
375	190	5
400	200	6
425	220	7
450	230	8
475	240	9
500	260	10

LENGTH

U.S.	METRIC
1/8 inch	3 millimeters
1/4 inch	6 millimeters
1/2 inch	12 millimeters
1 inch	2.5 centimeters

comfort food

recipes
Rick Rodgers

photographs
Ray Kachatorian

weldon**owen**

CONTENTS

ON THE SIDE

SOMETHING SWEET

WHAT IS COMFORT FOOD?

How do you even begin to define comfort food? It means something different to every one of us. It conjures up memories of childhood and makes us nostalgic for the more relaxed times of our youth. It is both nurturing and decadent, feeding our souls and encouraging an indulgent streak. It lifts our spirits when we are down and nourishes us when we are happy, soothing and satisfying us, like wrapping us in a big, warm quilt. Comfort foods are the cherished recipes, passed down through generations, that were served at the family table.

Even though everyone's roll call of ultimate comfort foods will differ, certain dishes turn up on nearly every list. These are the recipes I have collected here. For every recipe, I've tried to provide the ultimate, over-the-top version, using the best ingredients possible. It might not be the exact dish you remember from childhood, but it is guaranteed to taste great, and in many cases may even exceed your expectations.

Some of the dishes reflect an earlier time when slow-simmered foods were daily occurrences, rather than a treat reserved for weekends. Others are easy to prepare whenever the mood strikes. You'll find recipes for every meal of the day, both down-home American cooking, like corned beef hash, grilled cheese sandwiches and tomato soup, and crispy fried chicken, and dishes borrowed from beyond our borders, such as French onion soup, lasagna Bolognese, and cheesy chicken enchiladas. Simply put, there is something here for everyone who takes pleasure in sitting down to a table laden with comfort food.

Rick Rodgers

RISE AND SHINE

On school days, breakfast always meant a quick meal of cereal and milk, with Mom trying to slip sliced bananas into the bowl for extra vitamins. But weekends were another story. On those days, she heated up the griddle to cook stacks of blueberry-studded pancakes or golden brown French toast. If we kids had been especially good that week, we were treated to a plate of crisp waffles. In the long run, we didn't care which of the three was served, as they were all topped by big pats of melting butter and rivers of maple syrup. Today, these are still among my favorite breakfast items. This chapter has plenty of options for a leisurely morning meal, when you have time to relax with family and friends. In addition to griddle treats, you'll find everything from a southern-style breakfast of cheese grits and panfried ham to spiced doughnuts and fluffy cinnamon buns, the ultimate in morning decadence.

Pancakes have been a popular American breakfast since colonial cooks discovered that one of their favorite old-country recipes tasted even better topped with the maple syrup of their new home. Here is perhaps the ultimate version, studded with blueberries, slathered with butter, and dripping with syrup.

BLUEBERRY PANCAKES

All-purpose flour, 1½ cups

Baking soda, ¾ teaspoon

Baking powder, 1½ teaspoons

Sugar, 2 tablespoons

Fine sea salt, ¼ teaspoon

Buttermilk, 1¾ cups, or as needed

Large eggs, 2

Unsalted butter, 3 tablespoons melted, plus butter for serving

Blueberries, 2 cups

Canola oil for cooking

Pure maple syrup for serving

MAKES 4 SERVINGS

Preheat the oven to 200°F. In a large bowl, sift together the flour, baking soda, baking powder, sugar, and salt. In a medium bowl, whisk together the 1¾ cups buttermilk, the eggs, and the 3 tablespoons melted butter. Pour the buttermilk mixture into the flour mixture and stir just until combined. Fold in the blueberries.

Place a griddle over high heat until hot. (To test, flick a little water onto it. It should skitter across the surface.) Lightly oil the griddle. For each pancake, pour about ¼ cup of the batter onto the griddle and cook until bubbles form on the surface, about 2 minutes. Flip the pancakes and cook until the bottoms are golden brown, 1–2 minutes more. Transfer to a baking sheet and keep warm in the oven. Repeat until all the batter is used. If the batter begins to thicken, thin it with a bit more buttermilk. Serve the pancakes piping hot, with plenty of butter and syrup.

PUT A SPIN ON IT   To dress up the maple syrup—and enjoy a double dose of berries—in a saucepan, gently simmer 2 cups blueberries with 1 cup pure maple syrup until the berries start to release their juices, about 5 minutes.

Quiche may well be the most versatile brunch dish. Rich with eggy custard and encased in a buttery crust, it can be made with a seemingly endless variety of herbs, meats, cheeses, and vegetables. It can also be served hot or at room temperature, making it an ideal choice when you have other dishes on the menu.

BACON AND LEEK QUICHE

Single-crust flaky pastry dough (page 248)

Applewood-smoked bacon, 4 thick slices, coarsely chopped

Unsalted butter, 1 tablespoon

Leeks, 2 small, white and pale green parts, chopped

Half-and-half, 1 cup

Large eggs, 2

Kosher salt, ½ teaspoon

Freshly ground pepper, ¼ teaspoon

Freshly grated nutmeg, ⅛ teaspoon

Gruyère cheese, 1 cup shredded

MAKES 6 SERVINGS

Place the dough on a lightly floured work surface and dust the top with flour. (If the dough is chilled hard, let it stand at room temperature for a few minutes until it begins to soften before rolling it out.) Roll out into a round about 12 inches in diameter and about ⅛ inch thick. Transfer to a 9-inch tart pan with a removable bottom, gently fitting the dough into the bottom and sides of the pan. Using scissors or a small knife, trim the dough, leaving a ½-inch overhang. Fold the overhanging dough over and into the pan, pressing it firmly against the dough on the sides of the pan; the dough should be doubly thick at the sides and rise about ⅛ inch above the pan rim. Line the dough with a piece of aluminum foil and freeze for 30 minutes.

Meanwhile, position a rack in the lower third of the oven and preheat to 375°F. Place the dough-lined pan on a baking sheet and fill the foil with pie weights or dried beans. Bake until the dough is set and beginning to brown, about 20 minutes.

Meanwhile, make the filling. In a frying pan, fry the bacon over medium heat, stirring, until crisp and golden, about 6 minutes. Using a slotted spoon, transfer to paper towels to drain. Pour out the fat and wipe the pan clean with paper towels. Add the butter to the pan and melt over medium heat. Add the leeks and cook, stirring occasionally, until tender, about 10 minutes. Transfer to a plate and let cool slightly.

Remove the baking sheet with the tart pan from the oven. Remove the foil and weights. In a bowl, whisk together the half-and-half, eggs, salt, pepper, and nutmeg until combined. Scatter the leeks, bacon, and Gruyère evenly in the pastry shell. Carefully pour the egg mixture into the shell. Return to the oven and bake until the filling is puffed and golden brown, about 30 minutes. Let cool slightly, then serve.

PUT A SPIN ON IT Instead of bacon, leeks, and Gruyère, make a ham, shallot, and Cheddar quiche. To make the filling, cook 1 cup chopped ham and ⅓ cup chopped shallots in 1 tablespoon unsalted butter over medium heat until the shallots are tender, 4–5 minutes. Replace the Gruyère with Cheddar cheese.

The shining chrome of a roadside diner is a welcoming beacon to hungry travelers, and its good reputation invariably depends on the quality of its breakfast. Indeed, folks will come from miles around to dig into a rib-sticking meal of tender, juicy steak, fried eggs, and crispy hash browns. Here's an excellent homemade version.

A DINER BREAKFAST

Baking potatoes, 3 large

Yellow onion,
1 small, minced

**Kosher salt and freshly
ground pepper**

Canola oil, 4 tablespoons

**Boneless beef rib-eye
or top loin steaks,**
4 small, ¼ inch thick

Unsalted butter,
2 tablespoons

Large eggs, 4

Country white bread,
8 thick slices

Sour cream for garnish

**Chopped fresh chives
for garnish**

MAKES 4 SERVINGS

To make the hash browns, using a food processor or stand mixer fitted with the shredding attachment or the large holes of a box shredder-grater, shred the unpeeled potatoes. A handful at a time, squeeze the potatoes to remove as much moisture as possible and place in a large bowl. Add the onion, 1½ teaspoons salt, and ¼ teaspoon pepper and mix well. In a frying pan, preferably cast iron, heat 2 tablespoons of the oil over medium-high heat until it shimmers. Add the potato mixture and spread into a thick cake. Reduce the heat to medium, cover, and cook until the underside is golden brown and crisp, about 6 minutes. Using a large, wide metal spatula, transfer the potatoes to a plate. Add the remaining oil to the pan and heat. Flip the potatoes back into the pan, browned side up. Continue cooking, uncovered, until golden brown and crisp on the other side, about 6 minutes more.

Meanwhile, preheat the broiler. Season the steaks with salt and pepper. Place the steaks on a broiler pan and broil, turning after 2 minutes, until the steaks are browned on the outside and medium-rare, about 4 minutes total, or until done to your liking. Transfer to a platter and tent with aluminum foil. Turn off the broiler.

Transfer the potatoes to a baking sheet and keep warm in the turned-off oven. Wipe out the frying pan with paper towels. Return the pan to medium heat, add the butter and heat until foamy. One at a time, crack the eggs into the pan. Season with salt and pepper, cover, reduce the heat to medium-low, and cook until the whites are set, about 2 minutes for sunny-side-up eggs. Or, carefully flip the eggs and cook to the desired doneness. Meanwhile, toast the bread.

To serve, divide the hash browns, steaks, and eggs evenly among 4 plates. Top the hash browns with sour cream and a sprinkle of chives. Serve with the toast.

PUT A SPIN ON IT   For potatoes O'Brien, add ½ cup finely diced red or green bell pepper to the potatoes along with the onion. You can also broil pork chops—smoked chops are especially good—instead of steaks.

A longtime American breakfast staple, corned beef hash, prepared from scratch and panfried until crisp, is a dish worth getting up for any day of the week. Top each serving with a poached egg—the rich yolk will slowly flow over the hash—and pass the ketchup and mustard or hot-pepper sauce.

REAL CORNED BEEF HASH

Yukon gold or red-skinned potatoes, 2 large

Kosher salt and freshly ground pepper

Cooked corned beef (page 97), 2 cups coarsely chopped

Yellow onion, 1 small, coarsely chopped

Red bell pepper, ½, seeded and coarsely chopped

Poached eggs (page 247), 6

Unsalted butter, 2 tablespoons

MAKES 6 SERVINGS

In a saucepan, combine the unpeeled potatoes with salted water to cover by 1 inch, cover the pan, and bring to a boil over high heat. Uncover, reduce the heat to medium-low and simmer until tender when pierced with a knife, about 20 minutes. Drain, rinse under cold running water, and let cool completely. Peel the potatoes and cut into ½-inch chunks. You should have about 2 cups of potato chunks.

In a food processor, combine the potatoes, corned beef, onion, and bell pepper. Pulse a few times, just until the ingredients are coarsely chopped and well mixed. Do not mince them. Season generously with salt and pepper.

Poach the eggs and keep them warm in hot water as directed.

In a large frying pan, melt the butter over medium-high heat. Divide the corned beef mixture into 6 equal portions, and shape each portion into a patty about ¾-inch thick. Place the patties in the hot pan and fry until browned on the bottom, about 4 minutes. Turn and brown the second sides, about 4 minutes more.

To serve, place a patty on each plate. One at a time, using a slotted spoon, remove the poached eggs from the hot water, resting the bottom of the spoon briefly on a clean kitchen towel to blot excess moisture, and place an egg on each patty.

PUT A SPIN ON IT To make red flannel hash, a New England favorite, substitute 1 or 2 cooked beets for 1 of the potatoes. For a spicy hash, add 1 jalapeño chile, seeded and chopped, to the food processor with the hash.

Hot, golden waffles, crisp on the outside and tender on the inside, are a spectacular way to kick off a weekend morning, whether you're at home in your slippers or in a booth at a bustling diner. The indentations are perfect for catching melted butter, maple syrup, or the juices from fresh fruit, such as this honeyed cherry compote.

BROWN BUTTER WAFFLES WITH CHERRIES

Cherries, 2 cups (about ½ pound)

Orange blossom or other mild honey, 3 tablespoons

Unsalted butter, 4 tablespoons

Whole milk, 2 cups

Large eggs, 2, separated

Pure vanilla extract, 1 teaspoon

All-purpose flour, 2 cups

Sugar, 3 tablespoons

Baking powder, 4 teaspoons

Fine sea salt, ¼ teaspoon

Canola oil for cooking if needed

MAKES 4 SERVINGS

Halve and pit the cherries and place in a bowl. Add the honey, stir to mix evenly, and let stand at room temperature for about 30 minutes to allow the cherries to release some of their juice.

Preheat the oven to 200°F. Have ready a rimmed baking sheet. Preheat a waffle iron.

In a small saucepan, melt the butter over medium-low heat and bring to a boil. Cook, stirring occasionally, until the milk solids in the bottom of the pan turn a toasty brown, about 3 minutes. Transfer to a bowl and let cool slightly. Add the milk, egg yolks, and vanilla, and whisk until combined.

In a large bowl, sift together the flour, sugar, baking powder, and salt. Add the milk mixture and whisk just until combined (a few small lumps are okay). In another bowl, using a clean whisk or a handheld mixer, whip the egg whites until soft peaks form. Scoop the whites onto the batter and, using the whisk, gently fold them in evenly.

If your waffle iron is not nonstick, lightly and evenly oil the grid. According to the manufacturer's direction, spoon the batter over the grid, close the lid, and cook until the waffle is golden brown, usually about 4 minutes. Transfer to the baking sheet and keep warm in the oven. Repeat with the remaining batter. Serve the waffles piping hot with a big spoonful of the cherries.

PUT A SPIN ON IT For diner-style waffles, stir 1 tablespoon malted milk powder into the dry ingredients after sifting, and serve with the classic duo of butter and pure maple syrup. For strawberries-and-cream waffles, substitute sliced strawberries tossed with sugar to taste for the cherries and top with dollops of whipped cream (page 248).

When I was a kid, I would wake up on Sunday mornings to the irresistible smell of waffles browning.

That warm, buttery aroma can still make me jump out of bed, ready for a plateful of waffles, the crisp indentations pooled with melting butter and maple syrup. Waffles were one of the first things my brothers and I learned to make on our own. We fought over who got to pour the thick batter—not too much!—into the waiting hot iron and were fascinated when that wet mass magically expanded into a crisp, sweet waffle. It seemed like an eternity until steam stopped escaping from the iron and the red light went off, the welcome sign that breakfast was finally ready. Now that I am an adult, I am only slightly less impatient. Pass the syrup, please!

From the humble diner to the upscale restaurant, omelets are now fixtures on American breakfast and brunch menus. With a few deft twists of the wrist, it is easy to transform a few eggs into a light-as-air morning main course. This recipe yields a large, fluffy omelet packed with melting cheese and fresh herbs—ideal for sharing.

HERB AND BRIE OMELET

Large eggs, 4

Heavy cream,
2 tablespoons

Kosher salt and freshly
ground pepper

Fresh flat-leaf parsley,
1 teaspoon minced

Fresh chives,
1 teaspoon minced

Fresh chervil or tarragon,
1 teaspoon minced

Unsalted butter,
1 tablespoon

Brie cheese,
3 ounces, thinly sliced

MAKES 2 SERVINGS

In a bowl, whisk together the eggs, cream, ¼ teaspoon salt, and a few grinds of pepper just until thoroughly blended. Do not overbeat. Add the parsley, chives, and chervil and whisk gently to combine.

In a nonstick frying pan, melt the butter over medium heat until it foams and the foam begins to subside. Tilt the pan to cover the bottom evenly with butter.

Add the egg mixture to the pan and cook until the eggs have barely begun to set around the edges, about 30 seconds. Using a heatproof spatula, lift the cooked edges and gently push them toward the center, tilting the pan slightly to allow the liquid egg on top to flow underneath, then cook for 30 seconds. Repeat this process two more times. When the eggs are almost completely set but still slightly moist on top, spread the Brie slices over half of the omelet.

Using the spatula, fold the untopped half of the omelet over the filled half to create a half-moon shape. Let the omelet cook for 30 seconds more, then slide it onto a warmed serving plate. Cut in half and serve at once.

PUT A SPIN ON IT Sauté ½ apple, peeled and diced, in 1 tablespoon unsalted butter until tender-crisp, and add to the omelet along with the Brie. Or, substitute sharp Cheddar cheese for the Brie and use 1 green onion, white and green parts, minced, instead of the herbs.

Juicy, nectar-sweet peaches are one of the joys of summertime eating. In this southern-inspired dish, they are tucked into crunchy cornmeal crepes and then warmed in the oven until piping hot, to create a breakfast to linger over. A dollop of buttery mascarpone and a dusting of sugar provide the perfect finishing touches.

PEACHES AND CREAM CREPES

Whole milk, 1 cup

All-purpose flour, 1/2 cup

Yellow cornmeal, preferably stone-ground, 1/2 cup

Large eggs, 2

Unsalted butter, 5 tablespoons, melted

Granulated sugar, 1 teaspoon, plus more to taste

Fine sea salt, 1/4 teaspoon

Peaches, 4, halved, pitted, and thinly sliced

Fresh lemon juice, 1 tablespoon

Canola oil for cooking

Mascarpone cheese, 1/2 cup, at room temperature

Heavy cream, about 2 tablespoons

Confectioners' sugar for garnish

MAKES 4 SERVINGS

To make the crepe batter, in a blender, combine the milk, flour, cornmeal, eggs, 2 tablespoons of the butter, the 1 teaspoon granulated sugar, and the salt. Process until smooth. Let stand at room temperature for about 30 minutes. Meanwhile, in a bowl, combine the peaches, lemon juice, and sugar to taste, and toss to coat evenly. Let stand at room temperature for about 30 minutes to allow the peaches to release some of their juice.

Lightly oil a 7-inch nonstick frying pan and place over medium-high heat until hot. Pour 1/4 cup of the batter into the pan and tilt the pan to cover the bottom evenly. Drizzle a little batter into any holes. Cook until the bottom is golden brown, about 1 minute. Flip and cook the other side until golden. Transfer to a plate. Repeat with the remaining batter, adding more oil to the pan as needed and stacking the crepes, separated by parchment or waxed paper, as they are ready. You should have 10 crepes, or 2 more than you need (the extra crepes are the cook's treat!).

Preheat the oven to 400°F. Lightly brush a rimmed baking sheet with some of the remaining 3 tablespoons butter. In a small bowl, using a fork, stir together the mascarpone and enough cream to create a creamy mixture, then stir in granulated sugar to taste. Set aside for serving.

Place 1 crepe on a work surface. Spoon one-eighth of the peaches in an even layer on half of the crepe, then fold over the other half to cover. Fold the crepe in half again, to form a triangle. Place on the prepared baking sheet. Repeat with 7 more crepes and all of the peaches. Brush the tops of the filled crepes with the remaining butter. Bake just until hot throughout, about 5 minutes. To serve, place 2 crepes on each plate. Crown the crepes with a dollop of the mascarpone cream, and then sift confectioners' sugar over the top. Serve at once.

PUT A SPIN ON IT In the summer, swap out the peaches for other stone fruits, such as nectarines, apricots, or plums. Sliced bananas, lightly sautéed in butter with a little brown sugar, are delicious other times of the year.

The Italian frittata, which resembles a French quiche minus the crust, is casual fare, typically served directly from the pan in which it is cooked. Plump and golden, it shows how no more than a few eggs, a handful of vegetables, and a sprinkling of cheese can become a simple yet hearty meal to start the day.

POTATO AND PEPPER FRITTATA

Yukon gold potatoes, 2

Olive oil, 2 tablespoons

Yellow onion,
½ cup chopped

Red bell pepper, 1

Large eggs, 8

Fresh rosemary,
1 teaspoon minced

Kosher salt, ¾ teaspoon

Freshly ground pepper,
¼ teaspoon

Parmesan cheese,
3 tablespoons
freshly grated

MAKES 4-6 SERVINGS

Thinly slice the unpeeled potatoes. In an ovenproof frying pan, heat the oil over medium heat. Add the potatoes and turn to coat with the oil. Cover and cook, stirring occasionally, until almost tender, about 20 minutes. Uncover and stir in the onion. Cook, stirring occasionally, until the onion is tender and the potatoes are lightly browned, about 5 minutes.

Meanwhile, preheat the broiler. Place the bell pepper on a baking sheet and broil, turning occasionally, until blackened on all sides, about 12 minutes. Transfer to a work surface and let cool until easy to handle. Leave the broiler on. Peel off the blackened skin; discard the stem, seeds, and ribs; and chop the pepper.

Stir the roasted bell pepper into the potato mixture in the frying pan. In a bowl, whisk together the eggs, rosemary, salt, and pepper. Pour the egg mixture into the potato mixture and cook over medium heat until the edges begin to set. Using a heatproof spatula, lift the cooked edges of the frittata, and tilt the frying pan to allow the liquid egg on top to flow underneath. Continue cooking, occasionally lifting the frittata and tilting it again, until the top is almost set, about 4 minutes more.

Sprinkle the top of the frittata with the Parmesan. Place under the broiler until the frittata puffs and is golden brown, about 1 minute. Cut into wedges and serve hot, warm, or at room temperature.

PUT A SPIN ON IT Frittatas are versatile, allowing you to experiment with many kinds of vegetables and cheeses. To make an asparagus and goat cheese frittata, omit the potatoes, onion, bell pepper, and Parmesan. Blanch asparagus spears, cut into 1-inch pieces, then sauté in the olive oil just until heated through. Add 1 shallot, chopped, and cook until tender. Add to the egg mixture. Just before broiling, top the frittata with crumbled fresh goat cheese.

Breakfast doesn't get any more down-home than this: fluffy scrambled eggs; salty ham with coffee-infused red-eye gravy; creamy, cheesy grits; and tender, flaky buttermilk biscuits. Coordinating all of the components will bring out your inner short-order cook. Read the entire recipe before you begin, so all the steps go smoothly.

A SOUTHERN BREAKFAST

Buttermilk Biscuits (page 162)

Whole milk, 1½ cups

Old-fashioned white hominy grits, preferably stone-ground, ¾ cup

Kosher salt, ½ teaspoon

Unsalted butter, 5 tablespoons

Garlic, 1 clove, minced

Smoked ham steak, 1 (about 1¼ pounds)

Brewed coffee, ¾ cup

Sugar, 1 teaspoon

Large eggs, 8

Heavy cream or whole milk, ⅓ cup

Freshly ground pepper, ⅛ teaspoon

Sharp Cheddar cheese, ½ cup shredded

MAKES 4 SERVINGS

Prepare the biscuits as directed. While the biscuits are baking, begin cooking the grits. In a heatproof bowl, whisk together 2 cups water, the milk, grits, and ¼ teaspoon of salt. Fill a saucepan with water to a depth of 1 inch and bring to a steady simmer. Rest the bowl in the top of the pan over (not touching) the water. Cook the grits, whisking occasionally, until tender and thickened into a porridge, 30–60 minutes, depending on the grits and according to package directions.

While the grits are cooking, in a large, heavy frying pan, preferably cast iron, melt 1 tablespoon of the butter over medium heat. Add the garlic and cook, stirring often, until fragrant but not browned, about 1 minute. Scrape the butter and garlic into a small bowl and set aside.

In the same pan, when the grits are about 10 minutes from being done, melt another tablespoon of the butter over medium-high heat. Add the ham and cook until the bottom is browned, 3 minutes. Turn and brown the other side, 2 minutes more. Transfer the ham to a platter and cover to keep warm. Pour out all but 1 tablespoon of the fat from the pan. Add the coffee and sugar and bring to a boil over high heat, scraping up the browned bits with a wooden spatula. Cook until the liquid is reduced by half (it will be thin "gravy"), 3 minutes. Remove from the heat.

While the gravy is simmering, make the scrambled eggs. In a bowl, whisk together the eggs, cream, the remaining ¼ teaspoon salt, and the pepper just until blended. In a nonstick frying pan, heat the remaining 3 tablespoons butter over medium-low heat. Pour in the eggs and cook until they begin to set, about 20 seconds. Stir with a heatproof spatula, scraping up the eggs on the bottom and sides of the pan and folding them toward the center. Repeat until the eggs are barely cooked into moist curds. Remove the pan from the heat and let the eggs stand in the pan to allow the residual heat to finish cooking them, about 1 minute.

When the grits are ready, add the reserved garlic-butter mixture and Cheddar and stir to combine. To serve, slice the ham and divide the ham, grits, and eggs among individual plates. Drizzle the ham with the gravy. Serve hot, with the biscuits.

Southern cooks know how to lay out a rib-sticking spread, and never more so than at breakfast time.

In the South, breakfast is more than just a meal, it's a way of life. Southerners understand the importance of tucking away a hearty repast first thing in the morning so they'll be ready for whatever the day may bring. The first time I was in Nashville, a friend insisted we drive well out of the city proper to a café famous for its breakfast of country ham and red-eye gravy, creamy hominy grits, fried eggs, homemade berry jam, and, of course, a mountain of flaky, featherlight biscuits. Greedily, we dug in, relishing the juxtaposition of flavors and textures—sweet and salty, chewy and buttery—as we cleaned our plates. And then, even though we were stuffed, we ordered another plate of hot biscuits!

Cooks in many countries use the same method for reviving day-old bread: they dip it in eggs and milk or cream and then quickly panfry it. Our contemporary French toast is a descendant of *pain perdu* (literally "lost bread"), popularized in the kitchens of New Orleans. This luscious version is topped with caramelized bananas.

FRENCH TOAST WITH CARAMELIZED BANANAS

Large eggs, 6

Half-and-half or whole milk, 1 cup

Granulated sugar, 1 tablespoon

Pure vanilla extract, 1 teaspoon

Finely grated orange zest, from 1 large orange

Freshly grated nutmeg, 1/8 teaspoon

Day-old challah or other egg bread, 6 slices

Canola oil for cooking

Firm but ripe bananas, 3

Unsalted butter, 2 tablespoons

Light brown sugar, 3 tablespoons firmly packed

Fresh orange juice, 1/2 cup, or as needed

Dark rum, 2 tablespoons (optional)

MAKES 4 SERVINGS

To make the French toast, preheat the oven to 350°F. Have ready a rimmed baking sheet. In a large, shallow bowl, whisk together the eggs, half-and-half, granulated sugar, vanilla, orange zest, and nutmeg. Cut the bread slices in half, add to the egg mixture, and turn gently to coat evenly. Let stand until the bread has soaked up some of the egg mixture, about 1 minute.

Place a griddle over medium-high heat until hot. Lightly oil the griddle. Remove the bread from the egg mixture, letting the excess liquid drip back into the bowl, and place on the hot griddle. Cook until the bottoms are golden brown, about 2 minutes. Flip and cook the other sides until golden brown, about 2 minutes more. Transfer to the baking sheet and bake until the center of the bread is heated through but still moist, about 10 minutes.

Meanwhile, make the caramelized bananas. Peel the bananas and slice diagonally. In a large frying pan, melt the butter over medium-high heat. Add the banana slices and cook, gently turning them occasionally, until they begin to brown, 2–3 minutes. Sprinkle in the brown sugar and cook until it melts, about 1 minute. Gently stir in the 1/2 cup orange juice and the rum, if using, and cook until the liquid has reduced slightly, about 1 minute. If the sauce seems too thick, add a little more orange juice until it is the desired consistency. Serve the French toast piping hot, topped with spoonfuls of the caramelized bananas.

PUT A SPIN ON IT Sliced apples, pears, nectarines, or peaches are all meltingly delicious when caramelized in butter and sugar. Just substitute an equal amount of whichever fruit you prefer for the bananas. If you like, match the fruit juice—apple juice or peach nectar—to the type of fruit you are using.

These pancakes, fragrant with spices, will take you back to a winter's day spent cutting out gingerbread men on a flour-dusted kitchen counter. Light and fluffy, and topped with butter and maple syrup, these breakfast treats usually disappear as quickly as you can make them, so be prepared to whip up a second batch.

GINGERBREAD PANCAKES

All-purpose flour, 1¼ cups

Baking powder, 1 teaspoon

Baking soda, ½ teaspoon

Kosher salt, ½ teaspoon

Ground cinnamon, 1 teaspoon

Ground ginger, ¾ teaspoon

Ground cloves, ⅛ teaspoon

Large eggs, 2

Dark brown sugar, ¼ cup firmly packed

Unsulfured light molasses, 2 tablespoons

Unsalted butter, 2 tablespoons, melted, plus more for serving

Brewed coffee, ¼ cup, at room temperature

Canola oil for cooking

Pure maple syrup for serving

MAKES 4-6 SERVINGS

Preheat the oven to 200°F. In a large bowl, sift together the flour, baking powder, baking soda, salt, cinnamon, ginger, and cloves. In a medium bowl, whisk together the eggs, brown sugar, molasses, the 2 tablespoons melted butter, coffee, and ½ cup water. Pour the egg mixture into the flour mixture and stir just until combined.

Place a griddle over high heat until hot. (To test, flick a little water onto it. It should skitter across the surface.) Lightly oil the griddle. For each pancake, pour about ¼ cup of the batter onto the griddle and cook until bubbles form on the surface, about 2 minutes. Flip the pancakes and cook until the bottoms are golden brown, 1–2 minutes more. Transfer to a baking sheet and keep warm in the oven. Repeat until all the batter is used.

Serve the pancakes piping hot, with plenty of butter and syrup.

PUT A SPIN ON IT Top the pancakes with sautéed autumn fruit, such as apples or pears. Peel, core, and thinly slice 3 apples or pears, sprinkle with 2 tablespoons sugar and ⅛ teaspoon ground cinnamon, and sauté in 2 tablespoons unsalted butter until golden and tender, about 4 minutes.

When you are a kid, the best cinnamon buns are rich, pillowy swirls laced with brown sugar and cinnamon, studded with buttery pecans, and iced with a sugary vanilla glaze—just like these. But they were a rare treat. One of the great things about being an adult is that you can make cinnamon buns any time you want.

CINNAMON BUNS

Whole milk,
1 cup plus
2 tablespoons

Active dry yeast,
1 envelope
(2½ teaspoons)

Large eggs, 3, at
room temperature

Granulated sugar, ¼ cup

Kosher salt, 2 teaspoons

All-purpose flour, 4½ cups

Unsalted butter,
10 tablespoons, at
room temperature

Canola oil for bowl

Dark brown sugar,
1 cup firmly packed

Ground cinnamon,
1 tablespoon

Pecans, ½ cup toasted
and chopped (optional)

Confectioners' sugar,
1 cup

Pure vanilla extract,
2 teaspoons

MAKES 10 BUNS

In a small saucepan, heat the 1 cup milk over medium heat just until warm to the touch. Pour into the bowl of a stand mixer. Sprinkle the yeast over the milk and let stand until softened, about 2 minutes, then whisk until the yeast dissolves. Whisk in the eggs, granulated sugar, and salt until the sugar dissolves. Add 2 cups of the flour and stir with a wooden spoon until moistened. Cut 6 tablespoons of the butter into chunks and add to the bowl. Fit the mixer with the dough hook attachment and knead the mixture on medium-low speed, adding the remaining flour ½ cup at a time, until the dough pulls away from the sides of the bowl. Reduce the speed to low and continue to knead until the dough is smooth and springy, about 5 minutes. Lightly oil a large bowl. Gather the dough into a ball, add to the bowl, turn to coat with the oil, and arrange smooth side up. Cover with plastic wrap and let rise at room temperature until doubled, 1½–2 hours.

Meanwhile, butter a 9-by-13-inch baking pan. In a small bowl, mix together the brown sugar and cinnamon, breaking up any lumps with your fingers.

On a lightly floured work surface, roll out the dough into a 15-by-10-inch rectangle. Spread with 2 tablespoons of the butter. Sprinkle evenly with the brown sugar–cinnamon mixture and then the pecans, if using, leaving a 1-inch border uncovered along one long edge. Press the nuts lightly to adhere. Starting at the long edge covered with filling, roll up the dough snugly like a jelly roll. Pinch the seam to seal, but leave both ends open. Using a sharp knife, cut the roll crosswise into 10 equal pieces, each about 1½ inches thick. Arrange, cut sides down, in the prepared pan. Cover with plastic wrap and let rise at room temperature until puffy, about 1 hour. (Alternatively, cover tightly with plastic wrap and refrigerate for up to 24 hours, then let stand at room temperature for 30 minutes before baking.)

Preheat the oven to 375°F. Melt the remaining 2 tablespoons butter and brush it on the rolls. Bake until golden brown, 25–30 minutes. Let the rolls cool in the pan for 10–15 minutes. Meanwhile, sift the confectioners' sugar into a bowl and whisk in the 2 tablespoons milk and the vanilla. Spread over the buns and serve.

Blintzes arrived in America with Jewish immigrants from eastern Europe. The crepelike wrappers can be stuffed with a variety of fillings—from mushrooms to meat—but this cheese version, served with fruit compote and sour cream, is the most popular morning choice. The club soda aerates and lightens the batter.

CHEESE BLINTZES

All-purpose flour, 1¼ cups

Whole milk, ¾ cup

Club soda or seltzer, ⅔ cup

Large eggs, 2 whole plus 2 yolks

Unsalted butter, 5 tablespoons, melted

Sugar, 8 tablespoons plus 1 teaspoon

Fine sea salt, ⅛ teaspoon

Canola oil for cooking

Farmer or ricotta cheese, 2 cups (1 pound)

Pure vanilla extract, 1 teaspoon

Finely grated lemon zest, from 1 lemon

Plums, 1 pound, pitted and sliced

Fresh lemon juice, 1 tablespoon

Sour cream for serving

MAKES 6 SERVINGS

To make the blintz batter, in a blender, combine the flour, milk, club soda, whole eggs, 2 tablespoons of the butter, 1 teaspoon of the sugar, and the salt. Process until smooth. Let stand at room temperature for about 30 minutes.

Lightly oil a 7-inch nonstick frying pan and place over medium-high heat until hot. Pour ¼ cup of the batter into the pan and tilt the pan to cover the bottom evenly. Drizzle a little batter into any holes. Cook until the bottom is golden brown, about 1 minute. Flip and cook the other side until golden. Transfer to a plate. Repeat with the remaining batter, adding more oil to the pan as needed and stacking the blintzes, separated by parchment, as they are ready. You should have 12 blintzes.

Preheat the oven to 350°F. To make the filling, in a bowl, mix together the ricotta, 6 tablespoons of the sugar, the egg yolks, vanilla, and lemon zest. Lightly butter a rimmed baking sheet with some of the remaining 3 tablespoons butter. Place 1 blintz, spotted side up, on a work surface. Place about 2 tablespoons of the ricotta filling just below the center of the blintz, fold in the sides, and then roll up from the bottom, enclosing the filling. Place on the baking sheet, seam side down. Repeat with the remaining blintzes and filling. (The blintzes can be prepared to this point up to 2 hours ahead, covered, and refrigerated.) Brush the blintzes with the remaining butter. Bake until heated through, about 10 minutes (or a little longer if the blintzes have been refrigerated).

Meanwhile, in a saucepan, combine the sliced plums, the remaining 2 tablespoons sugar, and the lemon juice over medium heat and cook, stirring occasionally, until the plums are heated through, about 5 minutes. Remove from the heat and keep warm. To serve, place 2 filled blintzes on each plate. Crown with a dollop of sour cream and a spoonful of the plum compote. Serve at once.

PUT A SPIN ON IT   Substitute 2 cups blueberries or pitted cherries for the plums. Or, skip the compote and serve the blintzes with a spoonful of preserves. You can also fry the filled blintzes in butter instead of baking.

An elegant breakfast classic, eggs Benedict has a muddled history, but every story connects it to society's upper crust. Many tasty variations exist, each embellishing the unassuming poached egg on a muffin with luxurious hollandaise sauce and other ingredients, such as crisp bacon paired with sautéed spinach, as in this version.

LEMONY EGGS FLORENTINE

Large egg yolks, 4

**Fresh lemon juice,
1 tablespoon**

**Kosher salt and ground
white pepper**

**Unsalted butter,
1 cup plus 1 tablespoon**

Spinach, 1¼ pounds

**Shallots, 3 tablespoons
finely chopped**

**Applewood-smoked
bacon, 8 thick slices,
halved crosswise**

English muffins, 4, split

**Poached eggs
(page 247), 8**

MAKES 4 SERVINGS

To make the hollandaise, in a blender, combine the egg yolks, 1 tablespoon water, the lemon juice, ¼ teaspoon salt, and ⅛ teaspoon white pepper. In a small saucepan, melt the 1 cup butter over medium heat. With the blender running, slowly add the warm melted butter through the vent in the lid, processing until the sauce is thick and smooth. Taste and adjust the seasoning. If the sauce is too thick, add a bit more water to thin it. Transfer the sauce to a bowl, cover, and set aside.

Stem the spinach, rinse well but do not dry, and coarsely chop. In a large saucepan, melt the remaining 1 tablespoon butter over medium heat. Add the shallots and cook, stirring occasionally, until tender, about 2 minutes. Stir in the spinach, cover, and cook until the spinach is tender, about 3 minutes. Season to taste with salt and white pepper. Drain the spinach mixture in a sieve, pressing gently to remove excess liquid. Return to the pan, cover, and set aside.

In a large frying pan, fry the bacon over medium heat, turning once, until crisp and browned, about 6 minutes. Transfer to paper towels to drain. Meanwhile, preheat the broiler. Place the muffins, cut sides up, on a baking sheet. Broil until toasted, about 1 minute. Poach the eggs and keep them warm in hot water as directed.

To serve, place 2 toasted muffin halves, cut sides up, on each plate. Top the 2 halves with one-fourth of the spinach and 4 pieces of bacon. One at a time, using a slotted spoon, remove the poached eggs from the hot water, resting the bottom of the spoon briefly on a clean kitchen towel to blot excess moisture, and perch 2 eggs on each serving of bacon. Spoon about 3 tablespoons of the hollandaise over each pair of eggs. Serve at once, passing the remaining hollandaise on the side.

PUT A SPIN ON IT For classic eggs Benedict, substitute sautéed slices of Canadian bacon or ham for the spinach and bacon. For eggs Monterey, top the muffins with crabmeat, briefly sautéed in butter, in place of the spinach and bacon. And for eggs Blackstone, swap the spinach for tomato slices.

Hollandaise sauce is unwaveringly democratic: anything you put it on instantly becomes better.

Long ago, I worked at a restaurant that was ridiculously busy during weekend brunches. Eggs Florentine—a toasted English muffin layered with buttery sautéed spinach, crisp bacon, a poached egg, and rich, lemony hollandaise—and its well-known and well-loved cousin, eggs Benedict, were always top sellers. I had to make hollandaise sauce fast, and no matter how much I made, the kitchen always seemed to need more. This was a time when there were no food processors, so I became an expert at whipping up a quart or two of sauce at a time by hand. In spite of putting together more orders of eggs Benedict and its kin than I can count, the dish still lures me with its elegant combination of a classic, sophisticated sauce cloaking a simple, humble poached egg.

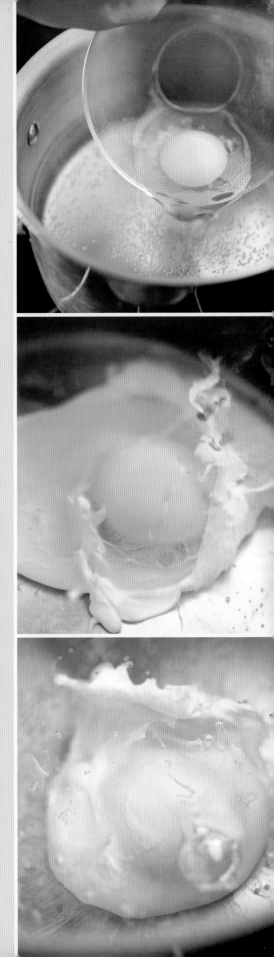

You may wonder if making your own doughnuts is worth the effort. Just one bite of these sugar-glazed deep-fried treats will prove it is. The spicy flavor is sure to bring back memories of crisp autumn mornings and relaxing breakfasts in flannel pajamas. Instead of the glaze, these are also delicious tossed with cinnamon-sugar.

SPICED CIDER DOUGHNUTS

Apple cider, 1 cup

All-purpose flour, 3¼ cups, plus more as needed

Granulated sugar, 1 cup

Baking powder, 2 teaspoons

Baking soda, 1 teaspoon

Ground cinnamon, ½ teaspoon

Freshly grated nutmeg, ½ teaspoon

Kosher salt, ½ teaspoon

Unsalted butter, 2 tablespoons cold, thinly sliced

Buttermilk, ½ cup

Large eggs, 2

Pure vanilla extract, 1 teaspoon

Canola oil for deep-frying

Confectioners' sugar, 1½ cups, sifted

MAKES 1 DOZEN DOUGHNUTS AND 1 DOZEN HOLES

In a small saucepan, bring the cider to a boil over high heat. Cook until reduced to ½ cup, 8–10 minutes. Let cool completely. In a bowl, sift together the 3¼ cups flour, the granulated sugar, baking powder, baking soda, cinnamon, nutmeg, and salt. Add the butter. Using a handheld mixer on low speed, beat until the mixture forms fine crumbs. In another bowl, whisk together the buttermilk, eggs, ¼ cup of the reduced cider, and the vanilla until combined. Add the buttermilk mixture to the flour mixture and stir until a soft dough forms. Turn out onto a floured work surface and knead until smooth, about 1 minute, adding up to ¼ cup more flour if needed. Line a rimmed baking sheet with parchment paper. Transfer the dough to the baking sheet and pat it out to a layer ½ inch thick. Freeze until slightly firm, 15 minutes.

Pour oil to a depth of at least 3 inches into a heavy, deep saucepan and heat over high heat to 350°F on a deep-frying thermometer. Set a large wire rack on another rimmed baking sheet and place near the stove. Return the dough to the work surface. Using a doughnut cutter 3 inches in diameter, and dipping the cutter into flour before each cut, cut out as many doughnuts as possible, pressing straight down and lifting straight up. Transfer the doughnuts and the holes to the parchment paper–lined baking sheet. Gather up the scraps and repeat rolling and cutting.

Using a metal spatula, carefully lower a few of the doughnuts into the hot oil, being sure not to crowd the pan. Deep-fry the doughnuts, turning them once at the halfway point, until golden brown, about 3 minutes. Using a wire skimmer, transfer to the rack to drain. Repeat until all of the doughnuts have been fried, then add the doughnut holes to the oil and deep-fry until golden brown, about 2 minutes. Let cool.

To make the glaze, in a small saucepan, bring the remaining ¼ cup reduced cider to a boil over high heat. Add the confectioners' sugar and whisk until smooth. Remove from the heat. Holding each doughnut or doughnut hole by its edges, briefly dip it, smooth side down, into the glaze, letting the excess drip back into the saucepan. Place on the wire rack, glazed side up, and let stand until the glaze is set, about 10 minutes. Serve warm or at room temperature.

MIDDAY MEALS

For most of my school years, when the noon bell rang, I hopped on my bike and rushed home for lunch. Usually, a freshly made sandwich awaited me. On the ride home, I would always try to guess what Mom might have made from her seemingly endless repertoire: a gooey peanut butter and jelly, a warm tuna melt, or my favorite, grilled cheese, which I dipped into creamy tomato soup. On wintry days, we swapped sandwiches for hearty bowls of soup. Few lunches are more satisfying than creamy clam chowder or chicken soup with dumplings. Soups and sandwiches are well represented in this chapter, but you'll also find some hearty, comforting salads, too, including two classics from my home state of California: the Cobb (the ultimate chef's salad) and the crab Louis (my all-time favorite). As Mom would say, "Don't forget to wash your hands before eating!" And as I would say, "Dig in!"

Proust had his tea and madeleines, but for many Americans, one bite of an egg salad sandwich, with a filling that dribbles out between the bread slices, is what transports them back to their childhood. Allowing the whole eggs to stand in the hot water, rather than boiling them, ensures against rubbery whites and gray-green yolks.

EGG SALAD SANDWICHES

Large eggs, 8

Mayonnaise (page 246 or purchased), 1/2 cup, plus more for the bread

Celery, 2 small stalks, finely chopped

Green onions, 2 small, white and green parts, finely chopped

Fresh flat-leaf parsley, 1 tablespoon minced

Dijon mustard, 1 teaspoon

Kosher salt and freshly ground pepper

Good-quality white bread, 8 slices

Butter lettuce, 4 leaves

MAKES 4 SANDWICHES

To hard-boil the eggs, place them in a saucepan just large enough to hold them. Add cold water to cover by 1 inch and bring just to a boil over high heat. Remove the pan from the heat and cover. Let stand for 15 minutes. Drain the eggs, then transfer to a bowl of ice water and let cool completely.

In a bowl, mix together the 1/2 cup mayonnaise, the celery, green onions, parsley, and mustard. Peel the eggs and chop finely. Add to the mayonnaise mixture and mix gently. Season with salt and pepper.

Spread 4 of the bread slices with equal amounts of the egg salad, then top each with a lettuce leaf. Spread mayonnaise on the remaining 4 breadslices, and place, mayonnaise side down, on each sandwich. Cut in half and serve.

PUT A SPIN ON IT Add chopped fresh herbs, such as tarragon, chervil, or chives, to the egg salad. For easy appetizers, spoon the egg salad into Belgian endive leaves, or for a lunchtime salad, mound it onto a bed of lettuce.

Once little known outside Hollywood, where it was one of the stars on the menu of the Brown Derby restaurant, Cobb salad is now served everywhere as a deceptively light lunch. Heaped with blue cheese, bacon, chicken, and avocado, it's a hearty meal that guarantees you won't be hungry until suppertime.

THE COBB

Large eggs, 2

White wine vinegar, ¼ cup

Dijon mustard, 1 teaspoon

Garlic, 1 clove, crushed

Olive oil, ¾ cup plus 1 tablespoon

Kosher salt and freshly ground pepper

Skinless, boneless chicken breast halves, 3 (about 6 ounces each)

Fresh flat-leaf parsley, 2 tablespoons minced

Fresh thyme, 2 teaspoons minced

Applewood-smoked bacon, 4 thick slices, chopped

Avocado, 1

Romaine lettuce hearts, 2, chopped

Cherry tomatoes, 2 cups, halved

Gorgonzola or other mild blue cheese, 1 cup crumbled

MAKES 4 SERVINGS

To hard-boil the eggs, place them in a saucepan just large enough to hold them. Add cold water to cover by 1 inch and bring just to a boil over high heat. Remove the pan from the heat and cover. Let stand for 15 minutes. Drain the eggs, then transfer to a bowl of ice water and let cool. Peel the eggs and cut into quarters.

To make the vinaigrette, in a blender, combine the vinegar, mustard, and garlic. With the blender running, slowly add the ¾ cup oil through the vent in the lid, processing until a thick dressing forms. Season with salt and pepper. Pour into a serving bowl.

Using a meat pounder, pound the chicken breasts until they are a uniform ½ inch thick. Season them with salt and pepper. Mix together the parsley and thyme, and sprinkle evenly over both sides of the breasts, pressing the herbs to help them adhere. In a large nonstick frying pan, heat the remaining 1 tablespoon oil over medium heat. Add the chicken and cook until the undersides are browned, about 5 minutes. Turn and cook until the second sides are browned and the breasts are opaque throughout, about 5 minutes more. Transfer to a plate and let cool.

Add the bacon to the frying pan and fry, stirring occasionally, until crisp and browned, about 4 minutes. Using a slotted spoon, transfer to paper towels to drain.

When ready to serve, slice the chicken breasts across the grain into strips. Halve, pit, peel, and cube the avocado. Divide the lettuce evenly among 4 individual plates, or heap it onto a platter. Arrange the chicken, bacon, tomatoes, avocado, eggs, and Gorgonzola on the lettuce. Drizzle with some of the dressing and serve, passing the remaining dressing on the side.

PUT A SPIN ON IT You can use sliced roast beef in place of the chicken. For delicious on-the-go wraps, arrange the salad ingredients on flour tortillas or sheets of lavash, dress them lightly with the vinaigrette, and then roll them up.

Meltingly tender onions, meaty stock, and rich, nutty melted cheese—these are the indispensable elements that make this boldly flavored soup a hallmark of French cuisine—and a favorite of American tables, too. Take the time to make your own stock and you will be rewarded with deep flavor and savory goodness.

FRENCH ONION SOUP

Unsalted butter,
2 tablespoons

Yellow onions,
2½ pounds, halved
and thinly sliced

All-purpose flour,
1 tablespoon

Dry white wine, 1 cup

Beef stock (page 244),
8 cups

Fresh thyme,
2 teaspoons minced,
or 1 teaspoon dried

Bay leaf, 1

**Kosher salt and freshly
ground pepper**

Crusty baguette, 1

Gruyère cheese,
2⅔ cups shredded

MAKES 8 SERVINGS

In a large, heavy sauté pan, melt the butter over medium heat. Add the onions, stir well, cover, and cook for 5 minutes. Uncover, reduce the heat to medium-low, and cook, stirring occasionally, until tender and deep golden brown, about 30 minutes.

Sprinkle the flour over the onions and stir until combined. Gradually stir in the wine, then the stock, and finally the thyme and bay leaf. Bring to a boil over high heat, reduce the heat to medium-low, and simmer, uncovered, until slightly reduced, about 30 minutes. Season with salt and pepper. Discard the bay leaf.

Meanwhile, preheat the broiler. Have ready eight 1½-cup broilerproof soup crocks. Cut the baguette into 16 slices, sizing them so that 2 slices will fit inside each crock. Arrange the bread slices on a baking sheet and broil, turning once, until lightly toasted on both sides, about 1 minute total. Set the slices aside. Position the oven rack about 12 inches from the heat source, and leave the broiler on.

Ladle the hot soup into the crocks. Place 2 toasted bread slices, overlapping if necessary, on top of the soup and sprinkle each crock evenly with about ⅓ cup of the Gruyère. Broil until the cheese is bubbling, about 2 minutes. Serve at once.

PUT A SPIN ON IT For an extra layer of flavor and complexity, instead of the yellow onions, use a mixture of roughly equal amounts red, white, and sweet (such as Vidalia) onions. Italy's Fontina cheese, from the Val d'Aosta, is a delicious alternative to the traditional Gruyère cheese.

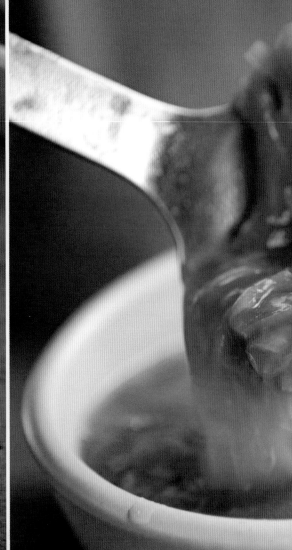

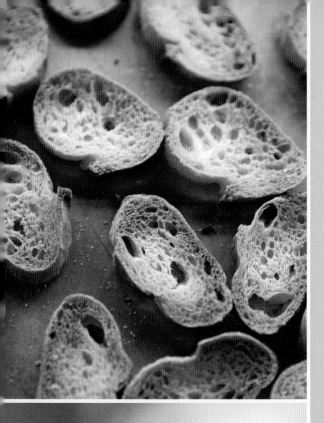

Unsure of what was hidden beneath the thick, golden topping of melted cheese, I plunged my spoon into the crock.

My high-school French teacher regularly took our class on field trips to expand our knowledge of French culture. One evening, she arranged for a proper meal *à la français* at an upscale restaurant in the city. The menu was pure French comfort food: a crock of cheese-blanketed onion soup, hearty coq au vin, and silky chocolate mousse. As I savored every wonderful bite, I had no inkling that this was the meal that would lead to my career. I was especially bowled over by the onion soup: that first spoonful of melt-in-your-mouth caramelized onions and rich, meaty broth literally changed my life. Years later, I studied French cuisine in Paris, and at my first meal in the City of Light, I raised a glass in toast to my French teacher, the resourceful Ms. Powell.

Chock-full of briny clams and tender chunks of potato, this creamy New England chowder seems custom-made to take the chill off of a cold afternoon. Before you add the clams to the pot, be sure to scrub them well and soak them to remove any trace of sand or other grit, which could spoil the soup.

CLAM CHOWDER

Littleneck clams,
4 dozen (about 4 pounds)

Kosher salt and freshly ground pepper

Red-skinned potatoes,
2 large

Applewood-smoked bacon,
4 thick slices, chopped

Yellow onion, 1 chopped

Celery, 2 small stalks, finely chopped

All-purpose flour,
3 tablespoons

Half-and-half, 2 cups

Fresh thyme,
½ teaspoon minced

Chopped fresh flat-leaf parsley for garnish

MAKES 6-8 SERVINGS

Scrub the clams under cold running water. Place in a large bowl, add salted cold water to cover, and let stand for 1 hour. Drain the clams and rinse well. Place the clams in a saucepan and add 1 cup water. Cover and bring to a boil over high heat. Cook, shaking the pan occasionally, until the clams have opened, about 4 minutes. Discard any unopened clams. Transfer the clams to a large bowl, reserving the cooking liquid in the pan. Remove the clam meat from the shells, setting the meat aside and discarding the shells. Line a fine-mesh sieve with dampened cheesecloth, place it over a 4-cup glass measuring cup, and strain the cooking liquid from the pan and the large bowl through the cheesecloth. Add cold water as needed to the measuring cup to total 4 cups liquid.

Meanwhile, dice the unpeeled potatoes and place in a large saucepan. Add salted water to cover by 1 inch, cover the pan, and bring to a boil over high heat. Uncover, reduce the heat to medium-low, and simmer until tender when pierced with a knife, about 20 minutes. Drain and set aside.

In a large saucepan, fry the bacon over medium-low heat, stirring occasionally, until browned, about 10 minutes. Using a slotted spoon, transfer to paper towels to drain. Add the onion and celery to the fat in the pan and cook over medium heat, stirring occasionally, until tender, about 5 minutes. Sprinkle in the flour and stir well. Stir in the reserved potatoes and clam liquid, the half-and-half, and the thyme. Bring to a simmer, reduce the heat to medium-low, and simmer until lightly thickened, about 5 minutes. Stir in the reserved clam meat and bacon, and season with salt and pepper. Ladle into warmed bowls, sprinkle with parsley, and serve.

PUT A SPIN ON IT To make fish chowder, omit the clams. Use 4 cups fish stock in place of the clam liquid and water. Add 1 pound skinned fish fillets, such as cod, haddock, or snapper, cut into 1-inch pieces, to the soup base along with the cooked potatoes. Simmer until barely opaque, about 5 minutes. Add the bacon, season, and serve as directed.

Up and down the West Coast, this seafood salad is considered the benchmark of the salad maker's art. A Louis (pronounced LOO-ee) is all about the seafood, so don't be tempted to add fancy salad greens or exotic vegetables, which will only detract from the mound of fresh, sweet crabmeat.

CRAB LOUIS

Large eggs, 4

Mayonnaise (page 246 or purchased), 1 cup

Ketchup-style chili sauce, ¼ cup

Green bell pepper, 2 tablespoons minced

Green onions, 2, white and green parts, minced

Fresh lemon juice, 1 tablespoon

Iceberg lettuce, ½ head

Romaine lettuce hearts, 2

Fresh-cooked lump crabmeat, 1 pound

Cherry tomatoes, ½ cup, halved

English cucumber, ¼, thinly sliced

Lemon, 1, cut into wedges

MAKES 4-6 SERVINGS

To hard-boil the eggs, place them in a saucepan just large enough to hold them. Add cold water to cover by 1 inch and bring just to a boil over high heat. Remove the pan from the heat and cover. Let stand for 15 minutes. Drain the eggs, then transfer to a bowl of ice water and let cool. Peel the eggs and cut into quarters.

To make the dressing, in a small bowl, whisk together the mayonnaise, chili sauce, bell pepper, green onions, and lemon juice. Cover and refrigerate until serving.

Tear the iceberg lettuce into bite-sized pieces, and coarsely chop the romaine hearts. In a large bowl, toss together the lettuces. Distribute the lettuces in a thick layer on a large platter or divide evenly among 4–6 individual plates. Pick over the crabmeat for shell shards and cartilage. Heap the crabmeat down the center of the lettuce. Arrange the tomatoes, cucumbers, and quartered eggs around the crab. Garnish with the lemon wedges and serve, passing the dressing on the side.

PUT A SPIN ON IT A Louis salad is often made with shrimp instead of crab, or with a combination of crab and shrimp. Use cooked, peeled, and deveined shrimp in the size you prefer (on the West Coast, tiny bay shrimp are usually the first choice). You can also top the salad with lightly cooked asparagus.

Throughout Louisiana, a po'boy, a soft French roll stuffed to the brim with the hot filling of your choice, is considered the best of all possible sandwiches. You can make it with spicy sausages or sliced roast beef dripping with gravy, but deep-fried oysters are what put this sandwich on the map.

FRIED OYSTER PO'BOYS

Shucked oysters, 1 pound

Yellow cornmeal, preferably stone-ground, 1 cup

All-purpose flour, 1 cup

Kosher salt, 1¼ teaspoons

Sweet paprika, preferably Hungarian or Spanish, ½ teaspoon

Dried basil, ½ teaspoon

Dried thyme, ½ teaspoon

Freshly ground black pepper, ½ teaspoon

Granulated garlic, ¼ teaspoon

Cayenne pepper, ⅛ teaspoon

Large eggs, 3

Canola oil for deep-frying

Soft French or Italian rolls, 4, split

Rémoulade (page 246)

Shredded iceberg lettuce for serving

Tomato slices for serving

MAKES 4 SANDWICHES

Drain the oysters in a sieve, then rinse well. In a food processor, process the cornmeal until finely ground, about 2 minutes. Pour into a bowl, add the flour, salt, paprika, basil, thyme, black pepper, garlic, and cayenne pepper, and whisk to combine. In another bowl, whisk the eggs until well blended.

Pour oil to a depth of at least 3 inches into a large, heavy saucepan and heat over high heat to 350°F on a deep-frying thermometer. Preheat the oven to 200°F.

Meanwhile, line a rimmed baking sheet with parchment paper. A few at a time, dip the oysters into the eggs, then toss in the flour mixture, shaking off the excess. Place on the prepared baking sheet.

Set a large wire rack on another baking sheet and place near the stove. In batches to avoid crowding, carefully slip the oysters into the hot oil and deep-fry, turning once, until golden brown, about 2½ minutes. Using a wire skimmer or slotted spoon, transfer the fried oysters to the rack and keep warm in the oven. Repeat with the remaining oysters.

Remove the oysters from the oven and turn on the broiler. Place the rolls, split side up, on a baking sheet, and toast in the broiler until lightly crisped, 1–2 minutes.

Spread the cut side of each roll half with about 2 tablespoons of the rémoulade. Place an equal number of oysters on the bottom half of each roll, and top with the tomato slices and lettuce. Place the top of the roll on top. Serve at once, passing the remaining rémoulade on the side.

PUT A SPIN ON IT   Not an oyster fan? Substitute 1 pound medium shrimp, peeled and deveined, for the oysters. Tartar sauce (page 105) or a mixture of ketchup and mayonnaise can stand in for the rémoulade.

Chicken soup is famous with moms the world over for its restorative properties, but this version, with its tender sage-flecked dumplings, will make you feel good even if you don't have the sniffles. Use a gentle hand when mixing the dough to ensure the dumplings will be light and delicate.

CHICKEN AND DUMPLINGS

Olive oil, 2 tablespoons

Yellow onion, 1, diced

Carrots, 2, diced

Celery, 1 stalk, diced

Chicken stock (page 244) or broth, 8 cups

Cooked, shredded chicken (from Chicken Stock, page 244 or purchased rotisserie chicken), 4 cups

Fine sea salt and freshly ground pepper

All-purpose flour, 1½ cups

Baking powder, 2 teaspoons

Fresh sage, 2 teaspoons minced

Whole milk, ¾ cup

MAKES 8 SERVINGS

In a soup pot, heat the oil over medium heat. Add the onion, carrots, and celery, cover, and cook, stirring occasionally, until the vegetables soften, about 5 minutes. Add the stock and bring to a boil over high heat. Reduce the heat to medium-low and simmer until the vegetables are tender, about 20 minutes. Add the chicken. Season with salt and pepper.

To make the dumplings, in a bowl, whisk together the flour, baking powder, and ½ teaspoon sea salt. Stir in the sage. Add the milk and stir to make a soft dough. Using a tablespoon, drop equal mounds of the dough onto the surface of the simmering soup. Cover and cook until the dumplings are firm, about 15 minutes.

Spoon the soup and dumplings into warmed large bowls and serve at once.

PUT A SPIN ON IT To make a classic chicken noodle soup, omit the dumplings and add cooked egg noodles or small pasta shapes, such as ditalini, along with the chicken, and heat through. For chicken and rice soup, add cooked long-grain rice and heat through. Don't add uncooked noodles or rice, as they will soak up too much liquid, making the soup too thick.

Perhaps more than any of its sandwich cousins, the tuna melt takes humble ingredients and transforms them into a special treat. You will need to outfit everyone at the table with a knife and fork to eat this open-faced lunchtime classic of zesty tuna salad and gooey melted cheese.

TUNA MELTS

White albacore tuna packed in oil or water, 3 cans (6 ounces each)

Mayonnaise (page 246 or purchased), ½ cup

Celery, ½ cup minced

Yellow or red onion, ¼ cup minced

Fresh flat-leaf parsley, 2 tablespoons minced

Freshly ground pepper

Firm white sandwich bread, 4 large slices

Tomato, 8 slices

Mild Cheddar cheese, 6 ounces, thinly sliced

MAKES 4 SANDWICHES

Preheat the broiler. Drain the tuna well and put in a bowl. Add the mayonnaise, celery, onion, and parsley and stir well. Season with pepper.

Arrange the bread slices on a rimmed baking sheet and broil, turning once, until very lightly browned on both sides, about 1 minute total. Spread equal amounts of the tuna mixture onto each toasted bread slice. Divide the tomato slices evenly among the sandwiches, then divide the Cheddar evenly on top. Return to the broiler and broil until the Cheddar melts, about 1 minute more. Serve at once.

PUT A SPIN ON IT   You can use rye bread or split English muffins for your tuna melts, and substitute sharp Cheddar, Gruyère, or Swiss cheese for the mild Cheddar. To impart a little tang to the tuna mixture, stir in 2 tablespoons chopped bread-and-butter pickles. If your idea of a tuna melt is not open faced, using untoasted bread, prepare the sandwiches as directed, topping them with a second slice of bread. Spread softened butter on the outside of each sandwich and cook it in a frying pan over medium heat until the cheese melts and the bread is golden brown on both sides.

Smoky, salty bacon makes almost everything taste better, and this hearty salad is no exception. It may even make kids happily eat their greens. Bacon has lots of presence here, so look for good-quality, thick-cut bacon for the tastiest results. And try not to eat all the crisp bacon bits while you assemble the salads.

WARM SPINACH AND BACON SALAD

Extra-virgin olive oil,
8 tablespoons

Button mushrooms,
1 pound, halved

Fresh lemon juice,
1½ tablespoons

Garlic, 2 cloves, thinly sliced

Fresh thyme,
1 teaspoon minced

Red pepper flakes,
¼ teaspoon

**Kosher salt and freshly
ground pepper**

Large eggs, 3

Baby spinach, 10 ounces

Applewood-smoked bacon,
8 thick slices, chopped

Balsamic vinegar,
3 tablespoons

Whole-grain mustard,
1 tablespoon

Red onion, 1 small,
thinly sliced

Cherry tomatoes,
1½ cups, halved

MAKES 6-8 SERVINGS

In a frying pan, heat 2 tablespoons of the oil over medium-high heat. Add the mushrooms and cook, stirring occasionally, until they give off their juices and are lightly browned, 5–6 minutes. Transfer to a bowl. Add 4 tablespoons oil, the lemon juice, garlic, thyme, and red pepper flakes, season with salt and pepper, and toss to coat. Let marinate for at least 1 hour or up to 24 hours.

To hard-boil the eggs, place them in a saucepan just large enough to hold them. Add cold water to cover by 1 inch and bring just to a boil over high heat. Remove the pan from the heat and cover. Let stand for 15 minutes. Drain the eggs, then transfer to a bowl of ice water and let cool. Peel and coarsely chop the eggs.

Put the spinach in a large bowl. In a large frying pan, fry the bacon over medium heat, stirring occasionally, until crisp and browned, about 7 minutes. Using a slotted spoon, transfer to paper towels to drain. Pour off all but 2 tablespoons of the fat in the pan. Off the heat, whisk the vinegar and mustard into the fat in the pan, then whisk in the remaining 2 tablespoons oil. Season to taste with salt and pepper and drizzle over the spinach. Toss to coat well.

Divide the dressed spinach among individual plates, top with the onion slices, tomatoes, marinated mushrooms, and chopped eggs. Sprinkle with the chopped bacon and serve at once.

PUT A SPIN ON IT You can top each serving with a poached egg (page 247) instead of chopped hard-boiled egg. The fruity flavor of cider vinegar in place of the balsamic vinegar pairs nicely with the smoky bacon.

Pancetta, garlic, vegetables, and herbs give this soup fragrance and flavor, and the beans and pasta make it hearty enough for even the healthiest appetite. Indeed, each and every ingredient adds character, including the Parmesan cheese rind that infuses the broth with depth and complexity, so don't omit it.

ITALIAN BEAN AND PASTA SOUP

Pancetta,
¼ pound, chopped

Extra-virgin olive oil,
1 tablespoon

Yellow onion,
1, finely chopped

Carrots, 2, diced

Celery, 1 stalk, diced

Garlic, 2 cloves, minced

Chicken stock (page 244)
or broth, 8 cups

Fresh cranberry beans,
1 pound, shelled

Fresh rosemary sprig, 1

Bay leaf, 1

Parmesan cheese rind,
2-inch piece

Small pasta shapes
such as *conchigliette*
or ditalini, ⅔ cup

Tomatoes, 2, seeded
and chopped

Kosher salt and freshly
ground pepper

Freshly grated Parmesan
cheese for serving

MAKES 6 SERVINGS

In a soup pot, cook the pancetta with the oil over medium heat, stirring occasionally, until the pancetta begins to brown, about 5 minutes. Add the onion, carrots, and celery and cook, stirring occasionally, until the vegetables have softened, about 8 minutes. Stir in the garlic and cook until fragrant, about 1 minute.

Pour in the stock and add the beans, rosemary, bay leaf, and Parmesan rind. Raise the heat to medium-high and bring to a boil. Reduce the heat to medium-low, cover, and simmer, stirring occasionally, until the beans are just tender, about 30 minutes.

Stir the pasta and tomatoes into the pot and simmer, stirring occasionally, until the pasta is al dente (check the package directions for cooking time). Discard the rosemary, bay leaf, and Parmesan rind.

Season the soup with salt and pepper, ladle into warmed bowls, and serve at once, passing the Parmesan cheese on the side.

PUT A SPIN ON IT If you can't find fresh cranberry beans, use dried: Rinse 1 cup dried cranberry beans and pick them over, discarding any misshapen beans or stones. In a large bowl, combine the beans with water to cover by 1 inch, and let stand at cool room temperature for at least 4 hours or up to 12 hours. (If the weather is warm, refrigerate the beans.) Drain the beans well before adding them to the pot, and increase the cooking time to 45–60 minutes. Hearty beef stock (page 244 or purchased) can be used in place of the chicken stock. Add a spoonful of basil pesto (page 245) to each bowl for a colorful garnish.

The best crab cakes are crispy on the outside, tender on the inside, and bursting with fresh seafood flavor. Too many versions lean heavily on fillers, but these plump cakes are loaded with sweet crabmeat, with just enough additional ingredients to flavor and bind them, ensuring that the crustacean remains the star.

CRAB CAKES WITH LEMON AIOLI

LEMON AIOLI

Mayonnaise (page 246 or purchased), 1 cup

Finely grated lemon zest, from 1 lemon

Fresh lemon juice, 2 tablespoons

Garlic, 1 clove, minced

Fine sea salt and freshly ground pepper

Fresh-cooked lump crabmeat, 1 pound

Panko or other dried bread crumbs, ¾ cup

Large egg, 1, beaten

Dijon mustard, 1 tablespoon

Worcestershire sauce, 2 teaspoons

Hot pepper sauce, ¼ teaspoon

Fresh flat-leaf parsley, 1 tablespoon chopped

Canola oil, ½ cup

Lemon wedges for serving

MAKES 4 SERVINGS

To make the aioli, in a small bowl, mix together the mayonnaise, lemon zest and juice, and garlic. Season with salt and pepper. Set aside ¼ cup of the aioli. Cover and refrigerate the remaining aioli until serving.

Line a rimmed baking sheet with parchment paper. To make the crab cakes, pick over the crabmeat for shell shards and cartilage. In a bowl, mix together ¼ cup of the panko, the reserved ¼ cup aioli, the egg, mustard, Worcestershire sauce, hot pepper sauce, and parsley. Add the crabmeat and mix gently until combined. Divide the mixture into 8 equal portions and shape each portion into a thick cake. Spread the remaining ½ cup panko in a shallow dish. Coat the cakes evenly with the panko, and transfer to the prepared baking sheet. Refrigerate for 15 minutes.

In a large frying pan, heat the oil over medium-high heat until it shimmers. Add the cakes and cook until the undersides are golden brown, 2–3 minutes. Flip the cakes and cook until the other sides are golden brown, about 2 minutes more. Using a slotted spatula, transfer to paper towels to drain briefly.

Serve the crab cakes at once with the lemon wedges and pass the remaining lemon aioli on the side.

PUT A SPIN ON IT   Instead of the aioli, serve the crab cakes with homemade mayonnaise (page 246) or a simple lemon vinaigrette. Or, make a creamy green goddess dressing: Whisk together 1 cup mayonnaise; 1 tablespoon *each* minced fresh tarragon, chives, and parsley; 1 teaspoon anchovy paste; 1 teaspoon Dijon mustard; and the grated zest of 1 lemon.

Growing up, my family often went to the wharf to buy freshly cooked crabs, pulled straight from giant sidewalk cauldrons.

It is a rite of passage for every young San Franciscan to learn how to cook, clean, crack, and eat a crab. In our family, Dad was the teacher of these all-important skills, just as he taught us how to properly mow the lawn or flip burgers on the grill. Nowadays, when I visit friends in the City by the Bay during winter—the local season for Dungeness—at least one get-together always features cracked Dungeness crab drizzled with fresh lemon juice or melted butter, a big green salad with a zesty vinaigrette, and a loaf of crusty sourdough bread, all washed down with a first-rate California Chardonnay. It just doesn't get any better than that.

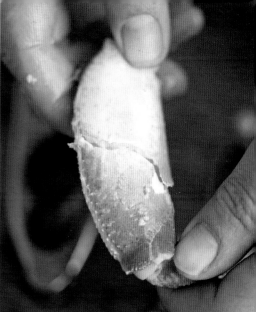

The peanut butter and jelly sandwich—better known as the PB & J—has been making lunch easy for countless moms over the years. The popular PB and banana variation trades out the jelly for bananas and adds honey for a touch of sweetness, while the grilled PB sandwich, with a layer of decadent chocolate, takes it over the top.

PB AND BANANA SANDWICHES

Whole-grain honey-wheat bread, 8 slices

Creamy or crunchy peanut butter, about ¾ cup

Bananas, 2 large

Honey, 8 teaspoons

MAKES 4 SANDWICHES

Place 4 bread slices on a work surface and spread with the peanut butter, dividing it equally. Peel and slice the bananas, and arrange the slices on top of the peanut butter, dividing them evenly. Drizzle 2 teaspoons honey over each banana-topped slice. Top with the remaining bread slices. Cut in half and serve.

PUT A SPIN ON IT Experiment with different types of bread—raisin bread or even cinnamon-swirl bread are good choices—or try different types of nut butters, such as almond or cashew.

GRILLED PB AND CHOCOLATE SANDWICHES

Good-quality white bread, 8 slices

Creamy or crunchy peanut butter, about ½ cup

Chocolate-hazelnut spread, such as Nutella®, about ½ cup

Unsalted butter, 4 tablespoons, at room temperature

MAKES 4 SANDWICHES

Place the bread slices on a work surface. Spread 4 of the slices with the peanut butter. Spread the other 4 slices with the chocolate-hazelnut spread, and place each slice, chocolate side down, on a peanut butter slice. Heat a griddle or 2 frying pans over medium heat until hot. Spread the outside of each sandwich with 1 tablespoon of the butter. Place on the griddle, reduce the heat to medium-low, and cook until the undersides are golden brown, about 3 minutes. Flip the sandwiches and brown the other side, 3 minutes more. Cut in half and serve.

PUT A SPIN ON IT Add a thin layer of jam—raspberry or apricot are delicious—or a layer of sliced banana. Spread the jam or the banana slices on the peanut butter before topping with the chocolate-hazelnut spread.

Many Americans have vivid memories of eating grilled American cheese sandwiches and bowls of canned tomato soup when they were kids. Here, that same classic pairing features the best Cheddar cheese and sourdough bread or *pain au levain* in the sandwiches and roasted tomatoes in the soup, for an over-the-top treat.

GRILLED CHEESE WITH CREAMY TOMATO SOUP

CREAMY TOMATO SOUP

Plum tomatoes, 4 pounds

Olive oil, 2 tablespoons

Unsalted butter,
1 tablespoon

Celery, 2 stalks,
finely chopped

Shallots, 1/3 cup
finely chopped

Chicken stock
(page 244) or broth,
1/2 cup, or as needed

Fresh thyme, 1 teaspoon

Sugar, 1/2 teaspoon

Heavy cream, 1/2 cup

Kosher salt and freshly
ground pepper

GRILLED CHEESE

Mild Cheddar cheese,
3/4 pound, thinly sliced

Sourdough bread or
pain au levain, 8 slices

Unsalted butter,
4 tablespoons, at
room temperature

MAKES 4 SERVINGS

To make the soup, preheat the oven to 400°F. Lightly oil a rimmed baking sheet. Cut the tomatoes in half lengthwise. Place them, cut side up, on the prepared baking sheet and brush with the 2 tablespoons oil. Roast until the tomatoes look somewhat shriveled, about 45 minutes. Let cool for about 20 minutes. Transfer the tomatoes and any juices to a food processor. Pulse until chopped, then rub the tomatoes and their juices through a coarse-mesh sieve placed over a bowl. You should have about 3½ cups tomato purée. Discard the contents of the sieve.

In a large saucepan, melt the butter over medium-low heat. Add the celery and cook, stirring occasionally, until tender, about 5 minutes. Add the shallots and cook, stirring occasionally, until softened, about 3 minutes. Stir in the tomato purée, ½ cup stock, and the thyme and bring to a simmer over medium-high heat. Reduce the heat to medium-low and simmer, uncovered, for about 15 minutes. Stir in the sugar. In 3 or 4 batches, transfer the soup to a blender and process until smooth. Transfer to a clean saucepan, add the cream, and heat until piping hot but not boiling. If the soup seems thick, thin with more stock. Season to taste with salt and pepper.

To make the grilled cheese sandwiches, heat a griddle or 2 large frying pans over medium heat until hot. For each sandwich, place one-fourth of the cheese on top of 1 bread slice and top with a second bread slice. Spread the outsides of each sandwich with 1 tablespoon of the butter. Place on the griddle, reduce the heat to medium-low, and cook until the undersides are golden brown, 3–4 minutes. Flip the sandwiches and brown the other side, 3–4 minutes more. Ladle the soup into warmed bowls. Serve at once, with the hot sandwiches alongside.

PUT A SPIN ON IT Grilled cheese sandwiches offer countless variations. Switch it up by using your favorite bread or different cheeses. For an over-the-top sandwich, add ham and tomato slices before grilling.

Few sights are more appetite sparking than a heap of plump, golden fried shrimp, their crunchy coating protecting the sweet tender meat beneath. Dip the shrimp, one by one, into the spicy cocktail sauce and savor every bite. This is one dish that you are allowed to eat with your fingers!

OVEN-FRIED SHRIMP

Ketchup-style chili sauce or ketchup (page 246), 1 cup

Prepared horseradish, 2 tablespoons drained

Finely grated lemon zest, from 1 lemon

Fresh lemon juice, 1 tablespoon

Hot pepper sauce

Panko or other dried bread crumbs, 1¼ cups

Sweet paprika, preferably Hungarian or Spanish, 1 teaspoon

Dried oregano, basil, and thyme, ½ teaspoon *each*

Granulated garlic, ½ teaspoon

Kosher salt, ½ teaspoon

Cayenne pepper, ⅛ teaspoon

Unsalted butter, 4 tablespoons, melted

Olive oil, 2 tablespoons

Large shrimp, 2 pounds, peeled and deveined

MAKES 4 SERVINGS

To make the sauce, in a small bowl, stir together the chili sauce, horseradish, and lemon zest and juice. Season with hot pepper sauce. Set aside.

Preheat the oven to 400°F. Lightly oil a large rimmed baking sheet. In a bowl, stir together the panko, paprika, oregano, basil, thyme, garlic, salt, and cayenne pepper. In another bowl, whisk together the butter and oil. In batches, toss the shrimp in the butter mixture to coat, then coat them with the panko mixture, shaking off the excess. Spread in a single layer on the prepared baking sheet.

Bake until the coating is golden brown and the shrimp are opaque throughout when pierced with the tip of a knife, about 10 minutes.

Transfer the sauce to individual bowls for dipping. Serve the shrimp at once, passing the sauce on the side.

PUT A SPIN ON IT For coconut shrimp, substitute 1½ cups unsweetened desiccated coconut for the panko mixture. Add 1 teaspoon curry powder to the butter mixture. Dip the shrimp in the butter mixture, then the coconut, and bake as directed. Serve with Thai sweet chili sauce for dipping.

When you're hungry for a rib-sticking meal, few sights are more encouraging—or aromas more enticing—than a big pot of simmering tomato sauce with meatballs. This rustic recipe combines the zesty sauce and tender meatballs inside crusty rolls, all covered with melted cheese. It would make any Italian nonna proud.

MEATBALL HOAGIES

Olive oil, 1 tablespoon

Yellow onion, ½ cup minced

Garlic, 2 cloves, minced

Coarse fresh bread crumbs, ¾ cup

Whole milk, ½ cup

Large egg, 1, beaten

Fresh flat-leaf parsley, 2 tablespoons minced

Dried oregano, 1½ teaspoons

Kosher salt, 1½ teaspoons

Freshly ground pepper, ½ teaspoon

Ground beef round, 1 pound

Ground pork and veal, ½ pound *each*

Marinara sauce (page 245), 6 cups

Crusty Italian rolls, 6, split

Provolone or mozzarella cheese, ½ pound

Freshly grated Parmesan cheese for sprinkling

MAKES 6 SANDWICHES

Preheat the oven to 400°F. Lightly oil a rimmed baking sheet. In a small frying pan, heat the oil over medium heat. Add the onion and cook, stirring occasionally, until softened, about 4 minutes. Add the garlic and cook until fragrant, about 1 minute more. Transfer to a large bowl and let cool to lukewarm.

Meanwhile, place the bread crumbs in a bowl. Add the milk and let stand for about 5 minutes. Transfer the mixture to a sieve and drain, pressing hard on the bread to extract the excess milk. Add the soaked bread crumbs, egg, parsley, oregano, salt, and pepper to the onion mixture and mix well. Add the ground meats and mix with your hands just until combined. Do not overmix, or the meatballs will be dense.

Using wet hands, shape the mixture into 18 meatballs, and arrange on the prepared baking sheet. Bake until the tops are browned, about 20 minutes, then turn and bake until cooked through, 15 minutes more. Remove from the oven.

In a large saucepan, bring the marinara sauce to a simmer over medium heat. Add the meatballs. Discard any fat on the baking sheet, add ½ cup boiling water to the baking sheet, and use a wooden spatula to scrape up any browned bits. Pour into the marinara sauce and stir. Simmer until the flavors are blended, about 20 minutes.

Preheat the broiler. Place the rolls, cut sides up, on another rimmed baking sheet. Place 3 meatballs on each roll, then spoon some of the sauce over the meatballs. Pour 2 cups of the remaining sauce into a bowl and keep warm. Reserve the remaining sauce for another use. Thinly slice the provolone and divide evenly among the sandwiches. Broil until the cheese melts, about 1 minute. Using a large, wide spatula, transfer the hoagies to individual plates. Sprinkle each sandwich with Parmesan cheese and serve, passing the sauce on the side.

PUT A SPIN ON IT For an even heartier meatball sandwich, add a topping of sautéed peppers and onions, such as the mixture used in Cheesesteaks (page 74), after you've melted the cheese.

The best fried chicken cutlets are always crisp, juicy, and perfectly seasoned—and surprisingly simple to make. Here, they are the stars of hearty sandwiches slathered with mayonnaise and topped with dill pickle slices and crisp lettuce, a nod to similar ones you might find in luncheonettes throughout the south.

FRIED CHICKEN SANDWICHES

Kosher salt, ½ teaspoon

Freshly ground pepper, ¼ teaspoon

Sweet or hot paprika, preferably Hungarian or Spanish, ¼ teaspoon

Boneless, skinless chicken breast halves, 4 (about 6 ounces each)

Large eggs, 2

Whole milk, ½ cup

All-purpose flour, 1½ cups

Peanut or canola oil for frying

Soft torpedo or sandwich rolls, 4, split

Mayonnaise (page 246 or purchased) for spreading

Dill pickles, 1 or 2, cut into 12 slices

Red-leaf lettuce, 4 large leaves

MAKES 4 SANDWICHES

Mix together the salt, pepper, and paprika. Using a meat pounder, pound the chicken breasts until they are a uniform ½ inch thick. Cut each breast half in half lengthwise, and sprinkle the pieces evenly with the salt mixture. Let stand at room temperature for 30 minutes, or wrap with plastic wrap and refrigerate overnight.

Have ready a rimmed baking sheet. In a shallow bowl, whisk together the eggs and milk. Put the flour into a second shallow bowl. One at a time, coat the chicken pieces with the flour, shaking off the excess, then dip into the egg mixture, allowing the excess to drip off. Coat with flour a second time, again shaking off the excess. Transfer to the baking sheet.

Preheat the broiler. Pour oil to a depth of ½ inch into a large cast-iron or other heavy frying pan and heat over medium-high heat to 375°F on a deep-frying thermometer. Set a large wire rack on another rimmed baking sheet and place near the stove.

In batches if necessary to avoid crowding, carefully slip the chicken pieces into the hot oil and cook, turning once, until golden brown on both sides, about 10 minutes total. Using tongs or a slotted spatula, transfer to the rack to drain.

Meanwhile, place the rolls, split side up, on a baking sheet and toast under the broiler until lightly crisped, about 1 minute. Transfer the toasted rolls to plates. Spread mayonnaise on the cut sides of the rolls. Divide the fried chicken, pickles, and lettuce evenly among the rolls. Serve at once.

PUT A SPIN ON IT   These sandwiches are also delicious topped with slaw instead of pickles and lettuce. Use either Creamy Coleslaw (page 180) or the more vinegary option offered as a "spin" with the Fish Tacos (page 83).

The cheesesteak, thin slices of griddled beef and cheese heaped on a toasted roll, is a Philadelphia treat that has made its way onto menus all across America. Partially freezing the beef makes it easier to slice thinly without an electric slicer. Have plenty of napkins on hand to catch the inevitable drips.

CHEESESTEAKS

Boneless beef top loin or rib-eye steak, 1¼ pounds, in one piece

Olive oil, 2 tablespoons

Yellow onion, 1 large, halved and thinly sliced

Red bell pepper, 1 large, seeded and thinly sliced crosswise

Garlic, 2 cloves, minced

Kosher salt and freshly ground pepper

Canola oil for cooking

Provolone cheese, 6 ounces, thinly sliced

Crusty French or Italian rolls, 4, split

MAKES 4 SANDWICHES

Freeze the meat until it is firm but not frozen, about 1 hour. Using a sharp, thin-bladed knife, cut the meat across the grain into slices ¼ inch thick. Using a meat pounder, pound the meat until it is a uniform ⅛ inch thick or thinner. Cut into pieces about 4 by 3 inches.

Meanwhile, in a frying pan, heat the olive oil over medium heat. Add the onion and bell pepper and stir well. Cover, reduce the heat to medium-low, and cook, stirring occasionally, until very tender, 25–30 minutes. Uncover and stir in the garlic. Cook until the garlic is tender, 2–3 minutes more. Season with salt and pepper. Set aside.

Preheat the broiler. Heat a large griddle or 2 frying pans over medium-high heat until hot. Lightly oil the griddle, or add 1 tablespoon oil to each frying pan and tilt to coat the bottoms evenly with the oil. Add the meat slices and cook until browned on the undersides, about 1 minute. Turn the meat slices and divide on the griddle into 4 equal mounds. Top each mound with an equal amount of the Provolone. Cook until the undersides of the mounds are browned and the cheese is beginning to melt, about 1 minute longer.

Meanwhile, place the rolls, split side up, on a baking sheet and toast in the broiler until lightly crisped, about 1 minute. Transfer the rolls to plates. Using a metal spatula, transfer each mound of beef and cheese onto a toasted roll bottom. Spoon an equal amount of the onion-pepper mixture onto each mound, place the top of the roll on top, and serve at once.

PUT A SPIN ON IT Mozzarella, mild Cheddar, and Monterey Jack cheese are all good choices to replace the provolone. Instead of the onion-pepper mixture, cook only one or the other. Or, top the mounds of beef and cheese with warm marinara sauce (page 245 or purchased).

This sandwich, a staple of natural-foods restaurants in the 1960s, could have disappeared like the Volkswagen bus. But, with its thick, juicy tomato slices, crunchy bacon, and buttery avocado, it has proven to have staying power, and is still one of the best ways to spend your lunch break.

BLTA SANDWICHES

Applewood-smoked bacon,
12 thick slices

Whole-wheat or multigrain bread,
8 slices

Mayonnaise (page 246 or purchased)

Avocados, 2 small

Kosher salt and freshly ground pepper

Beefsteak tomato,
8 slices

Red-leaf lettuce, 4 leaves

MAKES 4 SANDWICHES

Preheat the oven to 400°F. Spread the bacon in a single layer on a rimmed baking sheet. Bake until the bacon is crisp and browned, about 20 minutes. Transfer the bacon to paper towels to drain. (Alternatively, fry the bacon on a griddle or in a large frying pan over medium heat until crisp.)

Preheat the broiler. Arrange the bread on a baking sheet. Broil, turning once, until toasted on both sides, about 3 minutes. Transfer the bread to a work surface.

Spread mayonnaise on one side of each bread slice. Halve, pit, and peel the avocados. Place an avocado half, cut side down, on top of 4 of the bread slices. Slice the avocado directly on the bread, taking care not to cut into the bread, then fan out the slices. Season with salt and pepper. Top each avocado half with 3 bacon slices, cut to fit; 2 tomato slices; and 1 lettuce leaf. Place 1 bread slice, mayonnaise side down, atop each lettuce leaf. Cut each sandwich in half and serve.

PUT A SPIN ON IT These same sandwich ingredients can be transformed into a salad by using a little less bread and a little more lettuce. Cut 4 bread slices into cubes, coat with a drizzle of olive oil, and toast under the broiler to make croutons. Toss the sliced avocados and tomatoes, croutons, torn lettuce, and chopped bacon with your favorite vinaigrette (hold the mayo).

The perfect lunch? Few contenders can compete with a bacon, lettuce, and tomato sandwich, dressed up with buttery avocado.

Nothing is wrong with the traditional BLT, but I am prone to gilding the lily. In my college days, I worked at a restaurant whose fame was built on its irresistible avocado and bacon sandwich. Indeed, it was so popular that the kitchen went through at least three cases of avocados a day. The secret of the sandwich? Each component was top-notch: perfectly ripened avocado, juicy tomato, thick slices of crisp-yet-tender bacon, and garden-fresh lettuce. All of them were carefully layered between slices of firm whole-grain bread spread with thick swipes of mayo. And even though I made thousands of those best sellers during my four years there, I still cannot pass up a great BLTA sandwich.

Serve a New Englander a lobster roll and it's sure to conjure up memories of summers at the shore. These sandwiches are stuffed with lobster and more lobster, without a lot of filler, so wait until summertime, when lobsters are plentiful and reasonably priced, before making these deliciously rich rolls.

LOBSTER ROLLS

Live lobsters, 2
(1½–2 pounds each)

Mayonnaise (page 246 or purchased), ¼ cup

Fresh lemon juice, 2 teaspoons

Fresh tarragon, 1 teaspoon minced

Fresh flat-leaf parsley, 1 teaspoon minced

Celery salt

Freshly ground pepper

Hot dog buns, preferably New England–style split-top buns, 4

Unsalted butter, 4 tablespoons, at room temperature

MAKES 4 ROLLS

Fill a very large pot with lightly salted water and bring to a boil over high heat. Add the lobsters and cover. Return to a boil, then remove the lid. Boil until the lobsters are bright red, about 6 minutes. Drain and rinse under cold running water.

Place 1 cooked lobster, back side up, on a cutting board. Slip the tip of a large chef's knife into the lobster at the point where the head meets the body. Holding the lobster securely, cut the head in half lengthwise. Repeat at the other end of the lobster, cutting the body and tail in half lengthwise. Twist the legs and claws from the body. Discard any visceral matter from the body, then remove the meat from the body and tail shells. Using a lobster cracker or nutcracker, crack the claws and any large legs, and remove the meat from the shells. Repeat with the second lobster. Cut the lobster meat into chunks.

In a bowl, combine the lobster meat, mayonnaise, lemon juice, tarragon, and parsley and mix gently. Season with celery salt and pepper. Cover and refrigerate until chilled, at least 2 hours.

Heat a griddle or large, heavy frying pan over medium-high heat. Spread the outside top and bottom of the buns with the butter. Place the buns in the frying pan and cook, turning once, until golden brown on both sides, about 1 minute per side. Fill each bun with an equal amount of the lobster mixture. Serve at once.

PUT A SPIN ON IT Add 1 celery stalk, minced, to the lobster mixture or top the rolls with 1 cup shredded iceberg lettuce. To keep it simple, omit the mayonnaise, lemon, and herbs and serve the buns loaded with the lobster meat only and drizzled with plenty of melted butter. Or, change the seafood: use ¾ pound fresh-cooked lump crabmeat or cooked, peeled, and deveined shrimp, coarsely chopped, for the lobster meat.

These tasty tacos, filled with grilled fish and served with a tangy-sweet mango salsa, will have you dreaming of long, sunny days at the beach. The oil in the marinade coupled with oiling the cooking grate will help prevent the relatively delicate snapper fillets from sticking to the grate as you grill them.

FISH TACOS

MANGO SALSA

Mango, 1

Red onion,
2 tablespoons minced

Fresh cilantro,
2 tablespoons minced

Serrano chile, 1, seeds
and ribs removed, minced

Fresh lime juice,
3 tablespoons

Kosher salt

Finely grated lime zest,
from 1 lime

Fresh lime juice,
2 tablespoons

Extra-virgin olive oil,
2 tablespoons

Fresh cilantro,
1 tablespoon minced

Chili powder, 1 teaspoon

Garlic, 1 clove, minced

**Skinless red snapper
fillets, 1 pound**

Canola oil for grilling

Kosher salt

Corn tortillas, 8

MAKES 4 SERVINGS

To make the salsa, peel, pit, and dice the mango. In a small bowl, stir together the diced mango, onion, cilantro, chile, lime juice, and salt. Cover the salsa and let stand while preparing the snapper.

Prepare a grill for direct-heat cooking over medium heat. Meanwhile, in a shallow ceramic or glass bowl, whisk together the lime zest and juice, olive oil, cilantro, chili powder, and garlic. Add the snapper and turn to coat. Let stand while the grill is heating, no longer than 30 minutes.

Lightly oil the cooking grate. Remove the snapper from the marinade, season it with salt, and place on the grill. (You can use a perforated grill grid if you have one.) Cover and cook until opaque when flaked in the thickest part, about 5 minutes. (No need to turn the snapper.) Transfer to a cutting board. Do not worry if the snapper pieces fall apart when you remove them from the grill. Tent with aluminum foil to keep warm and let stand for 3 minutes.

Meanwhile, place the tortillas on the grill and cook, turning once, until heated through, about 1 minute total. Wrap in a cloth napkin or kitchen towel to keep warm.

Flake the fish into bite-sized pieces and transfer to a serving plate. Serve at once with the salsa and tortillas, allowing diners to fill their own tacos.

PUT A SPIN ON IT Fish tacos can be served with slaw instead of salsa: Mix together 4 cups finely shredded green cabbage; 1 green onion, white and green parts, minced; 1/3 cup mayonnaise (page 246 or purchased); 2 tablespoons fresh lime juice; and 2 tablespoons minced fresh cilantro. Season with salt and pepper, and let stand for about 30 minutes before serving.

Piled high with such delicatessen staples as corned beef, tangy sauerkraut, and creamy Russian dressing, this warm and cheesy sandwich has two very different cities claiming to be its birthplace: New York and Omaha. If you have homemade corned beef left over, by all means, use it.

REUBEN SANDWICHES

Mayonnaise (page 246 or purchased), 2/3 cup

Ketchup-style chili sauce or ketchup (page 246 or purchased), 1/4 cup

Bread-and-butter pickles, 2 tablespoons finely chopped

Cooked corned beef (page 97 or purchased), about 3/4 pound, sliced

Rye bread, 8 slices

Swiss cheese, 8 slices

Refrigerated sauerkraut, 1 cup well drained

Unsalted butter, 1/2 cup, at room temperature

MAKES 4 SANDWICHES

To make the Russian dressing, in a small bowl, mix together the mayonnaise, chili sauce, and chopped pickles. Set aside.

To make the sandwiches, preheat a griddle or 2 large frying pans over medium heat. Add the corned beef and cook, turning occasionally, just until heated but not browned, about 1 minute. Remove from the heat.

Lay the bread slices on a work surface and spread each slice with 1 tablespoon of the dressing. Trim the slices of Swiss to fit the bread slices, then place 1 cheese slice on each of 4 bread slices. Top each with one-fourth of the corned beef, followed by 1/4 cup of the sauerkraut, and then 1 more cheese slice. Top with the remaining bread slices, dressing side down. Spread the outside top and bottom of each sandwich with about 2 tablespoons of the butter.

Place the sandwiches on the griddle and reduce the heat to medium-low. Cook until golden brown on the bottoms, about 4 minutes. The sandwiches should cook fairly slowly to allow the bread to brown without burning while the cheese melts. Flip the sandwiches and brown the second sides, about 4 minutes more. Transfer to a cutting board and cut in half. Serve hot, passing the remaining dressing on the side.

 PUT A SPIN ON IT Use pastrami or smoked ham instead of the corned beef, and pumpernickel in place of the rye. Coleslaw (page 180) is excellent in place of the sauerkraut and cheese, especially with pastrami.

SUPPERTIME

My first memories of supper have me sitting on a phone book at the table, but the specifics of the menu are fuzzy. So many dishes made me feel good back then—and still do. It could have been a big plate of spaghetti and meatballs. Or, maybe it was a thick slice of meat loaf, perched on a mound of creamy mashed potatoes. When did I learn to love fried chicken or beef Stroganoff, all specialties of the Rodgers household? Nowadays, after a busy workday, I often crave long-simmered stews, pot roasts, and other melt-in-your-mouth braised dishes. In less hectic times, someone in the family would have prepared these in the afternoon for the evening supper, an impractical schedule for many of today's cooks. The solution is simple: make large batches of your favorites during the weekend when you have more time to cook, and freeze the leftovers. That way, culinary comfort is never far away.

In many homes, Monday-night supper calls for comfort food, as folks try to ease back into the workweek. A heaping plate of spaghetti crowned with plump meatballs is the perfect dish to serve. Make a double batch of the marinara sauce, so you have a container in the freezer, ready at a moment's notice.

SPAGHETTI AND MEATBALLS

Olive oil, 1 tablespoon

Yellow onion,
½ cup minced

Garlic, 2 cloves, minced

Coarse fresh bread crumbs, ¾ cup

Whole milk, ½ cup

Egg, 1 large, beaten

Fresh flat-leaf parsley,
2 tablespoons minced

Dried oregano,
1½ teaspoons

Kosher salt,
1½ teaspoons

Freshly ground pepper,
½ teaspoon

Ground beef round,
1 pound

Ground pork and veal,
½ pound *each*

**Marinara sauce
(page 245),** 6 cups

Spaghetti, 1 pound

Freshly grated Parmesan cheese for serving

MAKES 6 SERVINGS

Preheat the oven to 400°F. Lightly oil a rimmed baking sheet. In a small frying pan, heat the oil over medium heat. Add the onion and cook, stirring occasionally, until softened, about 4 minutes. Add the garlic and cook until fragrant, about 1 minute more. Transfer to a large bowl and let cool to lukewarm.

Meanwhile, place the bread crumbs in a small bowl. Add the milk and let stand for 5 minutes. Transfer the mixture to a sieve and drain, pressing hard on the bread to extract the excess milk. Add the soaked bread crumbs, egg, parsley, oregano, salt, and pepper to the onion mixture and mix well. Add the ground meats and mix with your hands just until combined. Do not overmix, or the meatballs will be dense.

Using wet hands, shape the mixture into 18 meatballs, and arrange on the prepared baking sheet. Bake until the tops are browned, about 20 minutes, then turn and bake until cooked through, 15 minutes more. Remove from the oven.

In a large saucepan, bring the marinara sauce to a simmer over medium heat. Add the meatballs. Discard any fat on the baking sheet, add ½ cup boiling water to the baking sheet, and use a wooden spatula to scrape up any browned bits. Pour into the marinara sauce and stir. Simmer until the flavors are blended, about 20 minutes.

Meanwhile, bring a large pot of salted water to a boil over high heat. Add the spaghetti and stir occasionally until the water returns to a boil. Cook according to the package directions until al dente. Drain in a colander. Return the pasta to the pot. Add about half of the sauce to the pasta, without the meatballs, and toss to combine. Divide the pasta among individual pasta bowls, and top each serving with more sauce and an equal number of the meatballs. Serve hot, with the Parmesan.

PUT A SPIN ON IT For a great baked dish, substitute ziti for the spaghetti and undercook it slightly. Toss the drained pasta with the meatballs and sauce, transfer to a baking dish, and top with 1 cup freshly grated Parmesan. Bake in a preheated 350°F oven until the cheese is browned, about 15 minutes.

The best shepherd's pies start with a languorously simmered lamb stew, redolent with rosemary and a hint of garlic. Capped with creamy mashed potatoes, the topping becomes golden brown in the oven. If you have trouble finding boneless lamb shoulder, look for it at butcher shops that cater to Mediterranean cooks.

SHEPHERD'S PIE

Boneless lamb shoulder, 2 pounds

Kosher salt and freshly ground pepper

Olive oil, 2 tablespoons

Unsalted butter, 8 tablespoons

Yellow onion, 1 large, diced

Carrots, 3, diced

Celery, 3 stalks, diced

Garlic, 2 small cloves, minced

All-purpose flour, 6 tablespoons

Beef stock (page 244) or broth, 3⅓ cups

Dry white wine, ⅔ cup

Fresh rosemary, 2 teaspoons minced

Baking potatoes, 3 pounds

Heavy cream, about ⅓ cup, warmed

Fresh or thawed frozen peas, 1 cup

MAKES 6 SERVINGS

Preheat the oven to 325°F. Trim the lamb of excess fat and cut into 1-inch cubes. Season with salt and pepper. In a Dutch oven, heat the oil over medium-high heat. In batches to avoid crowding, add the lamb cubes and cook, turning occasionally, until browned on all sides, about 5 minutes per batch. Transfer to a plate.

Add 4 tablespoons of the butter to the Dutch oven and melt over medium heat. Add the onion, carrots, celery, and garlic, cover, and cook, stirring occasionally, until the carrots are tender-crisp, about 5 minutes. Uncover, sprinkle with the flour, and stir well. Gradually stir in the stock and wine and then the rosemary. Bring to a boil over medium heat, stirring frequently. Return the lamb to the Dutch oven, cover, place in the oven, and cook until the lamb is tender, about 1½ hours.

About 30 minutes before the lamb is ready, oil six 2-cup ovenproof soup crocks or a 3-quart baking dish. Peel the potatoes and cut into chunks. In a saucepan, combine the potatoes with salted water to cover, cover the pan, and bring to a boil over high heat. Uncover, reduce the heat to medium, and simmer until the potatoes are tender, 20–25 minutes. Drain well. Return the potatoes to the pan and stir over medium-low heat for 2 minutes to evaporate the excess moisture. Cut 3 tablespoons of the butter into pieces and add to the potatoes. Using a handheld mixer or a potato masher, whip or mash the potatoes while adding enough cream to create a smooth mixture. Season with salt and pepper.

Season the lamb mixture with salt and pepper, stir in the peas, and pour into the prepared baking dish(es). Spread the mashed potatoes evenly on top. Cut the remaining 1 tablespoon butter into bits and use to dot the top. Bake until the top is lightly tinged with brown, about 20 minutes. Remove from the oven and let stand for about 5 minutes, then serve hot.

PUT A SPIN ON IT   For rancher's pie, substitute 2 pounds boneless beef chuck for the lamb, and fresh thyme for the rosemary. For an extra-rich topping, whip 6 ounces of fresh, rindless goat cheese into the potatoes.

These flavorful short ribs perfectly illustrate how braised meat cooked on the bone can turn out succulent and tender enough to cut with a fork. The bones also enrich the braising liquid, which marries delectably with the cheese-laced creamy polenta. A bold-flavored Syrah or Zinfandel is ideal for the pot and the table.

BRAISED SHORT RIBS WITH CREAMY POLENTA

Olive oil, 3 tablespoons

Meaty, bone-in, individual-cut short ribs, 6 pounds

Kosher salt, 4 teaspoons

Freshly ground pepper, 1 teaspoon

Yellow onion, 1, chopped

Carrots, 2, diced

Garlic, 6 cloves, chopped

All-purpose flour, 1/3 cup

Hearty red wine, 2 cups

Beef stock (page 244) or broth, 3 cups

Tomato paste, 2 tablespoons

Fresh rosemary, 1 tablespoon minced

Bay leaf, 1

Whole milk, 1 cup

Quick-cooking polenta, 1 1/3 cups

Parmesan cheese, 1/2 cup freshly grated, plus more for serving

MAKES 6 SERVINGS

Preheat the oven to 325°F. In a Dutch oven, heat 2 tablespoons of the oil over medium-high heat. Season the short ribs with 2 teaspoons salt and the pepper. In batches to avoid crowding, add the short ribs to the pot and cook, turning occasionally, until browned on all sides, 5–6 minutes per batch. Transfer to a plate.

Add the remaining 1 tablespoon oil to the pot and heat. Add the onion and carrots and cook, stirring occasionally, until the onion softens, about 5 minutes. Stir in the garlic and cook until fragrant, about 1 minute. Sprinkle in the flour and stir well. Slowly stir in the wine, then the stock. Stir in the tomato paste, rosemary, and bay leaf. Return the short ribs to the pot. The short ribs should be barely covered with liquid. If not, add hot water as needed. Bring the liquid to a boil. Cover the pot, place in the oven, and cook, moving the position of the ribs every 45 minutes or so to be sure that they are covered with liquid and are cooking evenly, until very tender, about 2½ hours. Transfer the ribs to a deep serving platter (don't worry if the meat separates from the bones), and tent with aluminum foil to keep warm.

Let the cooking liquid stand for 5 minutes. Skim off the fat from the surface and discard. Bring to a boil over high heat. Cook, stirring, until reduced by about one-fourth, about 10 minutes. Discard the bay leaf. Return the short ribs to the pot.

Just before serving, make the polenta: In a heavy saucepan, bring 3 cups water, the milk, and the remaining 2 teaspoons salt to a boil over high heat. Slowly whisk in the polenta and reduce the heat to medium-low. Cook, whisking often, until the polenta is thick, about 2 minutes. Stir in the ½ cup Parmesan. Divide the polenta among warmed deep serving bowls, top with the ribs and sauce and serve at once.

PUT A SPIN ON IT If you have leftover short ribs, you can easily turn them into a divine ragù. Simply remove the bones, shred the meat, stir it back into the sauce, and reheat until warm. Toss with freshly cooked pappardelle.

On a cold night, a bowl of meltingly tender short ribs spooned over creamy polenta is guaranteed to warm you to the bone.

In my hometown of San Francisco, the nights are often foggy and chilly, even in summer. My friends and I amassed a substantial repertoire of supper dishes designed to warm us up year-round, and we often cooked together. My dear friend Lillian was famous for her short ribs, falling-off-the-bone morsels of tender meat covered in a wine-rich sauce. At one potluck, I tried my hand at polenta, following a recipe provided by a friendly grocer in North Beach, the city's famed Italian neighborhood. We paired the meat and the polenta, and experienced for the first time what the Italians have known for centuries is a culinary marriage made in heaven.

Layers of tender pasta, slow-cooked meat sauce, and creamy béchamel—this satisfying lasagna is ideal for feeding a crowd, and is simply one of the most perfect comfort foods. Busy hosts will appreciate that it can be prepared in advance. Assemble it, then cover and refrigerate for up to 12 hours, before baking for 1 hour.

LASAGNA BOLOGNESE

Olive oil, 1 tablespoon

Pancetta, ¼ pound, diced

Yellow onions, 2 small

Carrot, 1, finely chopped

Celery, 1 stalk, finely chopped

Garlic, 2 cloves, minced

Ground beef, pork, and veal, 1 pound *each*

Dry white wine, 1 cup

Plum tomatoes, 1 can (28 ounces)

Dried basil and oregano, 1 teaspoon *each*

Kosher salt and freshly ground pepper

Bay leaves, 3

Heavy cream, ½ cup

Whole milk, 4 cups

Unsalted butter, ½ cup plus 1 tablespoon, diced

All-purpose flour, ½ cup

Fresh spinach pasta sheets, ¾ pound

Parmesan cheese, 1 cup freshly grated

MAKES 8 SERVINGS

To make the Bolognese sauce, in a large saucepan, heat the oil over medium heat. Add the pancetta and cook, stirring often, until lightly browned, about 8 minutes. Finely chop 1 onion, and add to the pan along with the carrot and celery. Cover and cook, stirring occasionally, until the vegetables soften, about 5 minutes. Stir in the garlic and cook until fragrant, about 1 minute. Add the ground meats and increase the heat to medium-high. Cook, stirring and breaking them up with a wooden spoon, until no longer pink, about 10 minutes. Add the wine and cook until it has almost evaporated, about 5 minutes. Crush the tomatoes with your fingers. Stir in the tomatoes and their juice, basil, oregano, 2 teaspoons salt, 1 teaspoon pepper, and 2 of the bay leaves and bring to a boil. Reduce the heat to low and simmer uncovered, stirring occasionally, until the tomatoes break down and a thick, meaty sauce forms, adding a little water if the sauce thickens too much, about 1¾ hours. Add the cream and simmer for 15 minutes more. Discard the bay leaves.

To make the béchamel, thickly slice the remaining onion and place in a saucepan. Add the milk and the remaining bay leaf and bring slowly to a simmer over medium heat. Cover, remove from the heat, and let stand 10 minutes. Discard the onion and bay leaf. In another saucepan, melt the ½ cup butter over medium heat. Whisk in the flour. Reduce the heat to medium-low and let bubble for 1 minute. Gradually whisk in the warm milk, raise the heat to medium, and bring to a gentle boil, whisking frequently. Reduce the heat to medium-low and simmer, whisking frequently, until smooth and lightly thickened, about 5 minutes. Season with salt and pepper.

Meanwhile, preheat the oven to 350°F. Butter a 10-by-15-inch baking dish. To assemble, cut the pasta sheets into 15-inch lengths. Spread ½ cup of béchamel in the bottom of the baking dish. Top with a layer of pasta, one-third of the Bolognese, one-fourth of the béchamel, and ¼ cup of the Parmesan. Repeat two more times with layers of pasta, Bolognese, bechamel, and Parmesan. Finish with a final layer of pasta, the remaining béchamel and Parmesan, and the 1 tablespoon diced butter. Bake, uncovered, until the béchamel is lightly browned and the sauce is bubbling, about 30 minutes. Let stand for 10 minutes, then cut into squares and serve hot.

A hefty corned beef brisket and a bushel of vegetables simmering in a pot on the stove top signals the St. Patrick's Day feast. But this simple-to-prepare celebratory supper is too good to serve just one day of the year. Plus, you can put any leftovers to delicious use in corned beef hash (page 15) or Reuben sandwiches (page 84).

CORNED BEEF AND CABBAGE

Fresh thyme, 3 sprigs

Fresh flat-leaf parsley, 5 sprigs

Corned beef brisket, 1 (about 3½ pounds)

Bay leaves, 2

Black peppercorns, 1 teaspoon

White boiling onions, 12

Carrots, 6, cut into large chunks

Small red-skinned potatoes, 2 pounds

Green cabbage, 1 small head, cut into 6–8 wedges

Heavy cream, 1 cup

Prepared horseradish, 3 tablespoons

Kosher salt

MAKES 6-8 SERVINGS

Tie together the thyme and parsley sprigs with kitchen string. Rinse the brisket, put it in a large Dutch oven, and add water to cover by 1 inch. Bring to a boil over medium-high heat, skimming off any foam that rises to the surface. Add the herb bundle, bay leaves, and peppercorns, reduce the heat to medium-low, cover, and simmer gently until almost tender, 2½–3 hours.

Add the onions, carrots, unpeeled potatoes, and cabbage wedges to the pot and return the liquid to a simmer. Cook until the vegetables and brisket are fully tender, about 25 minutes.

Meanwhile, in a bowl, using a whisk or a handheld mixer, beat the cream until soft peaks form. Using the whisk, fold in the horseradish, then season with salt. Cover and refrigerate the horseradish cream until ready to serve.

Using a slotted spoon, transfer the vegetables to a large platter. Transfer the brisket to a cutting board. Slice the meat across the grain and arrange on the platter with the vegetables. Serve hot, passing the horseradish cream on the side.

PUT A SPIN ON IT   Corning your own beef brisket is easy, but it takes some planning. To make the brine, in a large bowl, combine 8 cups water, 1½ cups kosher salt, ½ cup sugar, 3 tablespoons pickling spices, and 3 cloves garlic, crushed. Stir until the salt and sugar are dissolved. Submerge one 4 pound brisket in the mixture, cover, and refrigerate for 5–8 days. When you are ready to cook, remove the brisket from the brine, rinse well under running cold water, and then proceed with the recipe as directed.

Chicken potpie is both an example of the best of American home cooking and a kind of culinary miracle worker, with a creamy sauce and a flaky pastry lid that are guaranteed to calm even the most jangled nerves. Both the pastry and the filling can be made ahead and refrigerated for up to 8 hours before assembling and baking.

CHICKEN POTPIE

Unsalted butter,
6 tablespoons

Button mushrooms,
½ pound, quartered

Leeks, white and pale green parts,
1 cup chopped

Carrots, ½ cup finely diced

Fresh or thawed frozen peas, ⅓ cup

All-purpose flour,
⅓ cup plus 1 tablespoon

Chicken stock (page 244) or broth,
4½ cups

Dry sherry, ⅓ cup

Fresh tarragon,
2 teaspoons minced

Cooked, shredded chicken (from Chicken Stock, page 244 or purchased rotisserie), 4 cups

Kosher salt and freshly ground pepper

Double-crust flaky pastry dough (page 248)

Large egg, 1

MAKES 6 SERVINGS

To make the sauce and vegetables, in a large frying pan, melt 1 tablespoon of the butter over medium heat. Add the mushrooms and cook, stirring occasionally, until they begin to brown, about 6 minutes. Stir in the leeks and carrots, cover, and cook, stirring occasionally, until the leeks are tender, about 5 minutes. Remove from the heat and stir in the peas.

In a large saucepan, melt the remaining 5 tablespoons butter over medium-low heat. Whisk in the flour and let bubble gently for 1 minute. Gradually whisk in the stock and sherry and then the tarragon. Bring to a boil, whisking frequently. Stir in the shredded chicken and the mushroom-leek mixture and season with salt and pepper. Let cool until lukewarm, about 1 hour.

Preheat the oven to 400°F. Spoon the chicken mixture into six 1½-cup ovenproof soup crocks or ramekins.

Place the unwrapped dough on a lightly floured work surface and dust the top with flour. (If the dough is chilled hard, let it stand at room temperature for a few minutes until it begins to soften before rolling it out.) Roll it out into a rectangle about 20 by 13 inches and ⅛ inch thick. Using a 6-inch saucer as a template, use a knife to cut out 6 rounds. Beat the egg with a pinch of salt. Lightly brush each round with the egg. Place 1 round, egg side down, over each ramekin, keeping the pastry taut and pressing it around the ramekin edges to adhere. Place the ramekins on a rimmed baking sheet. Lightly brush the tops with the egg. Bake until the pastry is puffed and golden brown, about 25 minutes. Transfer each ramekin to a dinner plate and serve.

PUT A SPIN ON IT Use biscuit dough (page 162) in place of the pastry dough. Roll out the dough ½ inch thick, then cut out rounds to fit just inside the rim of each ramekin. Bake at 400°F until the biscuit topping is golden brown, about 20 minutes.

Ham owes its popularity not only to its smoky-salty flavor but also to its talent for feeding a lot of people with very little effort. This recipe, with a simple ginger and orange glaze, is no exception. Whip up a batch of homemade biscuits (page 162) and a dish of scalloped potatoes (page 196) for the ultimate comfort food menu.

BAKED HAM

Shank-end smoked ham,
1 (about 5 pounds)

Unsalted butter,
1 tablespoon

Fresh ginger,
2 tablespoons peeled
and minced

**Dark rum, bourbon, or
fresh orange juice,**
3 tablespoons

Bitter orange marmalade,
½ cup

Dijon mustard,
1 tablespoon

MAKES 12 SERVINGS

Position a rack in the lower third of the oven and preheat to 325°F. Line a roasting pan with aluminum foil, and place a roasting rack in the pan.

Using a sharp knife, score the fat on the ham in a crosshatch pattern, creating 1½-inch diamond shapes. Place the ham, flat side down, on the rack in the roasting pan. Add 2 cups water to the pan and cover loosely with aluminum foil. Bake until an instant-read thermometer inserted in the thickest part of the ham away from bone registers 125°F, about 1¼ hours.

Meanwhile, make the glaze. In a small saucepan, melt the butter over medium heat. Add the ginger and cook, stirring occasionally, until it softens, about 2 minutes. Add the rum and boil until it is reduced by half, about 2 minutes. Stir in the marmalade and mustard and bring to a boil, then remove from the heat and set aside to cool.

Remove the ham from the oven and discard the foil on top. Increase the oven temperature to 400°F. Spread the glaze all over the ham, forcing some of it into the scoring marks. Return to the oven and bake, uncovered, until the glaze melts onto the ham, about 15 minutes.

Transfer the glazed ham to a carving board. Let stand for 15 minutes, then carve into slices parallel to the bone. Serve hot or warm.

PUT A SPIN ON IT After the ham is sliced, be sure to save the ham bone for adding to your favorite recipe for split pea soup or a big pot of beans. Chop the leftover ham and stir it into the soup or beans, too.

Homemade gnocchi is the kind of hands-on dish that seems like it would take a family of gray-haired aunts to make. But these featherlight potato dumplings, tossed with fragrant basil pesto, are remarkably easy to shape. You can make the gnocchi up to 8 hours in advance and refrigerate them until 1 hour before cooking.

POTATO GNOCCHI WITH PESTO

Baking potatoes,
1⅔ pounds

Kosher salt

Large eggs, 2, beaten

All-purpose flour,
about 1⅓ cups,
or as needed

Basil pesto (page 245),
½ cup

**Freshly grated Parmesan
cheese for serving**

MAKES 4-6 SERVINGS

In a large saucepan, combine the unpeeled potatoes with salted water to cover by 1 inch, cover the pan, and bring to a boil over high heat. Reduce the heat to medium-low and simmer until tender when pierced with a knife, about 30 minutes. Drain and rinse with cold running water until easy to handle. Peel the potatoes and return them to the saucepan. Cook over medium-low heat, shaking the pan often, to evaporate the excess moisture, about 2 minutes.

Press the warm potatoes through a ricer or rub them through a coarse-mesh sieve into a bowl. Stir in the eggs and 2 teaspoons salt. Gradually stir in enough of the flour to make a soft dough, taking care not to add too much. Turn the dough out onto a lightly floured work surface and knead gently a few times until it is smooth, adding just enough flour to prevent sticking. Divide the dough into 4 equal portions.

Lightly flour a rimmed baking sheet. Using floured hands, transfer 1 portion of the dough to a lightly floured work surface. Using your palms, roll the dough to make a rope about ¾ inch in diameter. Cut the rope into 1-inch lengths and transfer to the prepared baking sheet. Repeat with the remaining dough.

Bring a large pot of salted water to a boil over high heat. Add half of the gnocchi to the water and simmer until they rise to the surface, then cook 1 minute longer. Using a skimmer, carefully transfer the gnocchi to a warmed serving bowl and cover to keep warm. Repeat with the remaining gnocchi, then scoop out ½ cup of the cooking water and discard the remainder.

Add the pesto and about ¼ cup of the reserved cooking water to the gnocchi. Toss gently, adding more water as needed to make a creamy sauce. Serve at once, passing Parmesan on the side.

PUT A SPIN ON IT Gnocchi will hold up to a variety of different sauces, from brown butter and sage or marinara sauce (page 245) to a hearty short-rib ragù (see "Put a spin on it," page 92) or Bolognese sauce (page 96).

Just about everybody likes crunchy fish fillets served with a heap of crisp fries, and you can successfully make this venerable British dish at home if you time the steps carefully. These fries—chips to the British—are "oven-fried" to ease the cook's workload. For a more authentic version, make the fries on page 161.

FISH AND CHIPS

TARTAR SAUCE

Mayonnaise (page 246 or purchased), 1 cup

Sweet pickle relish, 2 tablespoons

Nonpareil capers 1 tablespoon, rinsed

Fresh flat-leaf parsley, 1 tablespoon minced

Cake flour, 1 cup

Baking powder, 1½ teaspoons

Kosher salt and freshly ground pepper

Lager beer, ½ cup, or as needed

Large egg, 1, beaten

Canola oil, 5 tablespoons plus more for frying

Baking potatoes, 4 large

Skinless haddock or cod fillet, 1¼ pounds, cut into 4 pieces

Malt vinegar and lemon wedges for serving

MAKES 4 SERVINGS

To make the tartar sauce, in a bowl, mix together the mayonnaise, relish, capers, and parsley. Cover and refrigerate for at least 1 hour to allow the flavors to blend.

To make the batter, in a bowl, whisk together the flour, baking powder, and ½ teaspoon salt. Add the ½ cup beer, the egg, and 2 tablespoons of the oil and whisk just until the ingredients are combined (it should be slightly lumpy). The mixture should have the consistency of pancake batter; add more beer if needed. Let stand at room temperature for about 1 hour while you prepare the potatoes.

To make the chips, position racks in the center and upper third of the oven and preheat to 400°F. Cut each unpeeled potato in half lengthwise, then cut the halves lengthwise into wedges about ½ inch thick. Arrange the wedges in a single layer on 2 rimmed baking sheets, drizzle with the 3 tablespoons oil, and toss to coat. Place 1 sheet on each oven rack and bake for 20 minutes. Turn the potato wedges, then switch the pans between the racks, rotate the pans 180 degrees, and continue to bake until tender and golden brown, about 25 minutes more.

Just before the chips are finished baking, set a large wire rack on another rimmed baking sheet and place near the stove. Pour oil into a large saucepan to a depth of 3 inches and heat over high heat to 350°F on a deep-frying thermometer. Remove the chips from the oven. Reduce the oven temperature to 200°F. Combine the chips on a single baking sheet, season with salt, and return to the oven to keep warm.

In batches to avoid crowding, dip the fish pieces in the batter, letting the excess drip back into the bowl, and add to the hot oil. Deep-fry until golden brown, 3–4 minutes. Transfer to the rack and keep warm in the oven while frying the remaining fish. Serve the fish and chips hot, passing the tartar sauce, vinegar, and lemon wedges.

PUT A SPIN ON IT For an amazing fried fish sandwich, serve the fried fish and tartar sauce on a soft roll, such as a torpedo roll. Add some shredded lettuce and sliced tomatoes, if you like, and serve the chips on the side.

Meat loaf rarely gets points for good looks, but it sure can be delicious! Use beef, veal, and pork, a trio that yields an especially flavorful loaf that is also easy to slice. And don't neglect to make gravy from the pan drippings to spoon over the meat loaf and, of course, over a mountain of creamy mashed potatoes (page 190).

MEAT LOAF WITH GRAVY

Canola oil for greasing

Yellow onion, 1, minced

Dried bread crumbs,
½ cup

**Ketchup (page 246
or purchased)**, ½ cup
plus 3 tablespoons

Large eggs, 2, beaten

Worcestershire sauce,
2 tablespoons

**Kosher salt and freshly
ground pepper**

Ground beef, 1 pound

Ground pork and veal,
½ pound *each*

Unsalted butter,
about 1 tablespoon

All-purpose flour,
2 tablespoons

**Beef stock (page 244)
or broth, 2 cups**

MAKES 6 SERVINGS

Preheat the oven to 350°F. Lightly oil a small roasting pan.

In a large bowl, combine the onion, bread crumbs, the ½ cup ketchup, eggs, Worcestershire sauce, 1 teaspoon salt, and ½ teaspoon pepper. Add the meats and mix with your hands just until combined. Transfer the mixture to the prepared pan and shape it into a thick loaf about 9 inches long.

Bake the meat loaf for 45 minutes. Spread the top of the meat loaf with the remaining 3 tablespoons ketchup and bake until an instant-read thermometer inserted in the center registers 165°F, about 15 minutes longer. Remove from the oven and let stand in the pan for 5 minutes. Using a large, wide spatula, transfer the meat loaf to a platter and tent with aluminum foil to keep warm.

Pour the fat out of the roasting pan. Measure 2 tablespoons fat, adding butter as needed to supplement it, and return the fat to the pan. Heat the roasting pan over medium heat until the butter melts. Whisk in the flour and let bubble for 1 minute. Gradually whisk in the stock and bring to a boil. Reduce the heat to medium-low and simmer, whisking frequently, until a lightly thickened gravy forms, about 5 minutes. Season with salt and pepper. Strain through a sieve into a warmed sauceboat. Slice the meat loaf and serve hot, passing the gravy on the side.

PUT A SPIN ON IT Make a double batch of meat loaf so you will have leftovers for sandwiches. Serve the sliced meat loaf on thick bread slices or torpedo rolls with ketchup or grainy mustard and tomato slices.

This French classic is simply one of the most delicious stews around: chicken pieces slowly simmered in a rich red wine sauce with mushrooms and small onions until the meat nearly falls from the bones. Don't skimp on the wine. Use a good-quality light-bodied red, such as Pinot Noir or Beaujolais, that you also enjoy drinking.

COQ AU VIN

Whole chicken,
1 (about 4 pounds)

Pancetta, ¼ pound, diced

Canola oil, 1 teaspoon

Kosher salt and freshly ground pepper

Unsalted butter,
4 tablespoons

Cipollini or white boiling onions, 12

Button mushrooms,
½ pound, quartered

Shallots, ⅓ cup minced

Garlic, 2 cloves, minced

Cognac, 2 tablespoons

All-purpose flour, ⅓ cup

Light-bodied red wine,
2 cups

Chicken stock (page 244) or broth, 1 cup

Tomato paste, 2 teaspoons

Fresh thyme,
1½ teaspoons minced

Bay leaf, 1

Wide egg noodles, 1 pound

Chopped fresh flat-leaf parsley for garnish

MAKES 6 SERVINGS

Preheat the oven to 300°F. Cut the chicken into 2 drumsticks, 2 thighs, 2 wings, and 2 breast halves, reserving the back and giblets for another use. In a Dutch oven, brown the pancetta in the oil over medium heat, stirring, until browned, about 8 minutes. Transfer to paper towels to drain, leaving the fat in the pot. Increase the heat to medium-high. Season the chicken pieces with salt and pepper. In batches to avoid crowding, add the chicken pieces to the pot and cook, turning occasionally, until browned on all sides, about 5 minutes per batch. Transfer to a plate.

Add 1 tablespoon of the butter to the pot and melt over medium heat. Add the onions and cook, stirring occasionally, until browned on all sides, about 3 minutes. Transfer to the plate with the chicken. Add 2 tablespoons of the butter to the pot and melt. Add the mushrooms and cook, stirring occasionally, until lightly browned, 5–6 minutes. Stir in the shallots and garlic and cook, stirring, until softened, about 2 minutes. Add the Cognac and cook until almost evaporated, 1–2 minutes. Sprinkle in the flour and stir well. Slowly stir in the wine, stock, tomato paste, thyme, and bay leaf and bring to a simmer. Return the chicken, drumsticks and thighs first, to the pot, along with the onions and pancetta. Cover and bake in the oven until the chicken shows no sign of pink when pierced at the bone, 40–45 minutes.

While the chicken is cooking, bring a large pot of salted water to a boil over high heat. Add the egg noodles and stir occasionally until the water returns to a boil. Cook according to the package directions until al dente. Drain the noodles and return to the cooking pot. Add the remaining 1 tablespoon butter and toss to coat.

Discard the bay leaf from the chicken. Season with salt and pepper. Divide the noodles among dinner plates and top each serving with the chicken and sauce. Sprinkle with parsley and serve at once.

PUT A SPIN ON IT In Alsace, a similar dish is made using white wine instead of red. Substitute an off-dry Riesling or Pinot Blanc for the red wine, and omit the tomato paste and Cognac.

Plenty of cooks talk about their favorite braised beef or chicken dishes, but not about the pleasures of pork cooked in the same manner. This recipe will change that. Here, pork roast is braised with tangy sauerkraut and tart-sweet apples for a sumptuous Sunday supper. Accompany with small potatoes tossed in butter and parsley.

BRAISED PORK WITH SAUERKRAUT AND APPLES

Kosher salt and freshly ground pepper

Dried thyme, 2 teaspoons

Dried sage, 1 teaspoon

Bone-in center-cut pork loin roast, 1 (about 3½ pounds; 6 ribs)

Canola oil, 2 tablespoons

Granny Smith apples, 2

Yellow onion, 1, chopped

Refrigerated sauerkraut 2 pounds, well drained

Hard apple cider, ½ cup

Light brown sugar, 1 tablespoon firmly packed

Bay leaves, 2

Whole-grain mustard for serving

MAKES 6 SERVINGS

Position a rack in the lower third of the oven and preheat to 325°F. To prepare the pork, mix together 1 teaspoon salt, ½ teaspoon pepper, 1 teaspoon of the thyme, and the sage. Sprinkle the mixture evenly over the pork roast and rub it in. In a large Dutch oven, heat 1 tablespoon of the oil over medium-high heat. Add the pork and cook, turning occasionally, until browned on all sides, about 6 minutes. Remove from the heat and transfer the pork to a plate, leaving any fat in the Dutch oven.

To prepare the sauerkraut and apples, peel, halve, and core the apples, then cut into wedges. Add the remaining 1 tablespoon oil to the fat in the Dutch oven and heat over medium heat. Add the apples and onion and cook until the onion softens, about 5 minutes. Add the sauerkraut, cider, sugar, the remaining 1 teaspoon thyme, ¼ teaspoon pepper, and the bay leaves and stir well.

Return the pork to the Dutch oven and nestle it in the sauerkraut mixture. Cover and braise in the oven until an instant-read thermometer inserted in the center of the roast away from bone registers 145°F, about 1 hour.

Transfer the pork to a carving board. Discard the bay leaves. Cover the sauerkraut to keep warm. Let the pork stand for 10 minutes, then carve the pork roast into chops. Season the sauerkraut with more pepper and heap into a deep serving platter. Top with the chops and serve at once, passing the mustard on the side.

PUT A SPIN ON IT You can serve the sauerkraut mixture with sausages instead of the pork roast. Increase the cider to 1 cup, then bake the sauerkraut mixture for 1 hour. Using a fork, pierce your favorite smoked sausages, such as kielbasa, knackwurst, or bratwurst, and brown lightly in a frying pan. Bury the sausages in the sauerkraut and bake for 30 minutes more.

Pasta recipes are high on the list of soul-satisfying suppers, with this old-world classic among the most popular of the clan: briny fresh clams in a garlicky wine sauce, with nary a tomato in sight. Serve plenty of crusty bread alongside the dish to sop up every drop of the flavorful sauce.

LINGUINE WITH CLAMS

Littleneck clams,
3 dozen (about 3 pounds)

Kosher salt

Linguine, 1 pound

Extra-virgin olive oil,
¼ cup

Garlic, 3 cloves, minced

Red pepper flakes,
¼ teaspoon, or to taste

Dry white wine, ½ cup

Unsalted butter,
2 tablespoons

Fresh flat-leaf parsley,
3 tablespoons
finely chopped

MAKES 4 SERVINGS

Scrub the clams well under cold running water. Place in a large bowl, add salted cold water to cover, and let stand for 1 hour. Drain the clams and rinse well.

Meanwhile, bring a large pot of salted water to a boil over high heat. Add the linguine and stir occasionally until the water returns to a boil. Cook according to the package directions until al dente.

While the linguine is cooking, in a large saucepan over medium heat, heat together the olive oil, garlic, and red pepper flakes until the garlic softens and is fragrant but not browned, about 3 minutes. Add the clams and wine and cover. Increase the heat to high and cook, shaking the pan occasionally by its handle, until the clams have opened, about 4 minutes. Remove from the heat and discard any unopened clams. Add the butter and swirl the saucepan to melt the butter into the cooking liquid.

Drain the linguine and return it to its cooking pot. Pour the clams and sauce over the linguine and mix gently. Transfer to a serving platter or individual pasta bowls, dividing the clams evenly. Sprinkle with the parsley and serve at once.

PUT A SPIN ON IT   If you can't stand the idea of serving pasta without tomatoes, in a frying pan, sauté 2 cups whole grape or cherry tomatoes in 2 tablespoons olive oil over high heat until they are hot and begin to wilt, 3–4 minutes. Add them to the clams and their sauce along with the pasta.

A simple and bright sauce of crushed tomatoes is the perfect backdrop for this classic pie oozing with melted mozzarella and studded with savory pork sausage and sliced mushrooms. One secret to great pizza is great dough, and the key to great dough is a slow rise. For the best results, make the dough at least 9 or 10 hours before baking.

NEW YORK-STYLE SAUSAGE AND MUSHROOM PIZZA

Pizza dough (page 247)

Canned crushed plum tomatoes, 1 cup

Extra-virgin olive oil, 2 tablespoons

Dried oregano, 1 teaspoon

Cremini or button mushrooms, ½ pound, sliced

Kosher salt and freshly ground pepper

Sweet or hot Italian pork sausages, ½ pound, casings removed

All-purpose or bread flour and cornmeal for dusting

Fresh mozzarella cheese, 1 pound, thinly sliced

Parmesan cheese, 4 tablespoons freshly grated

MAKES TWO 12-INCH PIZZAS

The night before serving, prepare the pizza dough and refrigerate. Remove the dough from the refrigerator 1–2 hours before forming the pizzas. Position a rack in the lower third of the oven. Place a large pizza stone on the rack, and preheat the oven to 450°F, allowing at least 30 minutes for the oven to preheat fully.

To make the pizza sauce, in a bowl, mix together the tomatoes, 1 tablespoon of the oil, and the oregano. Set aside.

To prepare the toppings, in a large frying pan, heat the remaining 1 tablespoon oil over medium-high heat. Add the mushrooms and cook, stirring, until they give off their juices and are browned, about 8 minutes. Transfer to a bowl and season with salt and pepper. Add the sausages to the pan and cook over medium-high heat, stirring and breaking them up with a wooden spoon, until no longer pink, about 10 minutes. Transfer to the bowl with the mushrooms. Set aside.

Divide the dough in half and shape each half into a taut ball. Place 1 ball on a lightly floured work surface. Return the other dough ball to its bowl and cover. Roll, pat, and stretch the dough into a round about 12 inches in diameter. Generously dust a pizza peel with cornmeal. Transfer the dough to the peel and reshape into a round as needed. Spread with half of the sauce, leaving a ¾-inch border uncovered. Top with half of the mozzarella, then half of the mushroom mixture.

Slide the pizza off the peel onto the hot stone. Bake until the crust is golden brown, about 12 minutes. While the first pizza is baking, repeat with the remaining dough, tomato sauce, mozzarella, and mushroom mixture, so the second pizza is ready to bake when the first one comes out of the oven. Using a wide spatula or a rimless baking sheet, remove the baked pizza from the oven and transfer to a cutting board. Sprinkle with half of the Parmesan cheese. Slide the second pizza onto the hot stone and bake for about 12 minutes. Cut and serve the first pizza. When the second pizza is done, top with the remaining Parmesan cheese, cut, and serve.

These deliciously cheesy enchiladas are stuffed with tender chicken and bathed in a spicy, zesty green tomatillo sauce. Tomatillos, related not to tomatoes but to gooseberries, give the sauce its color and tartness; a jalapeño chile provides just the right amount of heat; and Monterey Jack cheese delivers a good dose of richness.

GREEN CHICKEN ENCHILADAS

Bone-in, skin-on chicken breast halves, 2 (about 1½ pounds total)

White onions, 2 cups chopped

Garlic, 6 cloves, crushed

Kosher salt

Black peppercorns, ½ teaspoon

Fresh cilantro, 6 sprigs, plus ⅓ cup coarsely chopped

Tomatillos, 2 pounds, husked

Jalapeño chile, 1, seeds and ribs removed, chopped

Olive oil, ½ cup plus 2 tablespoons, plus more as needed

Monterey Jack cheese, 2 cups shredded

Corn tortillas, 12

Chopped white onions, sour cream, chopped cilantro, and crumbled *cotija* **cheese for serving**

MAKES 6 SERVINGS

Place the chicken breast halves, skin side down, in a saucepan. Add ½ cup of the onion, 2 cloves of the garlic, 1 teaspoon salt, and water to cover. Bring to a simmer over high heat, skimming off any foam. Add the peppercorns and cilantro sprigs, reduce the heat to medium-low, cover partially, and simmer until the chicken is opaque throughout, about 25 minutes. Transfer the chicken to a cutting board, but keep the broth simmering. When the chicken is cool enough to handle, remove the skin and bones and return them to the simmering broth. Dice the chicken meat and set aside. Continue simmering the broth 30 minutes more. Taste and adjust the seasoning with salt, then strain through a fine-mesh sieve into a clean container. Let stand for 5 minutes, then skim off any fat from the surface.

Bring a large saucepan of salted water to a boil over high heat. Add the tomatillos, reduce the heat to medium-low, and simmer gently (do not boil) until they are tender, about 10 minutes. Transfer the tomatillos to a bowl, taking care that they don't burst. In batches, in a blender, combine the tomatillos, the remaining 1½ cups onions, the chopped cilantro, the remaining 4 garlic cloves, and the chile and process until smooth. In a large saucepan, heat the 2 tablespoons oil over medium-high heat. Add the tomatillo purée (it will splatter, so be careful) and 1 cup of the reserved broth and bring to a boil. (Reserve the remaining broth for another use.) Boil, stirring frequently, until the sauce is slightly reduced, about 10 minutes. Remove from the heat.

Preheat the oven to 350°F. Lightly oil a 9-by-13-inch baking dish. To assemble the enchiladas, spread ⅓ cup of the sauce in the dish. Mix 1½ cups of the cheese with the reserved chicken. Pour 2 cups of the sauce into a pie dish, and place near the stove. In a frying pan, heat the ½ cup olive oil over medium heat. Using tongs, dip 1 tortilla in the oil for a few seconds to soften, and then into the tomatillo sauce. Place the tortilla on a work surface, add a few tablespoons of the filling down the center, and roll up the tortilla. Place it, seam side down, in the baking dish. Repeat with the remaining tortillas and filling. Spread the remaining sauce on top, and sprinkle with the remaining cheese. Bake until the cheese is melted and the sauce is bubbling, 30–35 minutes. Serve warm with onions, sour cream, cilantro, and *cotija*.

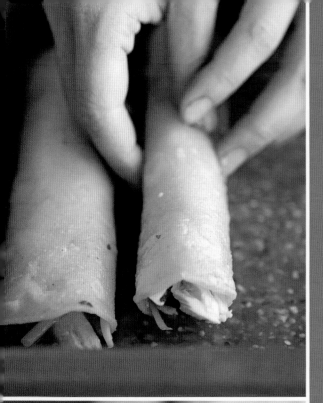

Tex-Mex food is neither authentically Mexican nor purely Texan, but it is one of the best-tasting "cuisines" in the world.

The summer before I started college, I used my high-school graduation cash to attend the University of Guadalajara. I was already nurturing a strong interest in food, and visions of flautas and tostadas danced in my head as I made my way south. Because I had grown up in California, I thought I knew authentic Mexican food. However, I soon discovered that what I grew up with and loved to eat was actually Tex-Mex cooking, a delicious hybrid. My first meal with the Garcias, my host family, was revelatory. Señora Garcia prepared the real thing: handmade corn tortillas, guacamole made in a stone mortar, and tangy chicken enchiladas. Although I didn't learn much at school that session, I did learn a lot about cooking real Mexican food.

What makes chili Texan? Most Lone Star chili masters eschew beans and tomatoes. To them, chili is all about meat—beef only—and the chile seasoning. And Lone Star fans of the real deal claim that toppings—sour cream, cheese, onions—turn their bowl of red into a salad bar. But you can opt for everything if you'd like.

TEXAS BEEF CHILI

Whole cumin seeds,
2 teaspoons

Pure ancho chile powder,
¼ cup

Spanish smoked paprika,
1 tablespoon

Dried oregano, 2 teaspoons

Boneless beef chuck roast,
4 pounds

**Kosher salt and freshly
ground pepper**

Olive oil, 3 tablespoons

Yellow onion,
1 large, chopped

Jalapeño chile, 1, seeds
and ribs removed, chopped

Red bell pepper, 1 large,
seeded and chopped

Garlic, 4 cloves, chopped

Lager beer, 1½ cups

Beef stock (page 244),
broth, or water, 1 cup

Yellow cornmeal,
2 tablespoons

**Shredded Cheddar cheese,
chopped red onions,
sour cream, and minced
jalapeño chiles for serving**

MAKES 8 SERVINGS

Heat a frying pan over medium heat. Add the cumin seeds and heat, stirring often, until toasted (you may see a wisp of smoke), about 1 minute. Transfer to a mortar and finely grind with a pestle (or use a spice grinder). Transfer to a bowl and add the ancho chile powder, paprika, and oregano. Mix well and set aside.

Cut the beef into ½-inch cubes. Season with salt and pepper. In a Dutch oven, heat 2 tablespoons of the oil over medium-high heat. In batches to avoid crowding, add the beef cubes and cook, turning occasionally, until browned, about 5 minutes per batch. Transfer to a plate.

Add the remaining 1 tablespoon oil to the pot. Add the onion, jalapeño, bell pepper, and garlic and reduce the heat to medium. Cover and cook, stirring occasionally, until the onion softens, about 5 minutes. Uncover, add the spice mixture, and stir well for 30 seconds. Stir in the beer and stock. Return the beef to the pot, cover, and reduce the heat to low. Simmer until the beef is fork-tender, 1½–2 hours.

Remove the chili from the heat and let stand for 5 minutes. Skim off any fat that rises to the surface. Return the pot to medium heat and bring to a simmer. Transfer about ½ cup of the cooking liquid to a small bowl, add the cornmeal, and whisk well. Stir into the chili and cook until lightly thickened, about 1 minute. Season with salt and pepper. Spoon the chili into warmed bowls and serve hot, with bowls of Cheddar, onions, sour cream, and jalapeños on the side for sprinkling on top.

PUT A SPIN ON IT At the risk of making some Texans hoppin' mad, add 1 cup cooked kidney or pinto beans to your chili and heat through just before serving. You can also add 1 cup or so of chopped canned tomatoes, but, again, don't tell any Texans. Ancho chiles are relatively mild, so if you want a hotter chili, add some cayenne pepper. This chili is excellent served with corn bread (page 186) or warmed tortillas to capture every last bit of the brick-red sauce.

A big platter of this crispy, tender, golden brown chicken would be a hit at almost any potluck or picnic. Immersing the chicken pieces in the buttermilk brine for several hours gives the chicken loads of flavor and helps keep the meat moist as it fries. The acid in the buttermilk also helps to tenderize the chicken.

BUTTERMILK FRIED CHICKEN

Buttermilk, 4 cups

Fine sea salt and freshly ground black pepper

Dried oregano, thyme, rosemary, and sage, 2 teaspoons *each*

Granulated garlic, 1 teaspoon

Cayenne pepper, ½ teaspoon

Whole chicken, 1 (about 3½ pounds)

Canola oil for deep-frying

All-purpose flour, 1⅓ cups

Baking powder, 1 teaspoon

MAKES 4 SERVINGS

To make the buttermilk brine, in a large bowl, whisk together the buttermilk and ⅓ cup salt. In a mortar, crush together the oregano, thyme, rosemary, and sage with a pestle (or pulse in a spice grinder) until finely ground. Whisk the ground herbs, garlic, and cayenne pepper into the buttermilk mixture. Cut the chicken into 2 thighs, 2 drumsticks, 2 wings, and 2 breast halves, reserving the back and giblets for another use. Cut each breast half crosswise to make 4 breast portions, for a total of 10 chicken pieces. Add to the buttermilk brine, making sure that the chicken is submerged. (If it isn't, transfer everything to a smaller bowl.) Cover and refrigerate for at least 4 hours or up to 6 hours.

Pour oil to a depth of at least 3 inches into a large, heavy saucepan and heat over high heat to 350°F on a deep-frying thermometer. Set a large wire rack on a rimmed baking sheet and place near the stove. Have ready a second rimmed baking sheet. While the oil is heating, in a large bowl, whisk together the flour, baking powder, and ½ teaspoon black pepper. Remove half of the chicken from the buttermilk brine, letting the excess brine drip back into the bowl. Add the chicken to the flour mixture and toss to coat evenly, then transfer to the second baking sheet.

When the oil is ready, in batches to avoid crowding, carefully slip the chicken pieces into the hot oil. The temperature will drop, but adjust the heat to keep the oil bubbling steadily at about 325°F. Deep-fry the chicken pieces, turning them occasionally with tongs, until they are golden brown and show no sign of pink when pierced at the thickest part, about 12 minutes. Using a wire skimmer, transfer the chicken to the rack to drain. Repeat with the remaining chicken. Serve warm.

PUT A SPIN ON IT Chicken Maryland is served with cream gravy: After frying the chicken, in a saucepan, heat 2 tablespoons of the cooking oil over medium heat. Whisk in 2 tablespoons flour, simmer for 1 minute, then whisk in 2 cups heated half-and-half. Bring to a boil, then simmer until thickened, about 5 minutes. Season with salt and pepper. Serve the gravy over the chicken.

Baked ziti is covered-dish cooking at its best, and is just the thing to take to a friend who needs a bit of cheering up. This version is more generously proportioned than most, with enough flavorful Italian sausage, roasted eggplant, tangy tomato sauce, and lush ricotta to satisfy even the heartiest appetite.

BAKED ZITI WITH SAUSAGE

Eggplants, 2 small
(about ¾ pound each)

Olive oil, 4 tablespoons

Sweet or hot Italian pork sausages, 1 pound, casings removed

Yellow onion, 1, chopped

Garlic, 2 cloves, minced

Hearty red wine, ½ cup

Crushed plum tomatoes,
1 can (28 ounces)

Dried oregano,
2 teaspoons

Red pepper flakes,
½ teaspoon

Kalamata olives,
½ cup pitted and coarsely chopped

Kosher salt

Ziti or other tubular pasta, 1 pound

Ricotta cheese, 2 cups

Parmesan cheese,
½ cup freshly grated

MAKES 6 SERVINGS

Preheat the oven to 400°F. Lightly oil a 3-quart baking dish or 6 individual baking dishes. Cut the eggplants into bite-sized cubes. Spread the cubes on a large rimmed baking sheet. Drizzle with 3 tablespoons of the oil and toss to coat. Roast, stirring occasionally, until tender and lightly browned, about 30 minutes.

Meanwhile, in a large, heavy saucepan, heat the remaining 1 tablespoon oil over medium-high heat. Add the sausages and cook, stirring and breaking them up with a wooden spoon, until no longer pink, about 10 minutes. Using a slotted spoon, transfer to a plate. Pour off all but 2 tablespoons of the fat in the pan.

Add the onion to the pan and cook over medium heat, stirring, until tender, about 5 minutes. Stir in the garlic and cook until fragrant, about 1 minute. Add the wine, stir to loosen any browned bits on the pan bottom, and bring to a boil. Stir in the tomatoes, oregano, and red pepper flakes and bring to a boil. Return the sausage to the pan and stir in the eggplant. Reduce the heat to medium-low and simmer until thickened, about 20 minutes. Stir in the olives and remove from the heat.

Meanwhile, bring a large pot of salted water to a boil over high heat. Add the ziti and stir occasionally until the water returns to a boil. Cook according to the package directions until not quite al dente. (The pasta will cook again in the oven, so do not overcook it now.) Drain well. Add the ziti to to the sauce along with the ricotta, and stir until combined. Season with salt, taste, and adjust the seasoning with red pepper flakes. Spread the pasta mixture in the prepared baking dish(es) and sprinkle evenly with the Parmesan. Bake until the sauce is bubbling and the Parmesan is golden, about 20 minutes. Let stand for 5 minutes, then serve.

PUT A SPIN ON IT For a meatless version of this dish, substitute 1¼ pounds cremini mushrooms, quartered, for the sausage, and finely chopped fresh rosemary for the oregano. Sauté the mushrooms in the olive oil (you may need more oil) over medium-high heat until tender, about 8 minutes.

In the Carolinas, "real" barbecue is languidly cooked in a smoker with hi
but more people likely make it this way, in the oven. It takes forever, but
a mountain of meltingly tender meat, perfect for a big family gathering c
you want leftovers for other meals down the road.

PULLED PORK SANDWICHES

Bone-in pork shoulder,
1 (about 7½ pounds)

Sweet paprika, preferably Hungarian or Spanish,
2 teaspoons

Dried thyme, ¾ teaspoon

Dried oregano,
¾ teaspoon

Kosher salt and freshly ground black pepper

Cayenne pepper,
⅛ teaspoon

Cider vinegar, 2½ cups

Yellow onion, 1, chopped

Garlic, 5 cloves, minced

Light brown sugar,
¼ cup lightly packed

Ketchup (page 246 or purchased), ¼ cup

Red pepper flakes,
1 teaspoon

Canola oil, ⅓ cup

Green cabbage,
1 small head, shredded

Soft sandwich buns,
10, split

MAKES 10 SANDWICHES

Position a rack in the lower third of the oven and preheat to 325°F. Cut the rind off the pork shoulder, leaving a thin layer of fat. Using a sharp knife, score the fat in a crosshatch pattern, creating 1-inch diamonds. Mix together the paprika, thyme, oregano, 2 teaspoons salt, ½ teaspoon black pepper, and the cayenne pepper. Sprinkle the mixture evenly over the pork and rub it in. Place the pork in a large Dutch oven and add ½ cup of the vinegar, the onion, and two-thirds of the garlic. Cover and bake, turning the pork every hour or so, until it is fork-tender and an instant-read thermometer inserted in the thickest part away from the bone registers at least 190°F, 5–6 hours.

Meanwhile, to make the barbecue sauce, in a bowl, whisk together the remaining 2 cups vinegar, the remaining garlic, the sugar, ketchup, and red pepper flakes. The sauce will be thin. Measure out ¼ cup sauce, then transfer the remaining sauce to a covered container and set aside at room temperature. To make the coleslaw, in a bowl, whisk together the ¼ cup barbecue sauce and the oil. Add the cabbage and mix to coat evenly. Season with salt and pepper. Cover and refrigerate for at least 2 hours to allow the cabbage to soften and the flavors to mingle.

When the pork is ready, transfer it to a carving board and tent with aluminum foil to keep warm. Let stand for at least 20 minutes. Meanwhile, skim the fat from the cooking liquid, then boil the liquid over high heat until reduced to about ¾ cup. Using 2 forks, pull the pork shoulder into shreds. (Once the pork has been pulled apart into large chunks, it may be easier to use a knife to help shred the meat.) Transfer to a serving bowl and moisten with the reduced cooking liquid. To serve, heap the pulled pork and a spoonful of the slaw onto the bottom half of each bun and cover with the bun top. Serve at once, passing sauce on the side.

PUT A SPIN ON IT If you don't have a large Dutch oven, cook the pork in a roasting pan, tightly covered with aluminum foil. For a real treat, add a layer of pulled pork to your favorite grilled cheese sandwich.

Never underestimate the appeal of fried food. When the homely squid is coated and fried to a crunchy golden brown, it becomes one of the most appealing of all seafood dishes, especially when paired with marinara sauce seasoned with pepper flakes. Be sure to let the oil return to 350°F between batches to guarantee crisp, tender calamari.

FRIED CALAMARI WITH SPICY MARINARA

Olive oil, 2 tablespoons

Garlic, 3 cloves, minced

Canned crushed plum tomatoes, 1½ cups

Dried oregano, 3 teaspoons

Red pepper flakes, ¼ teaspoon, or more to taste

Canola oil for deep-frying

All-purpose flour, ½ cup

Yellow cornmeal, preferably stone-ground ½ cup

Fine sea salt, 1 teaspoon

Cayenne pepper, ¼ teaspoon

Squid (calamari), 1 pound, cleaned

Chopped fresh flat-leaf parsley for garnish

Lemon wedges for serving

MAKES 4-6 SERVINGS

To make the spicy marinara, in a saucepan, heat the olive oil and garlic together over medium-low heat until the garlic softens and is fragrant but not browned, about 3 minutes. Stir in the tomatoes, 1 teaspoon of the oregano, and the red pepper flakes, increase the heat to medium, and bring to a simmer. Return the heat to medium-low and simmer, uncovered, until lightly thickened, about 10 minutes. Remove from the heat and keep warm.

Meanwhile, pour canola oil to a depth of 3 inches into a large, heavy saucepan. Heat over high heat to 350°F on a deep-frying thermometer. Preheat the oven to 200°F. Set a large wire rack on a rimmed baking sheet and place near the stove. In a bowl, whisk together the flour, cornmeal, the remaining 2 teaspoons oregano, the salt, and cayenne pepper. Cut the squid bodies crosswise into ¼-inch-wide rings; leave the tentacles whole. Toss one-third of the squid rings and tentacles in the flour mixture to coat evenly, shaking off the excess.

In 3 batches, carefully add the coated squid to the hot oil and deep-fry until golden brown, about 2 minutes. Using a wire skimmer, transfer to the rack and keep warm in the oven while you coat and fry the remaining squid.

Spoon the spicy marinara into individual dipping bowls. Transfer the fried calamari to a warmed platter and sprinkle with the parsley. Serve at once, passing the marinara sauce and lemon wedges on the side.

PUT A SPIN ON IT Shelled shrimp also fry up golden and crunchy using this method. Dip them first into plain flour and then into beaten eggs before coating them with the flour-cornmeal mixture.

Tender eggplant under a cloak of garlicky tomato sauce and melted cheese: who doesn't love eggplant Parmesan? Even picky eaters who think they don't like eggplant like this dish. In this simplified version, the breaded eggplant is "oven-fried" instead of panfried, which means less oil and less mess, but no less flavor.

EGGPLANT PARMESAN

Eggplants, 2 small
(about ¾ pound each)

Kosher salt

Extra-virgin olive oil,
¼ cup

Large eggs, 3

Whole milk, 2 tablespoons

All-purpose flour, 1 cup

Dried oregano, 1 teaspoon

Freshly ground pepper,
½ teaspoon

Fine dried bread crumbs,
2 cups

Parmesan cheese,
¾ cup freshly grated

Marinara sauce
(page 245), 3 cups

Fresh mozzarella cheese,
1 pound, sliced

MAKES 4-6 SERVINGS

Thinly slice the eggplants crosswise diagonally. Place a large wire rack on a rimmed baking sheet. Sprinkle both sides of each eggplant slice with salt. Set the slices on the rack and let stand for about 30 minutes. Wipe the slices with paper towels to blot the moisture and remove excess salt.

Preheat the oven to 425°F. Drizzle a large rimmed baking sheet with the oil. In a shallow bowl, whisk together the eggs and milk. In a second shallow bowl, stir together the flour, oregano, and pepper. In a third shallow bowl, combine the bread crumbs and ¼ cup of the Parmesan. One at a time, coat the eggplant slices with the flour mixture, shaking off the excess, then dip into the egg mixture, coating evenly and allowing the excess to drip off. Finally, dip into the bread crumb mixture, patting gently to help it adhere. Transfer to the prepared baking sheet. Bake for 15 minutes. Turn the eggplant slices over and continue to bake until golden brown, about 15 minutes more. Let cool until easy to handle, 5–10 minutes. Leave the oven on.

Lightly oil a 9-by-13-inch baking dish. Spread 1 cup of the marinara sauce in the bottom of the prepared dish. Layer half of the eggplant slices, overlapping them to fit, on top of the sauce, then spoon 1 cup of the sauce evenly over the slices. Top with half of the mozzarella, and sprinkle with ¼ cup of the Parmesan. Repeat with the remaining eggplant, marinara sauce, mozzarella, and Parmesan.

Bake until the cheese is melted and the sauce is bubbling, about 30 minutes. Let stand for 10 minutes, then serve hot.

PUT A SPIN ON IT For an eggplant Parmesan panini, brush 2 slices *pain au levain* or other rustic bread on both sides with olive oil. On 1 bread slice, layer mozzarella slices, oven-fried eggplant slices, marinara sauce, and more mozzarella slices, in that order. Top with a second bread slice. Using a panini grill, toast the sandwich until the bread is browned and the cheese is melted.

In Italy, scampi are shrimplike crustaceans known elsewhere as Dublin Bay prawns or langoustines. American cooks use the same term to describe sautéed jumbo shrimp in a buttery, white wine sauce. This version is more garlicky and saucy than most, and is delicious served over pasta, rice, or even grits.

GARLICKY SHRIMP SCAMPI

Jumbo or extra-large shrimp, 1½ pounds

All-purpose flour, ½ cup

Fine sea salt and freshly ground pepper

Olive oil, 2 tablespoons, plus more as needed

Unsalted butter, 12 tablespoons

Garlic, 3 cloves, minced

Dry white wine, ¼ cup

Finely grated lemon zest, from 1 lemon

Fresh lemon juice, 2 tablespoons

Fresh flat-leaf parsley, 2 tablespoons finely chopped

Lemon wedges for serving

MAKES 4 SERVINGS

Peel and devein the shrimp, leaving the tail segment intact. In a shallow bowl, stir together the flour, ½ teaspoon salt, and ¼ teaspoon pepper.

In a large, nonreactive frying pan, heat the oil over medium-high heat. Toss half of the shrimp in the flour mixture to coat evenly, shaking off the excess. Add to the hot oil and cook, turning occasionally, until opaque throughout when pierced with the tip of a knife, about 3 minutes. Transfer to a plate and tent with aluminum foil to keep warm. Repeat with the remaining shrimp, adding more oil as needed.

Reduce the heat to medium-low. Heat 2 tablespoons of the butter and the garlic together in the pan, stirring frequently, until the garlic softens and is fragrant but not browned, about 2 minutes. Add the wine and the lemon zest and juice and bring to a boil over high heat. Cook until reduced by half, about 1 minute. Reduce the heat to very low. One tablespoon at a time, whisk in the remaining 10 tablespoons butter, letting each addition soften into a creamy emulsion before adding more.

Return the shrimp to the sauce and mix gently to coat well. Remove from the heat and season the sauce with salt and pepper. Transfer to a warmed serving dish and sprinkle with the parsley. Serve at once, passing the lemon wedges on the side.

PUT A SPIN ON IT Scallops are good with this sauce, too. Small bay scallops will cook in about the same amount of time as the shrimp. If you opt for large sea scallops, sear them in an ovenproof frying pan over high heat for about 1 minute on each side, then slip the browned scallops, still in the pan, into a preheated 400°F oven and cook until barely opaque throughout, about 4 minutes. Transfer to a plate, cover to keep warm, and proceed with the recipe to make the sauce.

In this beloved southern recipe, meaty bone-in pork chops are literally smothered in vegetables and stock, then simmered until the vegetables have melted into a sauce tailor-made for spooning over rice. This is a purposely mellow version, so if you crave spicy food, jazz it up with a teaspoon or so of Cajun seasoning.

SMOTHERED PORK CHOPS

Center-cut bone-in pork loin chops, 4, each about 1 inch thick

Kosher salt and freshly ground pepper

Canola oil, 2 tablespoons

Unsalted butter, 2 tablespoons

Yellow onion, 1 large, chopped

Green bell pepper, 1 small, seeded and diced

Celery, 3 stalks, diced

Green onions, 4, white and green parts, chopped

Garlic, 3 cloves, minced

Fresh thyme, 1 teaspoon minced

All-purpose flour, 3 tablespoons

Chicken stock (page 244) or broth, 2½ cups

Heavy cream, ¼ cup

Hot pepper sauce

Steamed rice for serving

MAKES 4 SERVINGS

Season the pork chops with salt and pepper. In a very large frying pan, heat the oil over medium-high heat. Add the chops to the pan and cook until the undersides are browned, about 3 minutes. Turn and brown the second sides, about 3 minutes more. Transfer to a plate.

Add the butter to the pan and reduce the heat to medium. When the butter has melted, add the onion, bell pepper, celery, green onions, and garlic and stir with a wooden spoon to loosen any browned bits in the pan. Cover and cook, stirring occasionally, until the vegetables are tender, about 8 minutes. Stir in the thyme. Sprinkle in the flour and stir well. Gradually stir in the stock and bring to a simmer.

Return the pork chops to the pan and reduce the heat to medium-low. Cover and simmer until the pork shows no sign of pink when pierced at the bone, about 20 minutes. Transfer the pork chops to a deep serving platter and tent with aluminum foil to keep warm.

Stir the cream into the gravy in the pan and bring to a boil. Cook until thickened, about 1 minute. Season to taste with salt and hot pepper sauce. Pour the gravy over the pork, and serve at once with the steamed rice.

PUT A SPIN ON IT Chicken breasts are another excellent candidate for the smothered treatment. Sear boneless, skinless chicken breast halves for about 2 minutes on each side, then simmer them in the sauce for about 15 minutes.

Folks can't eat these tasty ribs without licking their fingers. The double-cooking method—first rubbed with pungent spices and slowly baked, then finished outdoors on a hot grill with a zesty glaze—results in extra flavorful and tender meat that will pull away from the bone with the slightest tug of the teeth.

BABY BACK RIBS

Baby back ribs, 2 racks
(about 5 pounds total)

Kosher salt, 2 teaspoons

Spanish smoked paprika,
1 teaspoon

Dried oregano, 1 teaspoon

Dried thyme, 1 teaspoon

Granulated garlic,
½ teaspoon

Onion powder, ½ teaspoon

Freshly ground pepper,
½ teaspoon

Ketchup-style chili sauce,
½ cup

Peach or apricot
preserves, ½ cup

Unsulfured dark molasses,
2 tablespoons

Cider vinegar,
1 tablespoon

Dijon mustard,
1 tablespoon

Hot pepper sauce,
½ teaspoon

Canola oil for grilling

MAKES 4-6 SERVINGS

Preheat the oven to 350°F. Cut each rib rack into 2 or 3 sections. Mix together the salt, paprika, oregano, thyme, granulated garlic, onion powder, and pepper. Sprinkle the mixture on both sides of the ribs and rub it into the meat.

Arrange the ribs, overlapping slightly if necessary, in a large roasting pan. Cover tightly with aluminum foil, place in the oven, and cook for 30 minutes. Remove the foil, turn the ribs, and return to the oven. Continue cooking until the ribs are tender and browned, about 30 minutes more.

Meanwhile, make the sauce. In a small saucepan, stir together the chili sauce, peach preserves, molasses, vinegar, mustard, and hot pepper sauce and bring to a simmer over medium-low heat. Remove from the heat and set aside.

While the ribs are cooking, prepare a grill for direct-heat cooking over medium-high heat. Lightly oil the cooking grate. Brush both sides of the ribs with the sauce. Place on the grill, cover, and cook, turning once, until shiny and glazed, about 3 minutes per side. (Alternatively, increase the oven temperature to 425°F. Pour off the fat in the roasting pan, then return the ribs to the pan. Brush the ribs with some of the sauce and cook until the ribs are shiny and glazed, about 5 minutes. Turn, brush with more of the sauce, and cook to glaze the other side, about 5 minutes more.)

Transfer the ribs to a carving board and let stand for 5 minutes. Cut between the bones into individual ribs, heap on a platter, and serve with any remaining sauce.

PUT A SPIN ON IT   Pork spareribs are also excellent prepared with this oven-barbecue method. They are larger, meatier, and a little tougher than baby back ribs, so they will take about 45 minutes of covered baking, another 45 minutes uncovered, and a final 15 minutes for the glazing.

Named after a nineteenth-century Russian count, this old-world dish has been popular on this side of the globe for decades. Countless versions fill the country's recipe boxes, but this one is particularly sensational: tender chunks of steak, sweet shallots, loads of sautéed mushrooms, and an outrageously rich sour cream sauce.

STEAK AND MUSHROOM STROGANOFF

Beef sirloin steak,
1½ pounds

Kosher salt and freshly
ground pepper

Wide egg noodles,
¾ pound

Canola oil, 2 tablespoons
plus more as needed

Button or cremini
mushrooms,
1 pound, sliced

Unsalted butter,
3 tablespoons

Shallots, ⅓ cup minced

Sour cream, 1½ cups,
at room temperature

Fresh dill, 1 tablespoon
minced, plus more
for garnish

MAKES 4 SERVINGS

Trim the steak of any surface fat. Cut the steak across the grain into slices ¼ inch thick, then cut the slices into 2-inch lengths. Season with salt and pepper.

Bring a large pot of salted water to a boil over high heat. Add the egg noodles and stir occasionally until the water returns to a boil. Cook according to the package directions until al dente.

While the noodles are cooking, brown the steak. In a large frying pan, heat the oil over medium-high heat until it shimmers. Add the steak in batches and cook, stirring frequently, until lightly browned and still quite rare, about 1½ minutes per batch, adding more oil to the pan as needed. Transfer the beef to a plate.

When all the steak is cooked, add the mushrooms and 2 tablespoons of the butter to the frying pan and cook over medium-high heat, stirring frequently, until the mushrooms are lightly browned, about 6 minutes. Add the shallots and cook, stirring occasionally, until they soften, about 2 minutes. Remove from the heat and stir in the steak, sour cream, and the 1 tablespoon dill. Return to medium heat and simmer, stirring constantly, until the sour cream is heated through, about 1 minute. Do not allow to boil. Season with salt and pepper.

When the noodles are ready, drain them and return to the cooking pot. Add the remaining 1 tablespoon butter and toss to coat. Divide the noodles among dinner plates and top each serving with the steak and sauce. Sprinkle with dill and serve.

PUT A SPIN ON IT You can also make this dish with 1½ pounds thin veal cutlets, cut into strips ½ inch wide. Or try leftover steak. You'll need about 2 cups of steak, cut into bite-sized cubes. Simply add it to the mushroom mixture along with the sour cream and heat through.

Filled with a mixture of creamy ricotta and sautéed spinach and onions, these calzone are fun to eat out of hand. Or, if you like, outfit diners with knives and forks and serve them with a side of tangy marinara sauce (page 245) for dipping, just like you might find at a classic Italian American pizzeria.

RICOTTA AND SPINACH CALZONE

Pizza dough (page 248)

Baby spinach, 10 ounces

Olive oil, 2 tablespoons, plus more for brushing

Yellow onion, 1, minced

Garlic, 2 cloves, minced

Parmesan cheese, ½ cup freshly grated

Fresh mozzarella cheese, ¼ pound, finely diced

Ricotta cheese, 1 cup

Kosher salt and freshly ground pepper

All-purpose or bread flour for dusting

MAKES 6 CALZONE

The night before serving, prepare the pizza dough and refrigerate. Remove the dough from the refrigerator 1–2 hours before forming the calzone.

To make the filling, rinse the spinach but do not dry it. In a large frying pan, heat the 2 tablespoons oil over medium heat. Add the onion and cook, stirring occasionally, until translucent, about 4 minutes. Stir in the garlic and cook until fragrant, about 1 minute. Add the spinach, cover, and cook until tender, about 3 minutes. Drain the spinach mixture in a sieve, pressing gently to remove excess liquid. Transfer to a bowl, add the Parmesan, mozzarella, and ricotta cheeses, and mix well. Season with salt and pepper.

Position racks in the center and lower third of the oven and preheat to 400°F. Oil 2 rimmed baking sheets. Divide the pizza dough into 6 equal portions, and shape each portion into a ball. Place the balls on a work surface and cover with a kitchen towel. Place 1 ball on a floured work surface, and roll out into a round 7 inches in diameter. Brush the edges of the round lightly with water. Place one-sixth of the cheese mixture on half of the round, leaving a 1-inch border uncovered. Fold the dough over so the edges meet, then crimp with a fork. Pierce the top of the calzone with the fork and transfer to a baking sheet. Repeat with the remaining dough and filling, putting 3 calzone on each baking sheet. Brush the calzone with olive oil.

Bake until golden brown, about 20 minutes. Transfer to wire racks and let cool for 10 minutes. Serve warm.

PUT A SPIN ON IT You can fill a calzone with just about any combination of meats, cheeses, and vegetables that you'd put on a pizza. For example, replace the spinach in this recipe with 1 cup sautéed sliced mushrooms or zucchini, or cooked and crumbled Italian sausage.

A delicious half-moon of crusty dough stuffed with cheese and countless other ingredients, the calzone knows no bounds.

Pizza is engrained in American food culture: everyone is familiar with the big, round pie topped with tomato sauce and melted mozzarella. But I had to go all the way to Rome to savor my first calzone. An Italian friend urged me to try it, explaining that it was like "an inside-out pizza," so we each ordered one. His description proved insufficient for what arrived: two mouthwatering turnovers, one filled with creamy ricotta cheese and salami, and the other with ricotta and fresh vegetables. After a failed attempt to eat my calzone out of hand, like a pizza, I finished my new-found favorite with a fork and knife. Fortunately, calzone appeared on the menu at my local pizza parlor not long after I returned home.

Every mom seems to have her own secret on how to transform a modest chuck roast into a scrumptiously tender pot roast supper. Some add lots of carrots, others favor parsnips or sweet potatoes. In this recipe, thickly sliced onions and paprika boost the flavor. You'll have lots of sauce, so make mashed potatoes (page 190) for soaking it up.

MOM'S HOME-STYLE POT ROAST

Yellow onions, 3

Beef chuck roast,
1 (about 2½ pounds)

Kosher salt and freshly
ground pepper

All-purpose flour, ¼ cup

Rendered bacon fat or
canola oil, 3 tablespoons

Garlic, 4 cloves, chopped

Sweet paprika, preferably
Hungarian or Spanish,
1 teaspoon

Beef stock (page 244)
or broth, 1½ cups

Canned plum tomatoes,
1½ cups, drained
and chopped

Fresh flat-leaf parsley,
2 tablespoons chopped,
plus more for garnish

MAKES 4-6 SERVINGS

Halve the onions through the stem, and cut the halves into ½-inch-thick half-moons. Set aside. Season the chuck roast with ¾ teaspoon salt and ½ teaspoon pepper. Spread the flour on a plate. Coat the roast with the flour, shaking off the excess.

In a Dutch oven, heat 2 tablespoons of the bacon fat over medium-high heat. Add the roast and cook, turning occasionally, until browned on both sides, about 5 minutes total. Transfer to a plate.

Add the remaining 1 tablespoon bacon fat to the pot and heat over medium-high heat. Add the onions, cover, and cook, stirring occasionally, until the onions soften, about 6 minutes. Stir in the garlic and paprika and cook until the garlic is fragrant, 1–2 minutes. Add the stock, tomatoes, and 2 tablespoons parsley and stir. Return the beef to the pot, nestling it in the onions. Bring the liquid to a boil, reduce the heat to medium-low, cover, and simmer until the beef is fork-tender, about 2 hours.

Transfer the pot roast to a deep serving platter. Season the onion mixture with salt and pepper. Skim off any fat from the surface. Spoon the onion mixture around the roast and sprinkle with more parsley. Serve at once.

PUT A SPIN ON IT   To make beef paprikash, simply add sour cream to the sauce. Transfer the pot roast to a platter and skim the fat from the sauce as directed. Stir 1 cup sour cream into the sauce and cook just until it is heated through; do not allow to boil. Season with salt and pepper. Pot roast also makes excellent hot sandwiches. Slice the roast and serve it along with plenty of the saucy onions on crusty rolls.

The poor sloppy Joe has gotten a bad rap. Perhaps the uninspired versions served by overworked school cafeteria staffers dulled whatever luster it ever possessed. Here's a recipe that returns the sloppy Joe to its rightful position as a dish to cherish when you want a quick and unpretentious supper on a bun.

REAL SLOPPY JOES

Canola oil, 1 tablespoon

Yellow onion, 1, diced

Celery, 1 stalk, diced

Green bell pepper, ¼ cup, finely diced

Ground beef, 1½ pounds

Tomato sauce, 1 cup

Ketchup-style chili sauce, ½ cup

Worcestershire sauce, 1 tablespoon

Dijon mustard, 1 tablespoon

Cider vinegar, 1 tablespoon

Light brown sugar, 1 tablespoon firmly packed

Kosher salt, 1 teaspoon

Freshly ground pepper, ¼ teaspoon

Sesame-seed sandwich buns, 6, split

MAKES 6 SANDWICHES

In a large frying pan, heat the oil over medium heat. Add the onion, celery, and bell pepper and cook, stirring occasionally, until the onion softens, about 5 minutes. Add the beef and increase the heat to medium-high. Cook, stirring and breaking up the beef with a wooden spoon, until it is no longer pink, about 10 minutes. Stir in ¼ cup water, the tomato sauce, chili sauce, Worcestershire sauce, mustard, vinegar, sugar, salt, and pepper and bring to a simmer. Reduce the heat to medium-low and simmer, stirring frequently, for about 20 minutes to blend the flavors.

Toast the buns. Place the bottom halves of the buns, cut side up, on warmed individual plates and top with the beef mixture, dividing it equally. Cover with the bun tops and serve right away.

PUT A SPIN ON IT Sloppy Joes are just as good when made with ground turkey or ground chicken. Some cooks like to add 1–2 cups cooked kidney or pinto beans to the beef mixture just before it is ready. Or, you can top the beef mixture with thin slices of Cheddar cheese before covering with the bun tops.

If someone mentions tacos and the first thing that comes to mind is bland ground meat in preformed taco shells, you're in for a treat. These authentic tacos are infinitely tastier: boldly seasoned slices of grilled steak and creamy guacamole rolled up in warm corn tortillas. This cut of beef tastes best grilled medium-rare.

CARNE ASADA TACOS

Chili powder, 2 teaspoons

Kosher salt, 1 teaspoon

Dried oregano, 1 teaspoon

Ground cumin, 1 teaspoon

Granulated garlic, ½ teaspoon

Skirt steak, 1½ pounds, cut into 2 or 3 pieces

CREAMY GUACAMOLE

Ripe avocado, 1, pitted, peeled, and diced

Sour cream, ¼ cup

Fresh lime juice, 1 tablespoon

Kosher salt

Fresh cilantro, 3 tablespoons chopped

Corn tortillas, 12

Lime, 1, cut into wedges

MAKES 6 SERVINGS

To prepare the steak, mix together the chili powder, salt, oregano, cumin, and garlic. Sprinkle the mixture on both sides of the steak and rub it into the meat. Let stand at room temperature while you make the guacamole and ready the grill.

To make the guacamole, halve, pit, peel, and coarsely dice the avocado. In a bowl, combine the avocado, sour cream, and lime juice, and mash the avocado with a fork to form a chunky purée. Season with salt and stir in the cilantro. Place a piece of plastic wrap directly on the surface of the guacamole and let stand at room temperature while you prepare the grill.

Prepare a grill for direct-heat cooking over high heat. Lightly oil the cooking grate.

Place the steaks on the grill and cover. Grill until the undersides are browned, about 2½ minutes. Turn the steaks and grill until the second sides are browned and the meat feels slightly resilient when pressed in the center, about 2½ minutes more for medium-rare. (Skirt steak is too thin to test with an instant-read thermometer, so use this "touch test" instead.) Transfer to a carving board, tent with aluminum foil to keep warm, and let stand for 5 minutes.

Grill the tortillas, turning once, until they are warm and pliable, about 1 minute. Wrap in a large cloth napkin or kitchen towel to keep warm.

With the carving knife held at a slight diagonal, cut the steaks across the grain into thin slices. Transfer to a bowl, adding any juices from the board.

Serve the steak, guacamole, and tortillas at once, passing the lime wedges on the side. Allow diners to fill their own tacos.

PUT A SPIN ON IT You can add all sorts of ingredients to these tacos to make them your own: fresh tomato salsa, shredded lettuce, dollops of *crema* or sour cream, or crumbled *cotija* or shredded Monterey Jack cheese. You can also opt for flour tortillas over corn.

Making a burger sounds like a simple endeavor, but to make a truly great one, each of the ingredients you use, from the beef to the bun to the tomato, should be of the best quality. The better the beef, the better the burger, so use organic free-range beef if possible. Also, don't use extra lean beef—burgers need a little fat to stay juicy.

THE ULTIMATE CHEESEBURGER

Ground beef round,
1½ pounds

Yellow onion, 1, plus
3 tablespoons minced

Worcestershire sauce,
1 tablespoon

**Kosher salt and freshly
ground pepper**

Hamburger buns, 4, split

Unsalted butter,
2 tablespoons, melted

Canola oil for brushing

Cheddar cheese, 4 slices

**Ripe beefsteak or
heirloom tomato,**
1 large, sliced

Butter or red-leaf lettuce,
4 leaves

**Ketchup (page 246
or purchased) for serving**

**Mayonnaise (page 246
or purchased) for serving**

**Bread-and-butter pickles
for serving**

MAKES 4 BURGERS

Prepare a grill for direct-heat cooking over medium-high heat. In a bowl, combine the beef, the 3 tablespoons minced onion, Worcestershire sauce, 1½ teaspoons salt, and ¾ teaspoon pepper and mix gently with your hands just until combined. Divide the mixture into 4 equal portions, and shape each portion into a patty about ¾ inch thick. Brush the cut sides of each bun with the butter.

Cut the whole onion into rounds about ¼ inch thick, but don't separate the rings. Brush the rounds with oil and season with salt and pepper.

Lightly oil the cooking grate. Grill the onion rounds, turning once, until slightly softened and grill marks are visible, about 3 minutes on each side. Grill the patties for about 3 minutes, then turn and place a cheese slice on top of each patty. Cook on the second sides for an additional 3 minutes for medium-rare, or until done to your liking. During the last 2 minutes of cooking the patties, place the buns, cut sides down, on the grill and toast until lightly browned.

Transfer the buns, cut side up, to plates. Place a patty on the bottom half of each bun and top with the grilled onions, tomato slices, and lettuce. Serve at once, allowing diners to add ketchup, mayonnaise, and pickles as desired.

PUT A SPIN ON IT Mix it up by changing the toppings: Use crumbled blue cheese instead of Cheddar, or Beer-Battered Onion Rings (page 166) instead of grilled onions. And sautéed mushrooms or crisp bacon slices are welcome additions to any burger.

Back in the day, Swiss steak was a supermarket staple. You would pick out a round steak and the butcher would put it through the "Swissing" machine, a contraption that perforated the tough meat to tenderize it. Nowadays, Swiss steaks, sometimes labeled "cube steaks," are harder to find, but this dish makes the search worthwhile.

CHICKEN-FRIED STEAK WITH CREAM GRAVY

Swiss steak or cube steak, 1½ pounds, no more than ⅛ inch thick

Kosher salt and freshly ground pepper

All-purpose flour, 1¼ cups plus 2 tablespoons

Whole milk, 2½ cups

Large eggs, 2

Canola oil for frying

MAKES 4 SERVINGS

Cut the steak into 4 equal pieces. Season the steaks with 1 teaspoon salt and ¼ teaspoon pepper. In a shallow bowl, combine the 1¼ cups flour with ½ teaspoon each salt and pepper. In a second shallow bowl, whisk together ½ cup of the milk and the eggs. One at a time, coat the steak pieces with the flour mixture, shaking off the excess, then dip into the egg mixture, coating evenly and allowing the excess to drip off. Return to the flour mixture to coat evenly, again shaking off the excess. Transfer the coated steak pieces to a plate.

Preheat the oven to 200°F. Set a wire rack on a rimmed baking sheet and place near the stove. Pour canola oil to a depth of about 1 inch into a large, heavy frying pan (preferably cast iron), and heat over medium-high heat until the oil shimmers. Add the steaks and cook until the undersides are golden brown, about 1½ minutes, then turn and cook until the other sides are browned, about 1½ minutes more. Transfer to the rack and keep warm in the oven while making the gravy.

Carefully pour the hot fat from the frying pan into a bowl and set aside. Wipe out the pan with paper towels. In a saucepan, heat the remaining 2 cups milk over medium heat to just below a boil and remove from the heat. Return 2 tablespoons of the fat to the pan and heat over medium-low heat. Whisk in the remaining 2 tablespoons flour and let bubble gently for 2 minutes. Gradually whisk in the hot milk and bring to a boil over high heat. Reduce the heat to medium-low and simmer, whisking frequently, until lightly thickened, about 3 minutes. Season with salt and pepper and pour into a sauceboat. Serve the steaks at once, passing the gravy on the side.

PUT A SPIN ON IT Be sure to make mashed potatoes (page 190), so you can pour a ridiculous amount of the gravy on top. For a spicy version, heat things up with smoky ground chipotle chile. Add ⅛ teaspoon of the ground chile to the steak seasoning and ⅛ teaspoon to the gravy.

Few dishes say supper like a beautifully roasted chicken, with burnished skin the color of chestnuts and juicy meat. This lemon-and-herb scented version is cooked in a frying pan instead of a roasting pan, which makes the drippings especially dark and flavorful—the perfect start to a successful gravy.

ROAST LEMON CHICKEN

Whole roasting chicken,
1 (about 6½ pounds)

Kosher salt and freshly ground pepper

Unsalted butter,
4 tablespoons, at room temperature

Fresh lemon thyme or regular thyme,
2 teaspoons minced

Lemon, 8 thin slices

Olive oil, 1 tablespoon

Chicken stock (page 244) or broth, about 2 cups

All-purpose flour,
2 tablespoons

Heavy cream, ¼ cup

MAKES 6-8 SERVINGS

At least 1 day before roasting the chicken, rinse the chicken under cold running water but do not dry it. Sprinkle the chicken inside and out with 2 tablespoons salt. Put it into a plastic bag and refrigerate for at least 16 hours and up to 48 hours. Remove the chicken from the refrigerator 1–2 hours before roasting.

Preheat the oven to 425°F. Rinse the chicken inside and out under cold running water. Pat the chicken very dry with paper towels. In a bowl, mix together the butter and thyme. Starting at the cavity, slip your fingers underneath the chicken skin and loosen it all over, being careful not to tear it and reaching as far as possible into the thigh area. Using your fingers, massage the butter under the skin to distribute it as evenly as possible. Slip the lemon slices under the breast skin, 4 slices on each side. Rub the chicken all over with the oil and season with ½ teaspoon pepper. Bend the wing tips and tuck them under the shoulders. Do not truss the chicken.

Place a large, heavy ovenproof frying pan (preferably cast iron) in the oven and heat until very hot, about 5 minutes. Twist a 12-inch length of aluminum foil into a rope, and fashion into a ring. Remove the pan from the oven and carefully place the ring in the pan. Place the chicken, breast side up, on top of the ring. Return the pan to the oven and roast, basting occasionally with the fat in the pan, until an instant-read thermometer inserted into the thickest part of the thigh away from the bone registers 165°F, about 1 hour and 20 minutes. Transfer the chicken to a platter and let stand for at least 15 minutes before carving.

Discard the foil ring. Pour the pan drippings into a large heatproof liquid measuring cup. Let stand for a few minutes, then spoon off and reserve the fat. Add enough stock to the drippings left in the cup to total 2 cups liquid.

Return the frying pan to medium heat. Add 2 tablespoons of the reserved fat and whisk in the flour. Let bubble for 1 minute. Gradually whisk in the stock mixture and the cream and bring to a boil. Reduce the heat to low and simmer, whisking frequently, until thickened, about 3 minutes. Season with salt and pepper and pour into a sauceboat. Carve the chicken and serve hot, passing the gravy on the side.

Two things set this old-fashioned beef stew apart from its rivals: browning the beef in bacon fat and adding lots of vegetables to the pot, both of which add flavor to the velvety sauce. The result is comfort food, grandmother style. This grandmother didn't cook with wine, but if you want to, just "put a spin on it" (see below).

HEARTY BEEF STEW

Boneless beef chuck,
3 pounds

Applewood-smoked bacon,
4 thick slices, chopped

Canola oil, 2 tablespoons

**Kosher salt and freshly
ground pepper**

Yellow onion, 1, chopped

Carrots, 3, cut into chunks

Celery, 3 stalks, cut
into ½-inch lengths

Garlic, 2 cloves, chopped

Unsalted butter,
2 tablespoons

All-purpose flour,
6 tablespoons

**Beef stock (page 244)
or broth,** 4 cups

Tomato paste,
2 tablespoons

Fresh flat-leaf parsley,
1 tablespoon chopped,
plus more for garnish

Fresh thyme and rosemary,
1 teaspoon *each,* minced

Bay leaf, 1

Red-skinned potatoes,
1¼ pounds

MAKES 6 SERVINGS

Position a rack in the lower third of the oven and preheat to 325°F. Cut the beef into 1½-inch cubes and set aside. In a large Dutch oven, cook the bacon in the oil over medium heat, stirring occasionally, until the bacon is crisp and browned, about 7 minutes. Using a slotted spoon, transfer to paper towels to drain and set aside. Pour the fat into a heatproof bowl. Return 2 tablespoons of the fat to the pot and heat over medium-high heat. Season the beef cubes with salt and pepper. In batches to avoid crowding, add the beef and cook, stirring occasionally, until browned on all sides, about 5 minutes per batch. Transfer the beef to a plate.

Add another 2 tablespoons of the fat to the pot and heat over medium heat. Add the onion, carrots, celery, and garlic and cook, stirring occasionally, until the onion softens, about 5 minutes. Stir in the butter and let it melt. Sprinkle with the flour and stir well. Gradually stir in the stock, and then stir in the tomato paste, the 1 tablespoon parsley, thyme, rosemary, and bay leaf. Return the beef to the pot and bring to a boil. Cover, place in the oven, and cook for 1½ hours.

Cut the unpeeled potatoes into 1-inch cubes, add them to the pot, stir, re-cover, and continue cooking until both the meat and potatoes are tender, about 45 minutes more. Season the stew with salt and pepper. Serve at once, garnished with parsley and the reserved bacon.

PUT A SPIN ON IT Substitute 1½ cups hearty red wine, such as Syrah or Zinfandel, for an equal amount of the beef stock. If you like, sauté ½ pound cremini mushrooms, quartered, in 2 tablespoons olive oil over medium heat until browned, about 5 minutes, and add them to the stew with the potatoes.

ON THE SIDE

The first time I went to a top-notch cafeteria in the South (and there are many), I was pleasantly overwhelmed by the choices of side dishes available. In fact, I passed up the baked ham and roast chicken to save room for more sides! After a cold first course of creamy potato salad and crisp coleslaw, I returned for my supper of warm scalloped potatoes, braised greens with bacon, macaroni and cheese, creamed spinach, and, of course, hot, flaky biscuits and corn bread. What made the cafeteria sides so special was easy to see: the cooks had taken as much care in their preparation as they had in the supposedly "more important" mains. I never forgot that lesson, and it is illustrated in the selection of accompaniments that appear in the following pages. With a little attention to detail, even seemingly everyday fare like mashed potatoes and baked beans can be worth second—maybe even third—helpings.

The traditional version of this casserole, made with cans of cream of mushroom soup and French-fried onions, is a celebration of American convenience foods and a standard offering on countless holiday menus. This updated recipe, made with fresh ingredients, is guaranteed to push that old formula aside.

THE ALL-NEW GREEN BEAN CASSEROLE

Green beans, 1¼ pounds

Kosher salt and freshly ground pepper

Unsalted butter, 2 tablespoons

Button mushrooms, 10 ounces, sliced

Shallots, 3 large, plus 3 tablespoons minced

All-purpose flour, ⅓ cup plus 3 tablespoons

Half-and-half, 1 cup

Chicken stock (page 244) or broth, 1 cup

Soy sauce, preferably mushroom soy sauce, 1 teaspoon

Canola oil for deep-frying

MAKES 6-8 SERVINGS

Preheat the oven to 350°F. Lightly butter a deep 2½-quart baking dish. Trim the green beans and halve crosswise. Bring a saucepan of salted water to a boil over high heat. Add the green beans and cook until tender-crisp, about 4 minutes. Drain and rinse under cold running water. Pat dry with paper towels and set aside.

In a saucepan, melt the butter over medium heat. Add the mushrooms and cook, stirring, until they give off their juices and are browned, 6–7 minutes. Stir in the 3 tablespoons minced shallots and cook until softened, 2–3 minutes. Sprinkle with the 3 tablespoons flour and stir well. Slowly stir in the half-and-half, stock, and soy sauce and then bring to a boil, stirring often. Reduce the heat to low and simmer, stirring, until thickened, 4–5 minutes. Stir in the green beans, season with salt and pepper, and transfer the mixture to the prepared baking dish. (The casserole can be prepared to this point up to 1 day ahead, covered, and refrigerated.) Bake until the liquid is bubbling, about 20 minutes (30 minutes if it has been refrigerated).

While the casserole is baking, pour oil to a depth of 2 inches into a heavy saucepan and heat over high heat to 350°F on a deep-frying thermometer. Line a baking sheet with paper towels and place near the stove. Cut the remaining 3 shallots crosswise into slices ⅛ inch thick and separate into rings. Place the remaining ⅓ cup flour in a small bowl. Toss the shallot rings in the flour to coat evenly, shaking off the excess. In batches to avoid crowding, add the shallots to the hot oil and deep-fry until golden brown, about 30 seconds. Transfer to the paper towels to drain.

Remove the casserole from the oven, scatter the fried shallots on top, and serve.

PUT A SPIN ON IT Substitute 1 head broccoli (about 1½ pounds) cut into florets, for the green beans. If you don't feel like frying the shallots, sprinkle ½ cup toasted sliced almonds over the casserole before serving.

Biting into hot corn on the cob slathered with butter is one of summer's great eating pleasures. Here, that classic is given a Latin accent with the addition of lime and cilantro to the butter and a sprinkle of ground chile at the table. Be careful not to overcook the corn, it tastes best when the kernels still carry some snap.

MEXICAN-STYLE CORN ON THE COB

CILANTRO-LIME BUTTER

Unsalted butter,
½ cup, at room temperature

Fresh cilantro,
2 tablespoons minced

Finely grated lime zest,
from 1 lime

Fresh lime juice,
1 tablespoon

Fresh corn, 6 ears

Pure ancho chile powder or other chile powder for serving

Kosher salt

MAKES 6 SERVINGS

To make the cilantro-lime butter, using a rubber spatula, in a small bowl, mash together the butter, cilantro, and lime zest and juice. Cover and let stand while you prepare the corn. (The butter can be prepared, covered, and refrigerated for up to 2 days. Bring to room temperature before serving.)

Remove the husks and silk from the ears of corn. Bring a large pot of water to a boil over high heat. Add the corn and cook until the kernels are tender-crisp, about 5 minutes. Drain well and transfer to a serving platter.

Serve the corn piping hot, with the cilantro-lime butter, chile powder, and salt on the side for diners to add as they like.

PUT A SPIN ON IT In Mexico, corn on the cob is often spread with *crema* (similar to sour cream) or mayonnaise, sprinkled with shredded *cotija* cheese, and seasoned with pure ground chile and a squeeze of lime juice.

Here, sweet cherry tomatoes and cherry-sized mozzarella balls, known as *ciliegine*, complement each other in this perfectly balanced, classic salad. On its own or heaped onto thick slices of grilled bread, it bursts with the flavors of summer. You can also use a rainbow of sliced heirloom tomatoes instead of cherry tomatoes.

TOMATO AND MOZZARELLA SALAD WITH PESTO

Basil pesto (page 245 or purchased), 3 tablespoons

Red wine vinegar, 1½ tablespoons

Extra-virgin olive oil, ¼ cup

Kosher salt and freshly ground pepper

Mixed red, yellow, and orange cherry tomatoes, about 4 cups

Small, fresh mozzarella balls, such as *ciliegine or bocconcino*, ½ pound

MAKES 4-6 SERVINGS

In a bowl, whisk together the pesto and vinegar. Whisking constantly, slowly add the oil until emulsified. Season to taste with salt and pepper.

Slice the tomatoes and mozzarella balls in half, add to the bowl, and toss gently. Season with salt and pepper and mound on a serving platter. Serve at once.

PUT A SPIN ON IT Tomatoes, mozzarella, and pesto are a classic panini combination. Instead of cherry tomatoes and small mozzarella balls, use heirloom tomato slices and thinly sliced fresh mozzarella. On 1 slice sourdough bread, spread the pesto vinaigrette, then layer mozzarella slices, tomato slices, and more mozzarella slices, in that order. Spread a second bread slice with more pesto vinaigrette and place, pesto side down, onto the mozzarella. Brush the outside of the bread with olive oil. Using a panini grill, toast the sandwich until the bread is browned and the cheese is melted.

TOMATO BRUSCHETTA

Tomato and mozzarella salad (above)

***Pain au levain*, sourdough, or other rustic country bread**, 6 slices, about ½ inch thick, halved crosswise

MAKES 4-6 SERVINGS

Prepare the tomato-mozzarella salad as directed and set aside.

Prepare a grill for direct-heat cooking over a medium-hot fire. Lightly oil the cooking grate. Alternatively, heat a heavy grill pan, preferably cast iron, over medium-high heat. Brush the bread with olive oil and grill, turning once, until toasted on both sides, about 2 minutes. Transfer the grilled bread slices to a serving platter. Mound the tomato salad on top and serve at once.

Skinny fries may have their fans, but when you want potatoes you can sink your teeth into, make a batch of these hefty steak fries. To ensure a perfectly crisp exterior and a light and fluffy interior, you need to soak, dry, and double fry the potatoes. To really take it over the top, serve them with the homemade ketchup (page 246).

THICK STEAK FRIES

Baking potatoes, 4 large

Canola oil for deep-frying

Sea salt

MAKES 4 SERVINGS

At least 3½ hours before serving, cut each potato in half lengthwise. Cut each half into wedges about ½ inch thick. Place the wedges in a large bowl and add ice water to cover. Let stand for at least 30 minutes or up to 1 hour. Drain the potatoes well. In batches, spin them dry in a salad spinner, then spread them on kitchen towels, wrap them up, and let stand for 30 minutes more to absorb any remaining moisture.

Pour oil to a depth of at least 3 inches into a large, heavy saucepan and heat over high heat to 315°F on a deep-frying thermometer. Set a large wire rack on a rimmed baking sheet and place near the stove.

In batches to avoid crowding, add the potatoes to the hot oil and deep-fry, stirring them occasionally with a wooden spoon to separate them, until they turn pale gold and are almost floppy, about 4 minutes. The potatoes should not be browned at this point, though they can be a little browned at the edges. Using a wire skimmer, transfer the potatoes to the rack to drain. Repeat with the remaining potatoes, allowing the oil to return to 315°F before adding the next batch. Remove the saucepan with the oil from the heat and set aside. Let the potatoes stand until completely cooled, at least 2 hours or up to 4 hours.

When ready to serve, preheat the oven to 200°F. Reheat the oil in the saucepan over high heat to 350°F. Transfer the potatoes to another baking sheet (no need to outfit this one with a rack), so the first baking sheet with its rack is free to hold the fully cooked fries. In batches to avoid crowding, add the potatoes to the hot oil and deep-fry until crisp and golden brown, 2–3 minutes. Transfer to the rack and keep warm in the oven while you fry the remaining potatoes. Transfer to a serving platter and sprinkle with salt. Serve at once.

PUT A SPIN ON IT Ketchup is the classic accompaniment for fries in the U.S., but the Belgians love mayonnaise with their fries. For a decadent treat, stir minced fresh herbs (rosemary and thyme are especially good), grated lemon zest, or minced garlic into homemade mayonnaise (page 246).

You don't have to be from Dixie to love these flaky, buttery biscuits. Crisp on the outside and tender on the inside, they are so easy to prepare that many southern cooks whip up a batch to serve with every meal, be it a hearty breakfast of fried eggs and cheesy grits (page 27), a hot soup lunch, or at supper alongside sliced baked ham.

BUTTERMILK BISCUITS

All-purpose flour, 1 cup

Cake flour, 1 cup

Baking powder, 2 teaspoons

Baking soda, ½ teaspoon

Kosher salt, ½ teaspoon

Unsalted butter, 6 tablespoons, chilled, plus more for serving

Buttermilk, ¾ cup

Butter and honey for serving (optional)

MAKES 6-8 BISCUITS

Preheat the oven to 400°F. Have ready an ungreased rimmed baking sheet.

In a bowl, sift together the all-purpose and cake flours, baking powder, baking soda, and salt. Cut the butter into tablespoons and scatter over the flour mixture. Using a pastry blender or 2 knives, cut the butter into the flour mixture just until the mixture forms coarse crumbs the size of peas. Add the buttermilk and stir just until the dough comes together. Knead the dough a few times in the bowl.

Turn out the dough onto a lightly floured work surface. Using a light touch, pat out the dough into a round ¾ inch thick. Using a 2½-inch round biscuit cutter or cookie cutter, cut out as many rounds as possible. Place them 1 inch apart on the baking sheet. Gather up the dough scraps, pat them out again, cut out more dough rounds, and add them to the baking sheet. Bake the biscuits until they have risen and are golden brown, 18–20 minutes. Serve hot with butter and honey, if desired.

PUT A SPIN ON IT   For savory biscuits, stir ½ cup shredded sharp Cheddar cheese, 1½ tablespoons minced fresh chives, and ¼ teaspoon freshly ground pepper into the flour and butter mixture before adding the buttermilk. You may need to use a little more buttermilk. The biscuits won't rise as high, but they will still be delicious.

Breakfast, lunch, and dinner—any meal is better when a big basket of flaky, hot-from-the-oven biscuits is on the table.

Perfect biscuits—tender rounds that break apart at the slightest tug—are a true test of the baker's art. I learned to make biscuits from a friend's grandmother, a grand southern lady who set a timer as we worked, explaining, "A dozen shouldn't take longer than five minutes to make. If you fuss over them, they'll be tough." She was correct, of course. If the dough is kneaded too much, the gluten in the flour will be overactivated, yielding hockey pucks instead of billowy biscuits. She also insisted that every serious baker should always keep a quart of buttermilk in the refrigerator. The acids present in the buttermilk help tenderize the gluten in the flour, another secret to light, tender biscuits.

You can serve these classic onion rings in their time-honored role: alongside a juicy cheeseburger or riding atop a grilled steak. But they are also a winning appetizer, especially when accompanied with a pint of cold, frothy beer. Sweet Vidalia onions, which are mellower than yellow onions, are a particularly tasty choice.

BEER-BATTERED ONION RINGS

Cake flour, 1 cup

Large egg, 1

Fine sea salt

**Cayenne pepper,
¼ teaspoon**

Lager beer, ¾ cup

**Vidalia or yellow onions,
2 large (about 1 pound
total weight)**

Canola oil for deep-frying

**Ketchup (page 246 or
purchased) for serving
(optional)**

MAKES 4-6 SERVINGS

In a bowl, whisk together the flour, egg, ½ teaspoon salt, and the cayenne pepper until blended. Add the beer and whisk just until combined. Do not worry if the batter has a scattering of lumps. Let stand for 30 minutes.

Meanwhile, cut the onions into thick rounds, and separate the rounds into rings.

Pour oil to a depth of at least 3 inches into a large, heavy saucepan and heat over high heat to 350°F on a deep-frying thermometer. Preheat the oven to 200°F. Set a large wire rack on a rimmed baking sheet and place near the stove.

In batches to avoid crowding, dip the onion rings into the batter to coat, letting the excess batter drip back into the bowl, and carefully add to the hot oil. Deep-fry until golden brown, about 3 minutes. Using a wire skimmer, transfer to the rack and keep warm in the oven while you fry the remaining onion rings.

Transfer the onion rings to a serving platter and sprinkle with salt. Serve at once with ketchup, if desired.

PUT A SPIN ON IT This batter also works well with other vegetables. Try broccoli or cauliflower florets, whole cremini or button mushrooms, or thawed frozen artichoke hearts. Finish with salt and a squeeze of fresh lemon juice.

For many of us, creamed spinach recalls special-occasion dinners at white-tablecloth steakhouses. It is a dish that people eat with gusto at restaurants but somehow forget to make at home. With shallots, garlic, and Parmesan cheese, this recipe is no shrinking violet, holding its own next to thick, juicy grilled steaks and roasts.

CREAMED SPINACH

Spinach, 3½ pounds

Heavy cream, 1 cup

Whole milk, 1 cup

Unsalted butter,
3 tablespoons

Shallots, ¼ cup minced

Garlic, 1 clove, minced

All-purpose flour,
3 tablespoons

Parmesan cheese,
½ cup freshly grated

**Kosher salt and freshly
ground pepper**

Freshly grated nutmeg

MAKES 6 SERVINGS

Remove the stems from the spinach leaves and chop the leaves coarsely. Fill the sink or a large bowl with cold water. Add the spinach and swirl it in the water to loosen any grit. Transfer the spinach, with any water clinging to it, to a large bowl.

In a large saucepan, bring ½ cup water to a boil over high heat. In batches, add the spinach to the pan and cover, letting each batch wilt before adding the next one. Cook until the spinach is tender, about 5 minutes. Drain the spinach in a large coarse-mesh sieve, then rinse briefly under cold running water. Let cool until easy to handle. A handful at a time, squeeze the spinach to remove any excess water and place in a bowl. Set aside.

In a small saucepan, bring the cream and milk to a simmer over medium heat. Remove from the heat. In the large saucepan you used for the spinach, melt the butter over medium heat. Add the shallots and garlic and cook, stirring frequently, until the shallots soften, about 2 minutes. Whisk in the flour. Reduce the heat to medium-low and let bubble for 1 minute. Gradually whisk in the hot cream mixture, raise the heat to medium, and bring to a boil, whisking frequently. Reduce the heat to medium-low and simmer until lightly thickened, about 5 minutes. Stir in the spinach and cook until heated through, about 5 minutes more.

Whisk in the Parmesan, and season with salt, pepper, and a pinch of the nutmeg. Transfer to a warmed serving dish and serve at once.

PUT A SPIN ON IT Just before serving, top the creamed spinach with a generous sprinkling of crisp-cooked chopped bacon or pancetta. You can make it even more hearty by adding mushrooms, such as button, cremini, or shiitake. Sauté 1 cup sliced mushrooms in 1 tablespoon unsalted butter until lightly browned, about 5 minutes. Add to the sauce along with the spinach.

Once you have tasted this dish of sweet, milky corn kernels bathed in cream and butter, you will never reach for its canned namesake again. Use only farm-fresh ears of corn here, and use them soon after you bring them home, before their natural sugars have the time to turn to starch.

CREAMED CORN

Fresh corn, 6 ears

Unsalted butter, 2 tablespoons

Yellow onion, 1 small, finely chopped

Sugar, ½ teaspoon

Kosher salt and freshly ground pepper

Heavy cream, ¾ cup

Fresh chives, 2 tablespoons minced

MAKES 4 SERVINGS

Remove the husks and silk from the ears of corn. Using a chef's knife, cut each ear in half crosswise. One at a time, stand the halves cut side down on a cutting board and slice the kernels from the cobs. Transfer the kernels to a bowl. Using the dull edge of the knife blade, scrape the milk and pulp from the corn cobs into the bowl.

In a large frying pan, melt the butter over medium heat. Add the onion and cook, stirring occasionally, until translucent, 5–6 minutes. Add the corn kernels with the pulp, the sugar, and ½ cup water, and season with salt and pepper. Bring to a boil, reduce the heat to low, cover, and cook, stirring occasionally, until the corn is tender but still has a bit of crunch, 8–10 minutes. Uncover and cook until the water evaporates, 2–3 minutes.

Add the cream to the pan, raise the heat to medium, and cook until the cream has thickened enough to coat the back of a spoon, about 3 minutes. Stir in the chives.

Transfer to a warmed serving bowl and serve at once.

PUT A SPIN ON IT Smoky flavor pairs wonderfully with the natural sweetness of corn. In a frying pan, fry 3 slices of bacon, coarsely chopped, over medium heat until crisp, about 7 minutes, then drain on paper towels. Use the bacon fat in place of the butter, and sprinkle the bacon over the corn just before serving. Or, for a version with smoke *and* spice, add 1 chipotle chile in adobo sauce, seeded and minced, and ½ teaspoon adobo sauce with the cream.

Collard greens are frankly quite bitter, but southern cooks know how to tame them. They lose their edge when simmered with smoky bacon and pungent garlic, and are perked up by a splash of vinegar and a shake of red pepper. The best part of a pot of greens is sopping up the cooking liquid with a thick wedge of corn bread (page 186).

BRAISED COLLARD GREENS WITH BACON

Collard greens, 4 pounds

Applewood-smoked bacon, 6 thick slices, coarsely chopped

Canola oil, 1 tablespoon

Garlic, 4 cloves, minced

Red pepper flakes, ¼ teaspoon

Cider vinegar, 2 tablespoons, plus more for serving

Kosher salt

MAKES 6-8 SERVINGS

Trim off and discard the thick stems from the collard greens. In batches, stack the leaves and cut crosswise into strips about ½ inch wide. Fill the sink or a large bowl with cold water. Add the greens and swirl them to loosen any grit. Transfer the collard greens, with any water clinging to them, to a large bowl.

In a large pot or a large, deep sauté pan, fry the bacon in the oil over medium heat until browned and crisp, about 8 minutes. Using a slotted spoon, transfer the bacon to paper towels to drain. Remove the pot from the heat, with the bacon fat still in it, and let cool slightly.

Return the pot to medium-low heat. Add the garlic and cook, stirring frequently, until softened, about 1 minute. Increase the heat to medium-high. Add a handful of the collard greens to the pot, cover, and cook until they wilt. Continue adding the greens, a handful at a time and allowing them to wilt before adding the next batch, until all of the greens are in the pot. Add the red pepper flakes, cover, reduce the heat to medium-low, and simmer, stirring occasionally, for about 15 minutes if you like the greens tender but still fresh, or up to 45 minutes if you like them well done.

Stir in the reserved bacon and the 2 tablespoons vinegar. Season with salt, then taste and adjust with red pepper flakes. Transfer the greens and their cooking liquid to a warmed serving bowl. Serve hot, passing vinegar on the side.

PUT A SPIN ON IT Other greens, such as dandelion, mustard, and kale, can be cooked in the same way, or you can use a combination of greens. Instead of using bacon, sauté the garlic in 2 tablespoons olive oil, bury a smoked ham hock or a smoked turkey wing in the greens, and cook for about 1½ hours to allow the meat to infuse the greens with smoky flavor. Don't worry: they can take the extended heat.

This mac and cheese is miles away from its neon-boxed cousin that you may have had as a kid. Once you have enjoyed a plate of this from-scratch version, bubbling hot from the oven, with its flavorful cheeses and buttery crown of crisp bread crumbs, you will be hard-pressed to return to its store-bought kin.

CREAMY MAC AND CHEESE

Unsalted butter, 7 tablespoons

Garlic, 1 clove, minced

Coarse fresh bread crumbs, 1½ cups

Kosher salt and freshly ground pepper

Elbow macaroni, 1 pound

All-purpose flour, ¼ cup

Whole milk, 3 cups, warmed

Sharp Cheddar cheese, 2 cups shredded

Fontina cheese, 2 cups shredded

Dry mustard, ½ teaspoon

MAKES 6 SERVINGS

In a large frying pan, melt 3 tablespoons of the butter over medium-low heat. Add the garlic and cook, stirring frequently, until tender but not browned, about 3 minutes. Add the bread crumbs and stir until coated with butter. Set aside.

Preheat the oven to 350°F. Butter a shallow 3-quart baking dish.

Bring a large pot of lightly salted water to a boil over high heat. Add the macaroni and stir occasionally until the water returns to a boil. Cook according to the package directions until not quite al dente. (The macaroni will cook again in the oven, so do not overcook it now.) Drain well and set aside.

Add the remaining 4 tablespoons butter to the pot used for the pasta and melt over medium heat. Whisk in the flour. Reduce the heat to medium-low and let bubble for 1 minute without browning. Gradually whisk in the milk, raise the heat to medium, and bring to a boil, whisking frequently. Remove from the heat and stir in the cheeses along with the mustard. Season with salt and pepper. Stir in the pasta. Spread in the prepared baking dish and sprinkle evenly with the buttered crumbs.

Bake until the crumbs are browned and the sauce is bubbling, about 20 minutes. Let cool for 5 minutes, then serve hot.

PUT A SPIN ON IT   Any tubular pasta will do: try penne, ziti, or *mostaccioli*. To give your mac and cheese a little personality, add chopped crisp bacon, cubes of smoked ham or cooked chicken, cooked peas, chopped blanched broccoli, sautéed wild mushrooms, or crumbled blue cheese.

You can make these golden brown fritters dotted with corn kernels with frozen corn any time of the year, but they are best if you wait until summertime when your local corn is in season. Any variety—white or yellow, standard or supersweet—can be used. Serve the fritters alongside everything from grilled fish to fried chicken.

FRESH CORN FRITTERS

Canola oil for deep-frying

All-purpose flour, 1½ cups

Baking soda, ¾ teaspoon

Fine sea salt, ¾ teaspoon

Freshly ground pepper, ¼ teaspoon

Corn kernels, 1½ cups (from about 4 ears)

Buttermilk, 1 cup

Large egg, 1

Maple syrup for serving

MAKES ABOUT 20 FRITTERS

Pour oil to a depth of at least 3 inches into a large, heavy saucepan and heat over high heat to 375°F on a deep-frying thermometer. Preheat the oven to 200°F. Set a large wire rack on a rimmed baking sheet and place near the stove.

While the oil is heating, in a bowl, sift together the flour, baking soda, salt, and pepper. In a blender, combine ½ cup of the corn kernels, the buttermilk, and egg and process until smooth. Pour the purée into the flour mixture and stir just until smooth. Fold in the remaining 1 cup corn kernels.

In batches to avoid crowding, add tablespoonfuls of the batter to the hot oil and deep-fry until golden brown, about 3 minutes. Using a wire skimmer, transfer to the rack and keep warm in the oven while you fry the remaining fritters.

Serve the fritters hot, with maple syrup on the side.

PUT A SPIN ON IT   To give the fritters a savory edge, add 2 tablespoons finely chopped fresh cilantro to the batter and serve with lime wedges instead of maple syrup. Or, make a spicy dip for the fritters: In a small bowl, mix together 1 cup plain yogurt; 1 clove garlic, minced; 1 serrano chile, minced; the finely grated zest of ½ lime; and salt to taste.

You can steam butternut squash on top of the stove, but the result doesn't hold a candle to thick chunks of squash that have been roasted until caramelized and meltingly tender. When cloaked with nutty brown butter and crispy fried sage, it brings up visions of autumn. This scrumptious squash is excellent alongside pork.

ROASTED BUTTERNUT SQUASH WITH BROWN BUTTER AND SAGE

Butternut squash,
1 (about 3¼ pounds)

Olive oil, 1 tablespoon

Kosher salt and freshly ground pepper

Unsalted butter,
2 tablespoons

Fresh sage, 24 leaves

MAKES 6-8 SERVINGS

Preheat the oven to 425°F. Using a sturdy vegetable peeler, peel the squash. Using a large, sharp knife, cut the squash crosswise where the bulbous part meets the narrower part, and trim off the blossom and stem ends. Cut the bulbous part in half vertically and scrape out and discard the seeds and fibers. Cut all of the squash into 1-inch chunks. Spread the pieces on a rimmed baking sheet. Drizzle with the oil and toss with your hands to coat. Season with salt and pepper.

Roast for 15 minutes. Stir the squash and continue roasting until tender and browned, 10–15 minutes more. Remove from the oven.

In a small frying pan, melt the butter over medium heat until the foam subsides. Add the sage and cook just until the butter turns a light hazelnut brown and the sage is crisp, about 30 seconds. Immediately pour the brown butter and sage over the squash on the baking sheet and toss to coat. Transfer to a warmed serving bowl and serve.

PUT A SPIN ON IT   Root vegetables, such as carrots, potatoes, parsnips, and turnips are also delicious served with brown butter and sage. Cut them all into 1-inch chunks. You can roast them together, mixing and matching the vegetables to suit your taste.

When the leaves on the trees turn burnt orange and begin to drop, it's time to put away the grill and turn on the oven.

For me, Thanksgiving is the ultimate fall holiday, and it always put me in a quandary: Should the menu consist of the tried-and-true favorites that my grandmother proudly served? Or, should I push the envelope with some new dishes? One year, I hit on roasted butternut squash as a side dish that could walk the line between the familiar and contemporary with ease. I stuck to a basic version, cutting the squash into cubes and roasting it with just a bit of olive oil. It tasted good but was too plain for a festive meal. I had fresh sage and butter on hand, so I quickly cooked up a finishing touch, frying the leaves until crisp in browned butter. The result that day was so perfect that it has been served alongside my holiday turkey ever since.

Many barbecue aficionados argue that a barbecue isn't a barbecue without a big bowl of cool, crisp coleslaw on the table. Indeed, nothing tastes better alongside a batch of spicy barbecued ribs. If you turn up your nose at too-sweet slaws, this one is for you. It gets its subtle sweetness from an unexpected source—grated apple.

CREAMY COLESLAW

Green cabbage, 1 head (about 2 pounds)

Celery, 2 stalks

Granny Smith apple, 1

Yellow or red onion, 1 small

Carrots, 2 small, peeled

Cider vinegar, 2 tablespoons

Fresh flat-leaf parsley, 2 tablespoons minced

Mayonnaise (page 246 or purchased), 1¼ cups

Kosher salt and freshly ground pepper

MAKES 6-8 SERVINGS

Cut the cabbage into wedges through the stem end, and cut out the core. Using a food processor or a stand mixer fitted with the thin slicing attachment, slice the cabbage into thin slivers. Transfer to a large bowl. Slice the celery with the slicing disk, and add it to the cabbage.

Replace the slicing attachment with the shredding attachment. Halve and core the apple but do not peel. Cut the apple and the onion into wedges. Shred the apple, onion, and carrots, and add to the cabbage and celery.

Sprinkle the vegetables with the vinegar and toss to coat evenly. Add the parsley and mayonnaise and mix well. Season with salt and pepper. Cover and refrigerate until chilled, at least 2 hours. Taste and adjust the seasoning with more vinegar, salt, and pepper before serving. Serve cold.

PUT A SPIN ON IT If you don't have a food processor, you can ready the vegetables by hand with a chef's knife and box shredder-grater. And if you prefer a sweeter coleslaw, stir in a bit of sugar until the flavor suits you. Thinly sliced red bell pepper and cucumber are also nice additions.

These soufflés are from the big family of warm, comforting cheese dishes. They are made with rich, tangy fresh goat cheese—be sure to use a rindless one—and rise beautifully in the oven, with the center forming a little "top hat." Serve alongside roast lamb for a feast, or pair with a green salad for a simple but special meal.

CHEESE SOUFFLÉS

Parmesan cheese,
3 tablespoons
freshly grated

Unsalted butter,
2 tablespoons
plus 1 teaspoon

Garlic, 1 clove, minced

All-purpose flour,
3 tablespoons

Whole milk,
1 cup, warmed

Fresh goat cheese,
6 ounces

Fresh thyme,
½ teaspoon minced

Fine sea salt, ⅛ teaspoon

Freshly ground pepper,
¼ teaspoon

Large eggs,
4, separated, plus
1 egg white

MAKES 6 SERVINGS

Preheat the oven to 375°F. Lightly butter six ¾-cup ramekins, then sprinkle with the Parmesan, tilt to coat the sides evenly with cheese, and tap out the excess.

In a saucepan, melt the 2 tablespoons butter over medium heat. Add the garlic and cook, stirring frequently, until fragrant but not browned, about 1 minute. Whisk in the flour. Reduce the heat to medium-low and let bubble for 1 minute without browning. Gradually whisk in the milk, raise the heat to medium, and bring to a boil, whisking frequently. Reduce the heat to medium-low and cook, whisking frequently, until very thick, about 3 minutes. Remove from the heat, crumble in the goat cheese, and whisk until it melts. Whisk in the thyme, salt, and pepper. Cut the 1 teaspoon butter into small pieces and dot the top of the cheese mixture. (The cheese mixture can be prepared up to 1 hour ahead and covered tightly. Reheat over low heat, whisking often, before proceeding.)

In a large bowl, whisk the egg yolks until blended. Gradually whisk the warm cheese mixture into the yolks. In another bowl, using a handheld mixer on high speed, beat the 5 egg whites until soft peaks form. Stir about one-fourth of the beaten egg whites into the yolk mixture to lighten it, then gently fold in the remaining whites just until combined. Divide the mixture evenly among the prepared ramekins, filling each one about three-fourths full. One at a time, insert a butter knife into each soufflé mixture and trace a circle about 1 inch deep and ¼ inch from the sides of the ramekin. (This creates the "top hat.")

Place the ramekins on a baking sheet and bake until the tops are puffed and golden brown and the soufflés quiver gently when jostled (the insides will be lightly set, and maybe a bit soft), about 20 minutes. Serve at once.

PUT A SPIN ON IT Have fun experimenting with different types of cheeses and herbs. For example, substitute 1 cup shredded sharp Cheddar or Gruyère cheese for the goat cheese. Rosemary is a good substitute for the thyme.

Old-time Italian American restaurants invariably include cheese-laden garlic bread on their menus. And their regular diners invariably order it, enjoying it alongside a big plate of spaghetti and meatballs. This version is dressed up with fresh herbs and Gruyère cheese for a more contemporary take on that much-loved classic.

GARLIC CHEESE BREAD

Unsalted butter,
6 tablespoons, at
room temperature

Garlic, 3 cloves, minced

Parmesan cheese,
3 tablespoons
freshly grated

Fresh basil,
1 tablespoon minced

Fresh chives,
1 tablespoon minced

Kosher salt, ¼ teaspoon

Italian bread, 1 loaf, split

Gruyère cheese,
¼ cup shredded

Fresh flat-leaf parsley,
1½ tablespoons minced

MAKES 6-8 SERVINGS

Preheat the oven to 450°F. Using a rubber spatula, in a small bowl, mash together the butter, garlic, Parmesan, basil, chives, and salt until well blended. Spread the mixture onto the cut sides of the bread, dividing it evenly, then sprinkle evenly with the Gruyère. Place the bread halves, cut sides up, on a rimmed baking sheet.

Bake until the edges of the bread are toasted and the cheese is melted and lightly golden brown, about 10 minutes. Sprinkle evenly with the parsley, cut crosswise into slices, and serve hot.

PUT A SPIN ON IT   Roasted garlic has a sweet, mellow flavor and makes superb garlic bread. Slice a head of garlic in half crosswise, drizzle the halves with olive oil, wrap them in aluminum foil, and place in a small, shallow pan. Bake in a preheated 400°F oven until the cloves are soft and creamy, about 35 minutes. Squeeze the cloves from their papery sheaths into the butter mixture in place of the raw garlic.

Although this salad has plenty of peppery arugula, what makes it stand out at the table is the interplay of the warm toasted bread, crunchy pine nuts, and slightly chewy pancetta. The vinaigrette is made special by sautéing the shallots, which helps distribute their flavor throughout the salad.

SAVORY BREAD SALAD

Pain au levain or country sourdough, 2 cups cubed

Olive oil, ½ cup plus 3 tablespoons

Pine nuts, ⅓ cup

Pancetta, ¼ pound, chopped

Shallots, 2 tablespoons minced

Red wine vinegar, 2 tablespoons

Kosher salt and freshly ground pepper

Baby arugula, 6 ounces

MAKES 4 SERVINGS

Preheat the oven to 350°F. Spread the bread cubes on a rimmed baking sheet and drizzle with 2 tablespoons of the oil. Bake until the bread is toasted but still slightly chewy, about 8 minutes. Let cool.

In a frying pan over medium-low heat, toast the pine nuts until golden, stirring continuously, about 5 minutes. Remove from the pan and set aside. In the same frying pan, combine the pancetta and 1 tablespoon of the oil over medium heat and cook, stirring occasionally, until the pancetta is browned and crisp, about 8 minutes. Using a slotted spoon, transfer to paper towels to drain. Pour off all but 1 tablespoon of the fat from the pan. Let the pan cool slightly.

Return the pan to medium heat, add the shallots, and cook, stirring frequently, until softened, about 2 minutes. Transfer to a small bowl and let cool. Add the vinegar to the cooled shallots, then slowly whisk in the ½ cup olive oil until well blended to make a vinaigrette. Season with salt and pepper.

In a large serving bowl, toss together the toasted bread cubes, arugula, toasted pine nuts, and pancetta. Add the vinaigrette and toss to coat evenly. Season with salt and pepper and serve at once.

PUT A SPIN ON IT For an entirely different but equally delicious bread salad, substitute toasted sliced almonds for the pine nuts, watercress for the arugula, and orange segments for the pancetta.

Corn bread is so simple to make—and tastes so delicious with lots of different dishes—that there is no excuse for not making it whenever you are in the mood. This jalapeño-spiked, Cheddar-flecked version is heartier than most and is the perfect accompaniment to a big bowl of meaty chili (page 118).

SPICY CORN BREAD

All-purpose flour, 1 cup

Yellow cornmeal, preferably stone-ground, 1 cup

Sugar, 2 tablespoons

Baking soda, ¾ teaspoon

Fine sea salt, ½ teaspoon

Cayenne pepper, ⅛ teaspoon

Sour cream or plain yogurt, ⅔ cup

Whole milk, ⅔ cup

Large eggs, 2

Unsalted butter, 6 tablespoons, melted

Sharp Cheddar cheese, ¾ cup shredded

Fresh or thawed frozen corn kernels, ¾ cup

Jalapeño chile, 1, seeds and ribs removed, minced

MAKES 8 SERVINGS

Preheat the oven to 400°F. Butter a heavy 10-inch ovenproof frying pan (preferably cast iron) or a heavy 10-inch cake pan.

In a large bowl, whisk together the flour, cornmeal, sugar, baking soda, salt, and cayenne pepper. In another bowl, whisk together the sour cream, milk, and eggs until blended. Make a well in the center of the flour mixture, pour in the sour cream mixture and melted butter, and stir just until combined. Do not overmix. Fold in the Cheddar, corn kernels, and jalapeño.

Pour the batter into the pan and smooth the top. Bake until the corn bread is golden brown and a knife inserted in the center comes out clean, about 20 minutes. Let cool in the pan for 5 minutes. Cut into wedges and serve hot or warm.

PUT A SPIN ON IT   You can easily make this same recipe into corn bread muffins: just spoon the batter into 12 buttered or paper-lined muffin cups. Bake for about 20 minutes. If you prefer a sweeter, plainer version of corn bread, omit the Cheddar and jalapeño, and increase the sugar to ¼ cup.

Southern cooks never pass up an opportunity to serve crispy, tangy, fried green tomatoes. (These are hard, unripened tomatoes, not ripe green-skinned heirloom varieties.) They are great with baked ham, and make a tasty breakfast topped with crisp bacon, especially if you add the bacon fat to the pan when you fry the tomatoes.

FRIED GREEN TOMATOES

All-purpose flour, ¾ cup

Kosher salt, 2 teaspoons

Freshly ground black pepper, ½ teaspoon

Cayenne pepper, ⅛ teaspoon

Whole milk, 1 cup

Large eggs, 2

Yellow cornmeal, preferably stone-ground, 1 cup

Green (unripened) tomatoes, 3 (about 7 ounces each)

Canola oil, 1 cup

Rémoulade (page 246) for serving

MAKES 6-8 SERVINGS

In a shallow dish, mix together the flour, salt, black pepper, and cayenne pepper. In a second shallow dish, whisk together the milk and eggs until blended. Spread the cornmeal in a third shallow dish. Have ready a baking sheet.

Core the tomatoes and cut crosswise into slices about ¼ inch thick. One at a time, dip the tomato slices into the flour mixture to coat evenly, shaking off the excess. Dip into the egg mixture, letting the excess drip back into the bowl, and then in the cornmeal, patting gently to help it adhere. Transfer to the baking sheet.

Preheat the oven to 200°F. Set a large wire rack on another rimmed baking sheet and place near the stove. In a large frying pan, heat the oil over medium-high heat until it shimmers. In batches to avoid crowding, add the coated tomato slices to the hot oil and cook until the undersides are golden brown, about 2 minutes. Turn the slices and fry until the other sides are browned, about 2 minutes more. Using a slotted spatula, transfer the tomatoes to the rack and keep warm in the oven while you fry the remaining tomatoes. Serve hot, passing the rémoulade on the side.

PUT A SPIN ON IT In New Orleans and elsewhere in the South, you will often see fried green tomatoes topped with a mound of fresh lump crabmeat. Serve with a dollop of the rémoulade or lemon aioli (page 62).

So many comfort foods call out for a side of mashed potatoes that you want to be sure you get them right. That means using the right potatoes, adding lots of sweet butter, and warming the milk so the potatoes don't cool. Those tips make the difference between a bowl of ordinary spuds and a creamy, fluffy masterpiece.

BUTTERY MASHED POTATOES

Baking potatoes,
3 pounds

Kosher salt and freshly
ground white pepper

Unsalted butter,
½ cup, at room
temperature plus
more for serving

Whole milk,
about ½ cup, warmed

Fresh chives,
3 tablespoons minced

MAKES 6 SERVINGS

Peel the potatoes and cut into chunks. In a large saucepan, combine the potatoes with salted water to cover, cover the pan, and bring to a boil over high heat. Uncover, reduce the heat to medium-low, and simmer until the potatoes are tender when pierced with a knife, about 20 minutes. Drain well. Return the potatoes to the pan and stir over medium-low heat for 2 minutes to evaporate the excess moisture.

Press the warm potatoes through a ricer into a large bowl. Cut the butter into slices and scatter over the potatoes. Whisk in the butter and enough of the milk to give the potatoes the texture you like. (Or, if you don't have a ricer, beat the potatoes in the pot with a handheld mixer on high speed. Add the butter and continue beating on high speed, adding milk as needed to create the desired texture. Be careful not to overbeat the potatoes.)

Mix in the chives and season to taste with salt and pepper. Transfer to a warmed serving bowl and serve at once with additional butter, if desired.

PUT A SPIN ON IT Give the mashed potatoes a boost of flavor with roasted garlic. Slice a head of garlic in half crosswise, drizzle the halves with olive oil, wrap them in aluminum foil, and place in a small, shallow pan. Bake in a preheated 400°F oven until the cloves are soft, about 35 minutes. Squeeze the cloves from their papery sheaths into the potatoes when you add the milk and whisk to combine.

At their best, baked beans, which have been at the center of the American table since colonial times, are both sweet and salty and have a tender bite—all of which add up to comfort food that never goes out of fashion. For the most traditional taste, look for Grade B maple syrup from Vermont, which boasts pronounced caramel flavors.

MAPLE BAKED BEANS

Great Northern or cannellini beans,
1 pound (about 2¼ cups)

Kosher salt, 2 teaspoons

Canola oil, 1 tablespoon

Yellow onion,
1 large, chopped

Pure maple syrup, 1 cup

Dark brown sugar,
⅓ cup firmly packed

Dry mustard, 1 teaspoon

Salt pork, ¾ pound

MAKES 8 SERVINGS

Rinse the beans and pick them over, discarding any misshapen beans or stones. In a large bowl, combine the beans with water to cover by 1 inch, and let stand at cool room temperature for at least 4 hours or up to 12 hours. (If the weather is warm, refrigerate the beans while soaking.)

Drain the beans, transfer to a large saucepan, and add water to cover. Cover and bring to a boil over high heat. Set the lid askew, reduce the heat to medium-low, and simmer until the beans are barely tender, 30–40 minutes. Stir in the salt during the last 10 minutes of cooking.

Meanwhile, in a large frying pan, heat the oil over medium heat. Add the onion and cook, stirring occasionally, until softened, about 5 minutes. Reduce the heat to low and cook, stirring occasionally, until the onion is very tender and turns a deep golden brown, about 25 minutes. Remove from the heat.

When the beans are ready, drain them in a colander, reserving the cooking liquid. Transfer the beans to a bowl. Add the cooked onion, maple syrup, brown sugar, and mustard and stir to combine.

Preheat the oven to 325°F. Trim off and discard the rind from the salt pork, then thinly slice. Line the bottom of a deep 2½- to 3-quart baking dish or Dutch oven with one-third of the salt pork. Add half of the beans, then half of the remaining salt pork. Top with the remaining beans and salt pork. Add enough of the reserved cooking liquid to barely cover the beans. Cover and bake for 2 hours. Uncover and continue baking until the cooking liquid has thickened to a glossy syrup, about 1½ hours more. Remove from the oven and let stand for 5 minutes. Serve hot.

PUT A SPIN ON IT If you can't find salt pork, use thick bacon slices, preferably applewood smoked. Or, bury a smoked ham hock or smoked turkey wing in the beans before you put them in the oven.

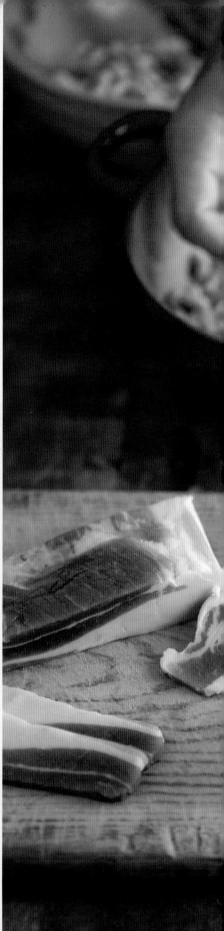

One of the best examples of New England cooking, baked beans should be at once slightly salty, darkly sweet, and a little tangy.

During New England's cold winters, our early ancestors didn't have much to feed themselves: some dried beans, some salt pork, maybe some onions from the root cellar, and a crock of molasses or maple syrup for sweetening. They likely combined this meager pantry of ingredients out of necessity, but the result has become a favorite staple of the American table. For many families, no backyard barbecue or baked ham supper is complete without a big pot of tangy-sweet baked beans on the menu, too. At one family reunion, my relatives brought three different versions of baked beans. And no one was surprised when they were the first side dishes to vanish from the buffet.

For many of us, it is unthinkable to eat baked ham without a huge scoop of creamy, cheesy scalloped potatoes alongside. Most old family recipes call for Cheddar cheese and milk, thickened with a sprinkling of flour, but this updated version takes it to a new level, with rich cream, nutty Gruyère, and meltingly tender leeks.

RICH SCALLOPED POTATOES

Unsalted butter,
2 tablespoons

Leeks, 3 cups chopped, white and pale green parts

Kosher salt, 2 teaspoons

Freshly ground pepper,
½ teaspoon

Baking potatoes,
3¾ pounds

Gruyère cheese,
2 cups shredded

Heavy cream, 3 cups

MAKES 8 SERVINGS

Preheat the oven to 350°F. Generously butter a 9-by-13-inch baking dish.

In a large frying pan, melt the butter over medium heat. Add the leeks and cook, stirring occasionally, until tender, about 7 minutes. Remove from the heat.

Mix together the salt and pepper. Peel the potatoes and thinly slice into rounds. Spread one-third of the potatoes in an even layer in the prepared baking dish and season with about one-fourth of the salt mixture. Top with one-third of the Gruyère and half of the leeks and season with about one-third of the remaining salt mixture. Top with half of the remaining potato slices, half of the remaining Gruyère, and the rest of the leeks, seasoning with half of the remaining salt mixture as you go. Finish with the remaining potatoes and Gruyère and season with the remaining salt mixture.

In a small saucepan, heat the cream over medium-high heat until it is simmering. Pour the hot cream evenly over the potatoes. Cover tightly with aluminum foil and place the baking dish on a rimmed baking sheet.

Bake for 1 hour. Remove the foil and continue baking until the potatoes are tender, coated with a creamy sauce, and golden brown on top, about 30 minutes longer. Let stand for about 5 minutes, then serve hot.

PUT A SPIN ON IT   For the classic all-American version of scalloped potatoes, omit the leeks and substitute sharp white Cheddar cheese for the Gruyère and whole milk for the cream. As you add the potatoes, sprinkle each layer with 1 tablespoon all-purpose flour, for a total of 3 tablespoons.

California is artichoke country, and many locals boil them up and eat them with plenty of melted butter or mayonnaise for dipping. But Italian Americans insist that stuffed artichokes, with a garlicky filling of bread crumbs and pine nuts, are the best way to show off these members of the thistle family.

STUFFED ARTICHOKES

Lemon, 1, halved crosswise

Artichokes, 4 (about 9 ounces each), with stems attached

Olive oil, 6 tablespoons

Coarse fresh bread crumbs, 2 cups

Pine nuts, 1/3 cup, toasted

Fresh flat-leaf parsley, 2 tablespoons minced

Garlic, 3 cloves, minced

Dried oregano, 1/2 teaspoon

Kosher salt and freshly ground pepper

Mayonnaise (page 246 or purchased) for serving

MAKES 4 SERVINGS

Squeeze the juice from 1 lemon half into a bowl, add 6 cups cold water, and then add the spent lemon half. Cut off the stem from each artichoke at the base. Rub the cut areas with the remaining lemon half. Using a paring knife, trim away the thick skin from each stem. Rub the peeled stems with the lemon half, then dice.

Add 1 tablespoon of the olive oil to a frying pan and heat over medium heat. Add the diced stems and 1/4 cup water, reduce the heat to medium-low, cover, and cook until the stems are tender and the water has evaporated, 8–10 minutes. Let cool slightly.

Meanwhile, cut 1 inch off the top of each artichoke. Using kitchen scissors, snip off any thorny tips that remain on the leaves. Rub the cut areas with the lemon half. One at a time, place the artichokes upside down on a work surface. Press hard on the artichoke bottom with the heel of your hand to loosen the leaves and force them far enough apart to hold the stuffing.

In a bowl, combine the bread crumbs, cooked stems, pine nuts, parsley, garlic, and oregano. Stir in 2 tablespoons of the olive oil. Season with salt and pepper. Using one-fourth of the bread crumb mixture for each artichoke, stuff the mixture between the outer few layers of thick leaves. Leave the thin inner leaves intact.

Pour 1 tablespoon of the olive oil into a saucepan just large enough to hold the artichokes upright in a single layer, and tilt to coat the pan bottom. Arrange the stuffed artichokes, bases down, in the saucepan and drizzle with the remaining 2 tablespoons olive oil. Add water to come 1/2 inch up the sides of the artichokes without immersing the stuffing. Bring to a boil over high heat. Reduce the heat to medium-low, cover, and simmer, adding more boiling water to the pan as needed to maintain the level, until a leaf can be easily pulled from an artichoke, about 1 hour.

Meanwhile, preheat the oven to 400°F. Lightly oil a rimmed baking sheet. When the artichokes are ready, using tongs, carefully transfer the artichokes, bases down, to the baking sheet. Bake until the stuffing is lightly browned, about 15 minutes. Transfer each artichoke to an individual bowl and serve with the mayonnaise.

Poppers can be hit or miss. Most people know them as popular bar food, and eat them at home only if they have picked up a package in the supermarket frozen-food aisle. But the crispy, spicy, smoky cheese-rich bites become memorable when you make them yourself. Make sure you have a cold beer on hand to wash away the heat.

JALAPEÑO POPPERS

Applewood-smoked bacon, 2 thick slices, finely chopped

Jalapeño chiles, 12 small

Cream cheese, 4 ounces, at room temperature

Sharp Cheddar cheese, ½ cup finely shredded

Monterey Jack cheese, ½ cup finely shredded

Hot pepper sauce, 1 teaspoon

Kosher salt and freshly ground pepper

Large eggs, 2

Whole milk, 1 tablespoon

Plain fine dried bread crumbs or panko, 1 cup

Vegetable oil for frying

MAKES 6 SERVINGS

In a frying pan, fry the bacon over medium heat, stirring occasionally, until crisp and browned, about 5 minutes. Transfer to paper towels to drain.

Using the tip of a paring knife, slit each chile on one side from the stem to the tip, then make a partial cut at the base of the stem, leaving the stem end intact. Gently open up the chile and remove the seeds with the knife or a small spoon.

In a small bowl, mix together the bacon, cream cheese, Cheddar, Monterey Jack, and hot pepper sauce until well blended. Season to taste with salt and pepper. Using a small spoon, fill the chiles with the cheese mixture, dividing it evenly. Close the filled chiles, pressing firmly on the seams so they retain their shape.

In a shall bowl, whisk together the eggs and milk. In a second shallow bowl, stir together the bread crumbs and a pinch each of salt and pepper. One at a time, dip the filled chiles into the egg mixture, allow the excess to drip off, then dip into the bread crumbs, patting gently to help them adhere. Transfer to a baking sheet. Let dry for about 10 minutes, then repeat, dipping the chiles first in the egg mixture and then in the crumbs to form a second coating.

Pour oil to a depth of at least 3 inches into a deep, heavy saucepan and heat over medium-high heat to 325°F on a deep-frying thermometer. Preheat the oven to 200°F. Line a rimmed baking sheet with paper towels.

In batches to avoid crowding, add the chiles to the hot oil and deep-fry, stirring occasionally with a wire skimmer, until golden brown, about 6 minutes. Using the skimmer, transfer to paper towels to drain and keep warm in the oven while you fry the remaining chiles. Serve the poppers hot.

PUT A SPIN ON IT The chiles can also be stuffed with a simple combination of Cheddar and Monterey Jack cheeses, omitting the cream cheese and bacon. For an extra (sweet) kick, set out Thai sweet chile sauce for dipping.

A big platter of deviled eggs, stuffed with an herb-flecked, fluffy, creamy filling, can round out countless comfort-food menus, from light lunches or suppers to picnics, potlucks, or backyard barbecues. Use homemade mayonnaise in the filling, and your deviled eggs will be legendary among family and friends.

DEVILED EGGS

Large eggs, 8

Mayonnaise (page 246 or purchased), ⅓ cup

Fresh chives,
1 teaspoon minced, plus more for garnish

Fresh tarragon,
1 teaspoon minced, plus more for garnish

Fresh flat-leaf parsley,
1 teaspoon minced, plus more for garnish

Finely grated lemon zest,
from 1 lemon

Kosher salt and freshly ground pepper

MAKES 16
DEVILED EGGS

To hard-boil the eggs, place them in a saucepan just large enough to hold them. Add cold water to cover by 1 inch and bring just to a boil over high heat. Remove the pan from the heat and cover. Let stand for 15 minutes. Drain the eggs, then transfer to a bowl of ice water and let cool completely.

Peel the eggs. Using a sharp, thin-bladed knife, cut each egg in half lengthwise. Remove the yolks, and set the egg white halves aside. Rub the yolks through a coarse-mesh sieve into a bowl. Add the mayonnaise, chives, tarragon, parsley, and lemon zest and whisk together until light and fluffy. Season with salt and pepper and whisk again.

Spoon the yolk mixture into a pastry bag fitted with a medium plain tip. Arrange the egg halves, hollow sides up, on a platter. Pipe the yolk mixture into the egg white halves. (Alternatively, use a teaspoon to fill the egg halves.) Cover lightly with plastic wrap and refrigerate until chilled, about 1 hour. (The eggs can be refrigerated for up to 8 hours before serving.)

Sprinkle with additional herbs and serve chilled.

PUT A SPIN ON IT For a devilishly spicy version, omit the herbs and lemon zest. Stir ½ chipotle chile in adobo, minced, into the mashed egg yolks. Or, go classic and add minced bread-and-butter pickles and 1 teaspoon yellow mustard instead of the herbs and lemon zest.

Nowadays, potato salad often seems to arrive with all sorts of "new" ingredients, which might be tasty, but just don't evoke the simple dish you remember. For those of you who think old ways are often the best ways, here is a recipe that makes nearly everyone reminiscent about family picnics and grandmother's potato salad.

OLD-FASHIONED POTATO SALAD

Red-skinned potatoes,
3 pounds

Kosher salt and freshly
ground pepper

White wine vinegar,
3 tablespoons

Mayonnaise (page 246
or purchased), 1 cup

Whole-grain mustard,
2 tablespoons

Celery, 4 stalks,
finely diced

Green onions,
4, white and green
parts, chopped

Fresh flat-leaf parsley,
2 tablespoons minced

MAKES 8 SERVINGS

Place the unpeeled potatoes in a large saucepan, add salted water to cover by 1 inch, cover, and bring to a boil over high heat. Set the lid askew, reduce the heat to medium-low, and cook at a brisk simmer until the potatoes are tender, about 25 minutes. Drain, then rinse the potatoes under cold running water until they are cool enough to handle.

Cut the potatoes into chunks about ½ inch thick and place in a large bowl. Sprinkle with the vinegar. Let cool completely.

In a small bowl, mix together the mayonnaise and mustard. Add to the potatoes along with the celery, green onions, and parsley and mix gently. Season with salt and pepper. Cover and refrigerate until chilled, at least 2 hours. Serve chilled.

PUT A SPIN ON IT   If you like hard-boiled eggs in your potato salad, by all means, add them. The same goes for chopped dill pickles or bread-and-butter pickles—you can even use pickle juice in place of the vinegar. You can also cook baking potatoes instead of red-skinned ones. They fall apart more easily, but some folks like that.

SOMETHING SWEET

I come from a family of dessert makers. My mom is our top pie baker, and when my great-aunts arrived from Europe they went to work in kitchens, where they learned how to prepare the American classics. As a kid, I always got to choose what kind of birthday cake I wanted, and with so many bakers around, I opted for something different every year, whether it was rich devil's food, creamy coconut, or lemony layers. My brothers went a different route and chose lemon meringue or banana cream pie instead of cake for their special days. In order to re-create these favorites and more, I spent many hours in the kitchen. The result is a treasure trove of sure-fire desserts: chocolaty brownies, shortcakes piled high with strawberries and cream, luscious layered butterscotch pudding, chewy chocolate chip cookies—they are all here, waiting to be joined by a tall glass of ice-cold milk.

There are chocolate chip cookies, and then there are these chocolate chip cookies: large, chewy, buttery, and with just the right amount of chips and nuts. Choose good-quality chocolate for the tastiest result. Store these gems in an airtight container at room temperature for up to 5 days—though they won't last that long.

CHOCOLATE CHIP COOKIES

Walnut pieces, 1 cup

All-purpose flour, 2¼ cups

Baking soda, 1 teaspoon

Kosher salt, 1 teaspoon

Unsalted butter, 1 cup, at room temperature

Granulated sugar, ⅔ cup

Light brown sugar, ⅔ cup firmly packed

Large eggs, 1 whole plus 1 yolk

Light corn syrup, honey, or maple syrup, 2 tablespoons

Pure vanilla extract, 2 teaspoons

Semisweet chocolate, 12 ounces, chopped into ½-inch chunks

MAKES ABOUT 3 DOZEN COOKIES

Preheat the oven to 350°F. Spread the walnuts in a single layer on a rimmed baking sheet. Place in the oven and toast, stirring occasionally, until they are fragrant and toasted, about 10 minutes. Let cool, then coarsely chop.

In a bowl, sift together the flour, baking soda, and salt. In another bowl, using a handheld mixer on medium-high speed, beat together the butter and the granulated and brown sugars until the mixture is light in texture, about 3 minutes. Beat in the whole egg and egg yolk, then the corn syrup and vanilla. Reduce the speed to low and gradually add the flour mixture, beating just until smooth and stopping to scrape down the bowl as needed. With a spoon, stir in the chopped chocolate and chopped walnuts, distributing them evenly throughout the dough. Cover and refrigerate until cold, at least 2 hours or up to 6 hours.

Position racks in the center and upper third of the oven and preheat to 350°F. Line 2 rimmed baking sheets with parchment paper. Drop rounded tablespoonfuls of the chilled dough onto the baking sheets, spacing them about 1 inch apart.

Place 1 sheet on each oven rack and bake, switching the pans between the racks and rotating them 180 degrees halfway through baking, until the cookies are lightly browned, 8–10 minutes. Let cool for 3 minutes on the baking sheets, then transfer to wire racks to cool slightly before serving.

PUT A SPIN ON IT If you want to make milk or white chocolate chip cookies, use chips rather than bar chocolate because they hold their shape better when baked. You can also make cookies with a mixture of semisweet, white, and milk chips. Try pecans, almonds, or peanuts in place of the walnuts.

You may have memories of finding small, individually wrapped pies tucked into your school lunch box. And while everyone has his or her favorite pie, surely blueberry is at or near the top of most lists. Be sure to have plenty of napkins ready, as part of the appeal is the delicious fruit juice that runs down your hands.

BLUEBERRY HAND PIES

Blueberries, 2 cups

Sugar, ¼ cup
plus 1 tablespoon

Fresh lemon juice,
1 tablespoon

Cornstarch, 2 teaspoons

**Double-crust flaky pastry
dough (page 248)**

Large egg, 1

MAKES 6 HAND PIES

In a saucepan, combine 1½ cups of the blueberries, the ¼ cup sugar, and lemon juice over medium heat and cook, stirring frequently, until the berries begin to give off their juices. Reduce the heat to medium-low and simmer, stirring occasionally, until all of the berries have burst, about 5 minutes.

Meanwhile, in a small bowl, stir together the cornstarch and 2 tablespoons water. Add the cornstarch mixture to the blueberry mixture and cook until the juices come to a boil and thicken. Remove from the heat and stir in the remaining ½ cup berries. Place the saucepan in a bowl of ice water and let the mixture cool, stirring frequently.

Preheat the oven to 375°F. Have ready an ungreased rimmed baking sheet. Place the unwrapped dough on a lightly floured work surface and dust the top with flour. (If the dough is chilled hard, let it stand at room temperature for a few minutes until it begins to soften before rolling it out.) Roll it out into a rectangle about 20 by 13 inches and ⅛ inch thick. Using a 6-inch saucer as a template, use a paring knife to cut out 6 rounds. Place about 3 tablespoons of the blueberry filling on one-half of a round, leaving a ½-inch border uncovered. Fold the dough over so the edges meet, then crimp them with a fork. Transfer to the baking sheet. Repeat with the remaining dough rounds and filling. Refrigerate the pies for 15 minutes.

In a bowl, beat the egg with 1 teaspoon water to make an egg wash. Lightly brush the pies with the egg wash, cut an X in the top of each pie, and sprinkle with the remaining 1 tablespoon sugar. Bake the pies until golden brown, about 20 minutes. Let the pies cool on the pan on a wire rack, then serve warm or at room temperature.

PUT A SPIN ON IT   To make a simple glaze, sift 1 cup confectioners' sugar into a bowl and whisk in 1–2 tablespoons water until the mixture has the consistency of a thin icing. Brush the icing over the cooled pies, then let set for a few minutes before serving.

Eating a cupcake brings out the kid in all of us. It's like having your very own little cake that you don't have to share with anyone. Topped with a thick layer of luscious cream cheese frosting and sprinkled with toasted coconut, these coconut cupcakes have a tender, moist crumb that literally melts in your mouth.

COCONUT CUPCAKES WITH CREAM CHEESE FROSTING

COCONUT CUPCAKES

All-purpose flour, 1¾ cups

Baking powder, 2 teaspoons

Fine sea salt, ¼ teaspoon

Granulated sugar, 1 cup

Unsalted butter, ½ cup, at room temperature

Large eggs, 3, separated

Vanilla extract, 1 teaspoon

Coconut milk, ½ cup

Sweetened dried coconut flakes, 1 cup

CREAM CHEESE FROSTING

Sweetened dried coconut flakes, ½ cup

Cream cheese, 6 ounces, at room temperature

Unsalted butter, 4 tablespoons, at room temperature

Lemon juice, 2 teaspoons

Vanilla extract, ½ teaspoon

Confectioners' sugar, 3 cups, sifted

MAKES 12 CUPCAKES

To make the cupcakes, preheat the oven to 350°F. Line 12 muffin cups with paper liners. In a bowl, sift together the flour, baking powder, and salt. In another bowl, using a handheld mixer on medium-high speed, beat together the sugar and butter until the mixture is light in texture, 2–3 minutes. Beat in the egg yolks, one at a time, then beat in the vanilla. Reduce the speed to low and add the flour mixture in 3 additions alternately with the coconut milk in 2 additions, beginning and ending with the flour mixture and scraping down the bowl as needed, beating just until smooth.

In another bowl, using the mixer on high speed, beat the egg whites until soft peaks form. Stir one-fourth of the whites into the batter to lighten it, then fold in the remaining whites, leaving some whites visible. Gently fold in the coconut flakes. Divide the batter evenly among the lined muffin cups, filling them about three-fourths full. Bake until a toothpick inserted in the center of a cupcake comes out clean, about 20 minutes. Let cool for 5 minutes in the pan, then turn out of the pan onto a wire rack and let cool completely. Leave the oven on.

To make the frosting, spread the coconut flakes on a rimmed baking sheet. Bake, stirring occasionally, until lightly toasted, about 10 minutes. Let cool completely. In a bowl, using the mixer on low speed, beat together the cream cheese, butter, lemon juice, and vanilla. Gradually beat in the confectioners' sugar until the icing is smooth. Spread the frosting on the cooled cupcakes, dividing it equally. Sprinkle with the toasted coconut, then serve.

PUT A SPIN ON IT   For coconut layer cake, divide the batter between 2 buttered and floured 8-inch round cake pans. Bake until the cakes begin to pull away from the sides of the pans, about 25 minutes. Make a double batch of the frosting and assemble the cake as directed for Devil's Food Layer Cake (page 226). Garnish with 1 cup toasted dried coconut flakes.

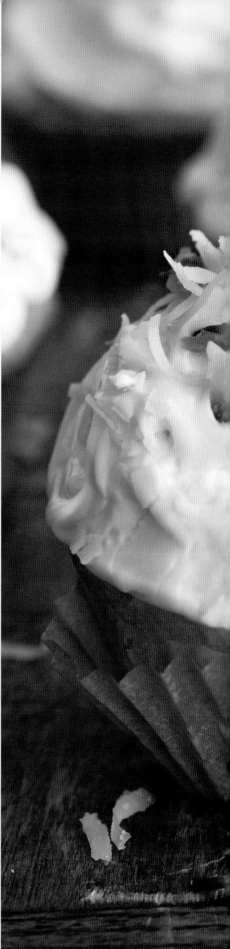

Cupcakes may be small, but they're never short on flavor, especially when crowned with a thick swirl of sweet frosting.

It is no surprise that cupcakes have experienced a comeback. For my generation, these pint-sized desserts bring back happy memories of childhood birthday parties. I recall neighborhood rumpus rooms filled with balloons, exciting games of pin the tail on the donkey, and, of course, big platters of birthday cupcakes. Coconut cupcakes have always been a personal favorite. I remember my mother carefully toasting the coconut until just golden, and not a shade darker. For a girl's birthday, mothers in my neighborhood would skip the toasting step and tint the coconut a pale pastel color. Toasted or not, I didn't care. I saw the cupcake as a repository for the frosting, which I carefully licked off before considering the cake beneath it. So don't skimp on the icing!

You would think that you would need only fresh berries, top-notch ice cream, and creamy whole milk to make an exceedingly good milkshake. But a great strawberry milkshake needs an extra boost of flavor, and strawberry preserves do the trick. For a classic soda fountain treat, there's nothing better than an old-fashioned malted.

STRAWBERRY MILKSHAKES

Whole milk,
⅓ cup, or as needed

Strawberry preserves,
¼ cup

Strawberries,
1½ cups sliced

Vanilla ice cream,
2½ cups

Whipped cream
(page 248)

MAKES 2 SERVINGS

In the following order, put the ⅓ cup milk, strawberry preserves, strawberries, and ice cream in a blender. Cover and process until smooth, adding more milk if necessary to achieve the consistency you desire.

Pour into 2 tall, chilled glasses, top each with a dollop of whipped cream, add a tall straw, and serve at once.

PUT A SPIN ON IT Other fruit flavors, such as banana and peach, also make delicious shakes. For a banana shake, omit the preserves and use 2 cups sliced bananas. For a peach shake, substitute peach preserves for the strawberry, and 1½ cups peeled, pitted, sliced peaches for the strawberries.

VANILLA MALTEDS

Whole milk,
⅓ cup, or as needed

Pure vanilla extract,
1 teaspoon

Malted milk powder,
2 tablespoons

Vanilla bean ice cream,
2½ cups

Whipped cream
(page 248)

MAKES 2 SERVINGS

In the following order, put the ⅓ cup milk, vanilla extract, malted milk powder, and ice cream in a blender. Cover and process until smooth, adding more milk if necessary to achieve the consistency you desire.

Pour into 2 tall, chilled glasses, top each with a dollop of whipped cream, add a tall straw, and serve at once.

PUT A SPIN ON IT You can easily turn this into a chocolate malted. Instead of the vanilla bean ice cream, use Double Chocolate Ice Cream (opposite) or your favorite premium-quality chocolate ice cream.

Rich, dense, and slow to melt, this ice cream is sweet and creamy enough to please kids and dark and chocolaty enough to seduce adults. Its deep flavor comes from using both cocoa powder (use natural, not Dutch process) and bittersweet chocolate in the base. Use the best-quality chocolate you can afford and you won't regret it.

DOUBLE CHOCOLATE ICE CREAM

Whole milk, 1½ cups

Heavy cream, 1½ cups

Bittersweet chocolate,
6 ounces, coarsely chopped

Large egg yolks, 4

Sugar, ½ cup

**Unsweetened natural
cocoa powder,**
2 tablespoons

Kosher salt

Pure vanilla extract,
2 teaspoons

MAKES ABOUT
1 QUART ICE CREAM

In a heavy saucepan, combine the milk and 1 cup of the cream and heat over medium heat just until the mixture comes to a simmer, about 5 minutes.

Meanwhile, put the chopped chocolate in a heatproof bowl. In another heatproof bowl, whisk together the egg yolks, sugar, cocoa, a pinch of salt, and remaining ½ cup cream until the sugar begins to dissolve.

Remove the saucepan from the heat. Gradually whisk about ½ cup of the hot milk mixture into the egg yolk mixture until well blended, then pour the egg mixture into the saucepan. Cook over medium heat, stirring constantly with a wooden spoon, until the mixture is thick enough to coat the back of the spoon and leaves a clear trail when a finger is drawn through it, 4–6 minutes. Do not allow it to boil. Pour the hot milk–egg yolk mixture over the chocolate and stir until the chocolate melts and the mixture is smooth. Strain through a fine-mesh sieve placed over a bowl. Stir in the vanilla. Place the bowl in a bowl of ice water and stir occasionally until cool. Cover with plastic wrap and refrigerate until cold, at least 3 hours or up to 24 hours.

Pour the cold ice cream base into an ice cream maker and freeze according to the manufacturer's instructions. Transfer the ice cream to a freezer-safe container. Press a piece of plastic wrap directly on the surface of the ice cream, cover, and freeze until firm, at least 3 hours or up to 3 days, before serving.

PUT A SPIN ON IT Orange pairs well with chocolate. Add 2 teaspoons finely grated orange zest to the milk and cream mixture as it heats (the zest is strained out later). Espresso is also a natural partner. Substitute ½ cup freshly brewed espresso for ½ cup of the milk.

If to you, baking brownies has meant using the recipe on the back of a brownie-mix box or can of cocoa powder, you are in for a treat. These thick, chewy, deeply chocolate brownies are dark, rich, and irresistible. You'll end up with a big pan of them, which means you will have plenty to share with your friends and neighbors.

DARK CHOCOLATE BROWNIES

All-purpose flour, 1 cup

Baking soda, ½ teaspoon

Fine sea salt, ½ teaspoon

Unsalted butter, ¾ cup

Unsweetened chocolate,
6 ounces, finely chopped

Granulated sugar, 1 cup

Light brown sugar,
1 cup firmly packed

Large eggs, 4,
at room temperature

Light corn syrup, honey,
or maple syrup, ¼ cup

Pure vanilla extract,
2 teaspoons

Semisweet or bittersweet
chocolate chips, 1 cup

MAKES 20 BROWNIES

Preheat the oven to 350°F. Butter a 9-by-13-inch baking pan. Press a 20-inch length of parchment paper into the bottom and up the sides of the pan, folding the parchment as needed to fit and allowing the excess to hang over the sides. Lightly butter the parchment and dust with flour, tapping out the excess.

In a bowl, sift together the flour, baking soda, and salt. In a saucepan, melt the butter over medium heat. Remove from the heat and add the unsweetened chocolate. Let stand for 3 minutes, then whisk until smooth. Whisk in the granulated and brown sugars until well blended. Whisk in the eggs, one at a time, then whisk in the corn syrup and vanilla until blended. Add the flour mixture and stir with a wooden spoon until combined. Stir in the chocolate chips, distributing them evenly. Spread the batter in the prepared pan and smooth the top.

Bake until a toothpick inserted into the center comes out with a few moist crumbs attached, about 25 minutes. Let cool completely in the pan on a wire rack. Run a knife around the inside of the pan to release the sides of the brownie. Lift up the whole brownie by the parchment "handles" and remove it from the pan.

Cut the brownie into 20 squares and serve. Leftovers can be stored in an airtight container at room temperature for up to 3 days.

PUT A SPIN ON IT If you think that brownies must have nuts, add 1 cup coarsely chopped toasted walnuts to the batter instead of the chocolate chips. For an outrageous brownie sundae, top a brownie with a big scoop of your favorite ice cream, drizzle with warm fudge sauce (page 225), and crown with a big dollop of whipped cream (page 248).

Cobblers celebrate ripe, juicy fruit of all kinds. No amount of sugar will improve the flavor of hard, flavorless, out-of-season fruits, so wait until you have the perfect specimens before you make a cobbler. Arguably, peaches make the best cobbler of all, and a scoop of vanilla ice cream makes a good thing even better.

PEACH COBBLER

Peaches, 5 pounds

Light brown sugar,
½ cup firmly packed

Cornstarch,
2 tablespoons

Half-and-half, ¾ cup

Large egg, 1

Pure vanilla extract,
1 teaspoon

All-purpose flour, 2 cups

Granulated sugar, ¼ cup,
plus more for sprinkling

Baking powder,
1 tablespoon

Fine sea salt, ½ teaspoon

Unsalted butter,
6 tablespoons

MAKES 8 SERVINGS

Preheat the oven to 375°F. Lightly butter a 9-by-13-inch baking dish. Have ready a bowl of ice water.

Bring a large pot of water to a boil over high heat. A few at a time, plunge the peaches into the boiling water just until the skins loosen, about 1 minute. Using a slotted spoon, transfer to the bowl of ice water. Peel, pit, and slice the peaches; you should have about 12 cups.

In a bowl, toss together the peaches, brown sugar, and cornstarch. Spread in the prepared baking dish, place the dish on a baking sheet, and bake for 15 minutes.

Meanwhile, in a bowl, whisk together the half-and-half, egg, and vanilla until well blended. In another bowl, sift together the flour, the ¼ cup granulated sugar, baking powder, and salt. Cut the butter into tablespoons and scatter over the flour mixture. Using a pastry blender or 2 knives, cut the butter into the flour mixture just until the mixture forms coarse crumbs the size of peas. Add the half-and-half mixture and stir just until the dough comes together.

When the filling has baked for 15 minutes, remove it from the oven. Drop the dough onto the filling in 8 heaping, evenly spaced spoonfuls. Return to the oven and bake until the peach juices are bubbling, the topping is golden brown, and a toothpick inserted into the topping comes out clean, 30–40 minutes more.

Transfer to a wire rack and let cool for at least 30 minutes, then serve.

PUT A SPIN ON IT Make your cobbler with 12 cups of your favorite fruit, adjusting the amount of sugar depending on the tartness of the fruit. Try blueberries, raspberries, and blackberries (don't use strawberries because they lose their color when baked); pitted sour cherries; peeled and pitted plums; or peeled, cored, and sliced apples or pears.

Most people would find it tough to choose a favorite pie, but banana cream pie would surely be on many short lists. Another diner classic that shines even more brightly when made at home, each bite features a heavenly medley of buttery crust, velvety vanilla filling, rich whipped cream, and slices of ripe, sweet banana.

BANANA CREAM PIE

Single-crust flaky pastry dough (page 248)

Whole milk, 3 cups

Cornstarch, 1/3 cup

Large egg yolks, 4

Sugar, 2/3 cup

Fine sea salt, 1/8 teaspoon

Vanilla bean, 1

Unsalted butter, 2 tablespoons, cut into tablespoons

Bananas, 2 large, peeled and thinly sliced

Whipped cream (page 248)

Semisweet chocolate curls (page 248) for serving (optional)

MAKES 8 SERVINGS

Place the unwrapped dough on a floured work surface and dust with flour. (If the dough is cold, let it stand for a few minutes to soften.) Roll out into a round about 12 inches in diameter and 1/8 inch thick. Transfer to a 9-inch pie dish, fitting the dough into the bottom and sides. Trim the dough, leaving a 3/4-inch overhang. Fold the overhang under, then flute the edge. Using a fork, pierce the dough all over, then line with aluminum foil and freeze for 30 minutes. Meanwhile, position a rack in the lower third of the oven and preheat to 375°F. Place the dough-lined pan on a baking sheet and fill the foil with pie weights. Bake until the dough looks dry and is barely golden, 12–15 minutes. Remove the foil and weights. Continue baking until the crust is golden brown, 12–15 minutes more. Transfer to a rack and cool completely.

In a small bowl, whisk together 1/2 cup of the milk and the cornstarch. In a heatproof bowl, beat the yolks until blended. Gradually whisk the milk mixture into the yolks. In a saucepan, combine the remaining 2 1/2 cups milk, the sugar, and salt. Using a paring knife, slit the vanilla bean in half lengthwise, scrape out the seeds into the saucepan, and add the pod. Place over medium heat and bring to a simmer, stirring to dissolve the sugar. Gradually whisk the hot milk mixture into the egg mixture, then return to the saucepan. Heat over medium heat until the mixture comes to a boil, whisking constantly. Reduce the heat to low and let bubble for 30 seconds. Remove from the heat and whisk in the butter. Strain through a medium-mesh sieve into a stainless-steel bowl to remove any bits of cooked egg white and the vanilla pod. Press a piece of plastic wrap directly onto the surface of the filling, and pierce the plastic a few times with a knife tip to allow the steam to escape. Place the bowl in a larger bowl of ice water and let cool until lukewarm.

Spread the banana slices in the cooled pie crust. Spread the filling on top. Press a clean piece of plastic wrap directly on the surface of the filling and refrigerate until chilled, at least 1 hour. Remove the plastic wrap. Spread and swirl the whipped cream over the filling. Refrigerate until ready to serve. When ready to serve, scatter the chocolate curls, if using, over the whipped cream topping, and serve in wedges.

In the past, most home cooks made pineapple upside-down cake with canned pineapple and enough brown sugar to set your teeth on edge. Nowadays, you can pick up a fresh pineapple in most markets and reduce the amount of topping to suit contemporary tastes. Be brave when inverting the cake—it's not that difficult.

PINEAPPLE UPSIDE-DOWN CAKE

Pineapple, 1

Light brown sugar,
1 cup firmly packed

Unsalted butter,
6 tablespoons, plus
½ cup at room temperature

All-purpose flour, 1½ cups

Baking powder,
1½ teaspoons

Fine sea salt, ¼ teaspoon

Granulated sugar, 1 cup

Large eggs, 2,
at room temperature

Pure vanilla extract,
1 teaspoon

Whole milk, ½ cup

MAKES 8 SERVINGS

Preheat the oven to 350°F. Cut off the crown and stem end of the pineapple. Holding the pineapple upright, pare off the skin, removing as little of the flesh as possible. With the pineapple on its side, cut shallow furrows to remove all of the brown "eyes." Cut the pineapple lengthwise into quarters, then trim away the fibrous core. Cut the fruit into chunks and set aside. You should have 2 cups.

In a 10-inch cast-iron frying pan, combine the brown sugar and the 6 tablespoons butter and heat over medium heat, stirring frequently, until the butter is melted and the mixture is bubbling. Spread the pineapple chunks evenly in the pan. Set aside.

In a bowl, sift together the flour, baking powder, and salt. In another bowl, using a handheld mixer on medium-high speed, beat together the granulated sugar and the ½ cup butter until the mixture is light in color and texture, about 3 minutes. Beat in the eggs, one at a time, then beat in the vanilla. Reduce the speed to low and add the flour mixture in 3 additions alternately with the milk in 2 additions, beginning and ending with the flour mixture and stopping to scrape down the bowl as needed, beating until smooth. Spread the batter evenly over the pineapple.

Bake the cake until golden brown and a toothpick inserted in the center comes out clean, about 35 minutes. Let cool in the pan on a wire rack for 5 minutes.

Run a knife around the inside of the pan to release the cake. Invert a platter or cake plate over the pan. Holding the platter and pan together, invert them and give them a good shake to unmold the cake. Lift off the pan. Let cool until warm, then serve.

PUT A SPIN ON IT Scatter ½ cup chopped pecans over the butter and brown sugar mixture in the frying pan just before adding the pineapple. You can also substitute 2 cups peeled, pitted, and sliced peaches or peeled, cored, and sliced apples or pears for the pineapple.

Here's how to make a creamy, rich rice pudding guaranteed to make any cook proud. Italian rice used for making risotto, such as Arborio or Carnaroli, is especially starchy and helps thicken this pudding without eggs. The recipe requires your patience and attention as it bakes, so make it on a day when you have time on your hands.

BAKED RICE PUDDING

Whole milk,
4 cups, or as needed

Arborio or Carnaroli rice,
⅓ cup

Sugar, ⅓ cup

Unsalted butter,
1 tablespoon

Cinnamon stick, ½

Pure vanilla extract,
1 teaspoon

Finely grated orange zest,
from 1 orange

Fine sea salt

Whipped cream
(page 248)

MAKES 4-6 SERVINGS

Preheat the oven to 300°F. Lightly butter a shallow 2-quart baking dish.

In a saucepan, combine the 4 cups milk, the rice, sugar, butter, and cinnamon stick and bring to a simmer over medium heat, stirring to dissolve the sugar. Pour into the prepared baking dish and distribute the rice evenly. Bake, stirring with a wooden spoon every 15–20 minutes, until the rice is very tender and has absorbed most of the milk, about 1½ hours.

Remove from the oven and stir in the vanilla, orange zest, and a pinch of salt. If the pudding seems too thick, stir in milk until it is the consistency you desire. Serve warm, or let cool to room temperature, cover, and refrigerate until chilled. Spoon into bowls, top with whipped cream, and serve.

PUT A SPIN ON IT   While some remember picking the raisins out of our rice pudding, others can't imagine rice pudding without dried fruit. If you wish, add ½ cup raisins or dried currants, cherries, cranberries, blueberries, or chopped figs, stirring them into the pudding with the vanilla.

Going to the ice cream parlor as a kid, banana splits always seemed like the ultimate decadence. With caramelized bananas, buttery toasted almonds, warm fudge sauce, and fresh cherries, it's clear that this is not your average banana split. But it's perfect for adult tastes. Buy the best ice cream you can find, or, better yet, make your own.

THE ULTIMATE BANANA SPLIT

HOT FUDGE SAUCE

Heavy cream, ¾ cup

Light corn syrup,
2 tablespoons

Semisweet chocolate,
6 ounces, finely chopped

Pure vanilla extract,
½ teaspoon

**Slivered blanched
almonds,** ½ cup

Unsalted butter,
1 tablespoon, melted

Kosher salt, ½ teaspoon

Firm, ripe bananas, 4

Sugar, 8 teaspoons

Vanilla ice cream,
about ½ gallon

**Whipped cream
(page 248)**

Cherries with stems, 4

MAKES 4 SERVINGS

Preheat the oven to 350°F. To make the hot fudge sauce, in a small saucepan, combine the cream and corn syrup and bring to a simmer over medium heat. Remove from the heat and add the chopped chocolate. Let stand for 3 minutes, then add the vanilla and whisk until smooth. Let cool to lukewarm.

Meanwhile, on a small rimmed baking sheet, toss together the almonds and butter, then spread in a single layer. Place in the oven and toast, stirring occasionally, until golden, about 10 minutes. Remove from the oven and sprinkle with the salt. Let cool on the baking sheet.

Halve the unpeeled bananas lengthwise. Sprinkle the cut sides of each banana half with 1 teaspoon sugar. Heat a large nonstick frying pan over medium heat. In batches to avoid crowding, add the banana halves, cut sides down, and cook just until the sugar is caramelized, about 30 seconds. Transfer to a plate.

To make each banana split, peel 2 banana halves and arrange, caramelized sides up, in a banana-split dish or an oblong bowl. Place 3 scoops of ice cream between the banana halves. Top with the hot fudge sauce, a sprinkle of the toasted almonds, and a large dollop of whipped cream. Perch a cherry on top and serve at once.

PUT A SPIN ON IT Many ice cream parlors make their banana splits with a scoop each of vanilla, strawberry, and chocolate, and you may wish to follow suit. Or, use your favorite flavor of ice cream. You can also substitute toasted peanuts or cashews for the almonds.

The secret behind this moist, rich chocolate cake is mixing the cocoa powder—use natural, not Dutch process—with boiling water, which allows the chocolate flavor to blossom and adds extra moisture to the crumb. This time-honored favorite, layered with velvety chocolate frosting, makes the ultimate birthday cake.

DEVIL'S FOOD LAYER CAKE

DEVIL'S FOOD CAKE

Boiling water, 1 cup

Unsweetened natural cocoa powder, ¾ cup

All-purpose flour, 1¾ cups

Baking soda, 1½ teaspoons

Fine sea salt, ¼ teaspoon

Sugar, 2 cups

Unsalted butter, ½ cup plus 2 tablespoons, at room temperature

Large eggs, 3

Pure vanilla extract, 1 teaspoon

Buttermilk, 1¼ cups

CHOCOLATE FROSTING

Confectioners' sugar, 3¾ cups

Unsweetened natural cocoa powder, 1 cup

Unsalted butter, ½ cup, at room temperature

Pure vanilla extract, 1 teaspoon

Heavy cream, about 1 cup

MAKES 10 SERVINGS

To make the cake, preheat the oven to 350°F. Lightly butter two 9-inch round cake pans. Line the bottom of each pan with a round of parchment paper. Dust the pans with flour, tapping out the excess.

In a small heatproof bowl, whisk together the boiling water and cocoa until smooth. Let cool completely. In a bowl, sift together the flour, baking soda, and salt. In a large bowl, using a handheld mixer on medium-high speed, beat together the sugar and butter until the mixture is light in color and texture, about 3 minutes. Beat in the eggs, one at a time, then beat in the vanilla and the cooled cocoa mixture. Reduce the speed to low and add the flour mixture in 3 additions alternately with the buttermilk in 2 additions, beginning and ending with the flour mixture and stopping to scrape down the bowl as needed, beating until smooth. Divide the batter evenly between the prepared pans and smooth the tops. Bake the cakes until they begin to pull away from the sides of the pans, 35–40 minutes. Transfer to wire racks and let cool in the pans for 15 minutes. Run a knife around the inside of each pan to release the cake. Invert the pans onto the racks, lift off the pans, and peel off the parchment paper. Turn each cake right side up and let cool completely.

To make the frosting, in a bowl, sift together the confectioners' sugar and cocoa. Using the mixer on low speed, mix in the butter until it is crumbly. Mix in the vanilla, and then gradually mix in enough of the cream to make a spreadable frosting.

Place 1 cake layer, bottom side up, on a cake plate. Using an icing spatula, spread the top of the layer with a generous ½ cup of the frosting. Place the second layer, top side down, on top of the first layer. Frost the top, then the sides, with the remaining frosting. Slice the cake into thick wedges and serve.

PUT A SPIN ON IT   For chocolate cupcakes, line 24 muffin cups with paper liners. Spoon the batter into the prepared cups. Bake until the tops spring back when pressed in the center, 20–25 minutes. Let cool before frosting.

Moist devil's food layered with luscious chocolate frosting is a masterpiece guaranteed to win over every chocolate lover.

My extended family was so large that hardly a weekend went by without someone hosting a birthday party for a relative. Chocolate was usually the cake of choice, so I became a connoisseur at an early age. My late cousin Trudy made the cake that set the standard: tender, moist layers with intense chocolate flavor, held together with a generous amount of dark, delicious frosting. She guarded her recipe closely, and some whispered that her specialty came from a boxed mix. In my family of bakers, where homemade croissants were served as dinner rolls, such talk was nothing short of heresy. She passed away without revealing the recipe, but I knew this recipe was a winner when another cousin remarked, "This cake is as good as Trudy's!"

There is nothing more homey, autumnal, and American than a warm apple pie cooling on the kitchen counter. Look for good baking apples, such as Mutsu, Pink Lady, or Empire, for making this traditional dessert, then top each slice with a scoop of vanilla ice cream or slices of sharp Cheddar cheese to stay with tradition.

APPLE PIE

Baking apples, 3 pounds

Light brown sugar,
⅓ cup firmly packed

Granulated sugar, ⅓ cup

Fresh lemon juice,
2 tablespoons

All-purpose flour,
2 tablespoons

Ground cinnamon,
½ teaspoon

Double-crust flaky pastry
dough (page 248)

Unsalted butter,
2 tablespoons,
thinly sliced

MAKES 8 SERVINGS

Position a rack in the bottom third of the oven and preheat to 400°F. Peel and core the apples and cut into thin wedges. In a large bowl, toss together the apples, brown and granulated sugars, lemon juice, flour, and cinnamon. Set aside.

Place the unwrapped dough on a lightly floured work surface and divide in half. Rewrap one half of the dough and set aside. (If the dough is chilled hard, let it stand at room temperature for a few minutes until it begins to soften before rolling it out.) Dust the top of the dough with flour and roll out into a round about 12 inches in diameter and ⅛ inch thick. Transfer to a 9-inch pie dish, gently fitting the dough into the bottom and sides of the dish. Using scissors or a small knife, trim the dough, leaving a ¾-inch overhang. Spread the apple mixture in the pie dish and scatter the butter slices on top.

Place the second half of the dough on a lightly floured work surface and dust the top with flour. Roll out into a round about 12 inches in diameter and ⅛ inch thick. Center the round over the apple filling. Trim the dough so it is even with the bottom crust. Fold the overhang under so the dough is flush with the pan rim, then press together to seal. Flute the edge decoratively. Cut a few slits in a decorative pattern in the top crust. Refrigerate the pie for 15 minutes.

Place the pie dish on a rimmed baking sheet. Bake for 15 minutes. Reduce the oven temperature to 350°F and continue baking until the crust is golden brown and the juices visible through the slits are bubbling, about 1 hour. Transfer to a wire rack to cool. Serve warm or at room temperature.

PUT A SPIN ON IT For homemade cherry pie, mix 4 cups pitted sour cherries with 1⅓ cups sugar, 3 tablespoons quick-cooking tapioca, 1 tablespoon fresh lemon juice, and ¼ teaspoon pure almond extract. Spread the mixture in the pastry-lined pan. Scatter the butter on top as directed for the apple pie, cover with the second dough round, and bake as directed.

Even at its simplest, bread pudding is scrumptious. Using challah or another egg bread, such as brioche or panettone, gives this version extra richness and substance, and then two things take it over the top: caramelized sugar, which adds incredible depth of flavor, and a scattering of bright red raspberries to finish.

CARAMEL BREAD PUDDING

Challah, 1 loaf
(about 1 pound)

Whole milk, 4 cups

Unsalted butter, ½ cup

Fine sea salt

Sugar, 1⅔ cups

Light corn syrup,
1 tablespoon

Large eggs, 5

Pure vanilla extract,
1½ teaspoons

Raspberries, 4 cups

Whipped cream
(page 248) or crème
fraîche for serving

MAKES 8 SERVINGS

Preheat the oven to 350°F. Cut the challah into 1-inch cubes; you should have about 8 cups. Spread the bread cubes on a rimmed baking sheet. Bake until the bread is dry around the edges but not toasted, 10–15 minutes. Let cool. Reduce the oven temperature to 300°F.

In a saucepan, heat the milk, butter, and a pinch of salt over medium heat, stirring frequently, until the butter is melted. Set aside and cover to keep warm. In a large saucepan, combine the sugar, corn syrup, and ¼ cup water and stir to moisten the sugar. Place over high heat and bring to a boil, stirring constantly. Stop stirring and cook, brushing down any crystals that form on the sides of the pan with a pastry brush dipped in cold water and occasionally swirling the saucepan by its handle, until the sugar turns a deep golden brown caramel. The caramel will have a toasty aroma, and you may see some wisps of smoke. Reduce the heat to low. Gradually and very carefully stir the warm milk mixture into the caramel; the mixture will boil furiously. Cook, stirring constantly, until the mixture is smooth and the caramel is completely dissolved. Remove from the heat.

In a very large heatproof bowl, whisk the eggs until blended. Gradually whisk in the caramel mixture, then the vanilla. Add the bread cubes and let stand, stirring occasionally, for 10 minutes.

Lightly butter a 3-quart baking dish. Pour the bread mixture into the dish. Place the dish in a large roasting pan. Place the roasting pan in the oven and add hot water to the pan to come halfway up the sides of the baking dish. Bake until a knife inserted in the center of the pudding comes out clean, about 40 minutes. Transfer to a wire rack and let cool for 10 minutes. Scatter the raspberries over the warm pudding. Serve in bowls, with a dollop of whipped cream on each serving.

PUT A SPIN ON IT   Instead of raspberries, top the bread pudding with another seasonal fruit, such as peaches, nectarines, blackberries, or blueberries, or a combination.

Spoon for spoon, is there any dessert more comforting than pudding? Of the trio of vanilla, chocolate, and butterscotch flavors, the last one arguably has the most dedicated fans. But many people have tasted only the boxed kind. Here is the real deal, infused with caramel and the rich flavor of butter.

REAL BUTTERSCOTCH PUDDING

Large egg yolks, 6

Cornstarch, ⅓ cup plus 1 tablespoon

Whole milk, 3 cups

Unsalted butter, 6 tablespoons

Fine sea salt

Sugar, 1¼ cups

Pure vanilla extract, 1 teaspoon

Whipped cream (page 248)

MAKES 4-6 SERVINGS

In a heatproof bowl, whisk together the egg yolks, cornstarch, and ½ cup of the milk until well blended. In a small saucepan, combine the remaining 2½ cups milk, the butter, and a pinch of salt and heat over medium heat, stirring frequently, until the butter is melted. Set aside and cover to keep warm.

In a large saucepan, combine the sugar and ¼ cup water and stir to moisten the sugar. Place over high heat and bring to a boil, stirring constantly. Stop stirring and cook, brushing down any crystals that form on the inside of the pan with a pastry brush dipped in cold water and occasionally swirling the saucepan by its handle, until the sugar turns a deep golden brown caramel. The caramel will have a toasty aroma, and you may see some wisps of smoke. Reduce the heat to low. Gradually and very carefully stir the warm milk mixture into the caramel; the mixture will boil furiously. Cook, stirring constantly, until the mixture is smooth and the caramel is completely dissolved. Gradually whisk the hot caramel mixture into the egg mixture. Return to the saucepan and heat over medium heat until the mixture comes to a full boil, whisking constantly. Strain through a coarse-mesh sieve placed over a bowl. Stir in the vanilla. Press a piece of plastic wrap directly onto the surface of the pudding, and pierce the plastic a few times with a knife tip to allow the steam to escape. Let cool to lukewarm, then refrigerate until cold, about 2 hours.

Layer the chilled pudding and whipped cream evenly in 4–6 parfait glasses or footed bowls. Serve at once, or chill for up to 8 hours before serving.

PUT A SPIN ON IT For a top-notch banana pudding, in individual bowls, layer the butterscotch pudding with sliced bananas, vanilla wafers, and whipped cream. Chill for a couple of hours to soften the cookies.

One of life's great pleasures is curling up with a favorite book and a cup of hot cocoa topped with marshmallows. Homemade marshmallows, which are surprisingly easy to make, only make this treat even better. So does adding coffee to the cocoa, which gives it a welcome hint of mocha flavor.

COCOA AND MARSHMALLOWS

MARSHMALLOWS

Canola oil for the pan

Confectioners' sugar for dusting

Unflavored gelatin, 2 envelopes (¼ ounce each)

Granulated sugar, 1 cup

Light corn syrup, ⅔ cup

Fine sea salt, ⅛ teaspoon

Vanilla bean, 1

HOT COCOA

Unsweetened natural or Dutch-process cocoa powder, ⅓ cup

Granulated sugar, ½ cup

Fine sea salt

Brewed hot coffee or boiling water, ⅓ cup

Whole milk, 4 cups

MAKES 4 SERVINGS
HOT COCOA AND
24 MARSHMALLOWS

To make the marshmallows, lightly oil an 8-inch square baking pan. Press a 16-inch length of aluminum foil into the bottom and up the sides of the pan, folding the foil to fit and allowing the excess to hang over the sides. Lightly oil the foil and generously dust the bottom and the sides of the pan with confectioners' sugar. Pour ⅓ cup water in the bowl of a stand mixer. Sprinkle the gelatin over the water. Fit the mixer with the paddle attachment. In a small saucepan, combine the granulated sugar, corn syrup, and ⅓ cup water. Attach a candy thermometer to the side of the pan and place over high heat. Bring to a boil, stirring to dissolve the sugar. Stop stirring and cook, brushing down any crystals that form on the sides of the pan with a pastry brush dipped in cold water and occasionally swirling the saucepan by its handle, until the syrup registers 240°F on the thermometer. With the mixer on low speed, gradually pour the hot syrup into the gelatin mixture. Add the salt, increase the speed to medium-high, and beat until the mixture is white, fluffy, and cooled to lukewarm, about 10 minutes. Using a paring knife, slit the vanilla bean in half lengthwise. Using the knife tip, scrape out the seeds into the mixer bowl and beat briefly to combine. Set aside the vanilla bean pod. Using a wet rubber spatula, immediately spread the mixture in the prepared pan. Let stand at room temperature until completely set, at least 4 hours.

Generously dust a work surface with confectioners' sugar. Gently invert the pan onto the work surface to unmold the marshmallow sheet, carefully lift off the pan, and peel off the foil. Using an oiled knife or pizza wheel, cut into 24 marshmallows.

To make the hot cocoa, in a saucepan, whisk together the cocoa, sugar, and a pinch of salt. Gradually whisk in the coffee. Add the reserved vanilla bean pod. Place over medium heat and bring to a boil, whisking frequently. Reduce the heat to medium-low and simmer for 2 minutes. Whisk in the milk and increase the heat to medium-high. Cook, whisking frequently, until very hot but not boiling. Discard the vanilla bean pod. Divide the hot cocoa among 4 warmed mugs and top each with 2 marshmallows. (Store the remaining marshmallows, dusted with confectioners' sugar, in an airtight container at room temperature for up to 1 week.) Serve at once.

Cheesecake isn't just a dessert—it is an event. This one is incredibly thick and rich, and also a little bit firm and dense, just as a proper New York–style cheesecake should be. It is at home on both an elegant holiday table and a casual weeknight supper menu. Take care not to overbake it, or it will crack as it cools.

CHERRY CHEESECAKE

Graham cracker crumbs,
1 cup

Slivered blanched
almonds, ½ cup

Sugar, 1½ cups
plus 3 tablespoons

Unsalted butter,
4 tablespoons, melted

Cream cheese,
2 pounds, at room
temperature

All-purpose flour,
2 tablespoons

Kosher salt

Sour cream, ½ cup

Pure vanilla extract,
1 tablespoon

Large eggs, 3,
at room temperature

Cherries, 1 pound,
pitted and halved

Cherry juice, ½ cup

Cornstarch, 1 tablespoon

MAKES 12 SERVINGS

To make the crust, preheat the oven to 350°F. Butter a 9-inch round springform pan. In a food processor, combine the cracker crumbs, almonds, and the 3 tablespoons sugar and process until finely ground. Drizzle in the butter and pulse until well blended and evenly moistened. Transfer to the prepared pan and press evenly into the bottom and about 1½ inches up the sides. Bake until golden and set, about 7 minutes. Let cool completely on a rack. Reduce the oven temperature to 300°F.

To make the filling, in a stand mixer fitted with the paddle attachment, combine the cream cheese, flour, and ¼ teaspoon salt. Beat on medium-high speed until smooth, stopping as needed to scrape down the bowl. Add 1¼ cups of the sugar, the sour cream, and the vanilla and beat until blended, again stopping to scrape down the bowl as needed. Add the eggs, one at a time, beating after each addition. Pour the filling into the cooled crust. Bake the cheesecake until the filling is set but the center still jiggles slightly when the pan is gently shaken, about 1 hour. (The filling will firm as it cools.) Transfer to a wire rack. Carefully run a sharp knife around the inside of the pan to loosen the cheesecake. Let cool to room temperature. Cover and refrigerate until cold, at least 3 hours.

Meanwhile, make the cherry topping. In a saucepan, combine the cherries, cherry juice, the remaining ¼ cup sugar, and a pinch of salt and cook over medium-high heat, stirring, until the cherries soften, 2–3 minutes. In a bowl, stir together the cornstarch and 1 tablespoon water, then add to the cherry mixture. Cook just until the liquid comes to a boil and thickens, about 3 minutes. Transfer to a bowl to cool.

To serve, unclasp and remove the pan sides. Slide the cheesecake onto a serving platter. Cut into wedges and serve with the cherry topping on each slice.

PUT A SPIN ON IT For a lemony cheesecake, add 2 teaspoons grated lemon zest to the filling with the vanilla. Instead of the cherry topping, serve the cheesecake with sliced, sugared strawberries.

If you love billowy meringue, this is the pie for you. It is piled extra high above a perfectly tart-sweet, silky smooth lemon filling. Fragrant Meyer lemons are becoming more widely available, so use them if they are around, although no one will turn down a slice of this pie if you use regular lemons.

MILE-HIGH LEMON MERINGUE PIE

Single-crust flaky pastry dough (page 248)

Large eggs, 8

Sugar, 2 cups plus 2 tablespoons

Cornstarch, ¼ cup

Fresh Meyer lemon juice, 1 cup

Fine sea salt, ¼ teaspoon

Unsalted butter, 4 tablespoons, cut into tablespoons

Finely grated Meyer lemon zest, from 3 lemons

MAKES 8 SERVINGS

Place the unwrapped dough on a floured work surface and dust with flour. (If the dough is chilled hard, let it stand for a few minutes to soften.) Roll out the dough into a round about 12 inches in diameter and ⅛ inch thick. Transfer to a 9-inch pie dish, fitting the dough into the bottom and sides. Trim the dough, leaving a ¾-inch overhang. Fold the overhang under, then flute the edge. Using a fork, pierce the dough all over, then line with aluminum foil and freeze for 30 minutes. Meanwhile, position a rack in the lower third of the oven and preheat to 375°F. Place the dough-lined dish on a baking sheet and fill the foil with pie weights. Bake until the dough looks dry and is barely golden, 12–15 minutes. Remove the foil and weights. Continue baking until the crust is golden brown, 12–15 minutes more. Transfer to a rack and cool while you make the filling. Raise the oven temperature to 400°F.

In a bowl, beat 3 of the eggs until blended. Separate the remaining 5 eggs, adding the yolks to the beaten whole eggs and putting the whites in a separate large bowl. Cover the whites and set aside at room temperature. Beat the yolks into the beaten eggs. In another bowl, whisk together 1½ cups of the sugar and the cornstarch, then whisk in the beaten eggs, the lemon juice, and salt. Transfer to a heavy, nonreactive saucepan, place over medium heat, and heat until the mixture comes to a full boil, whisking almost constantly. Reduce the heat to low and let bubble for 30 seconds. Be careful not to undercook or overcook the filling or it will separate as it cools. Remove from the heat and whisk in the butter. Strain through a coarse-mesh sieve into a bowl to remove any bits of cooked egg white. Stir in the lemon zest, then pour into the baked crust (the crust can be warm or cool).

Using a handheld mixer on high speed, beat the reserved egg whites until soft peaks form. One tablespoon at a time, beat in the remaining ½ cup plus 2 tablespoons sugar, beating until the egg whites become a meringue with stiff, shiny peaks. Using a spatula, spread the meringue evenly over the hot filling, making sure the meringue touches the crust on all sides (to prevent the meringue from shrinking). Swirl the meringue with the spatula to form peaks. Bake until the meringue is browned, about 5 minutes. Transfer to a rack and cool completely before serving, at least 3 hours.

Growing up, we had a much-loved lemon tree in our backyard, which made lemon meringue pie a frequent sight at our table.

This wonderful pie, my maternal grandmother's favorite, is a family classic. I remember all of us sitting around her kitchen table, each with our own big wedge of pie. Everyone had a different approach to eating the treat. I consumed it in stages, working my way through the billowy topping, then the tart yellow filling, and, finally the crisp crust. Grandma slowly nibbled her pie between sips of coffee, as if to prolong the enjoyment, and combined all three elements, meringue, filling, and crust, in each bite. The recipe remained the same for decades, until a Meyer lemon tree joined the Eureka tree in my parents' garden. Now, with the Meyer's perfumed flavor, an already perfect recipe is even better.

Even though strawberries are available year-round in supermarkets, you should wait to make this recipe until your local crop comes into season in the spring. Your patience will be rewarded with juicy berries that sing with flavor and take this beloved classic over the top. And don't be shy with the whipped cream.

STRAWBERRY SHORTCAKES

Strawberries, 1½ pounds, hulled and sliced

Sugar, 6 tablespoons

All-purpose flour, 2 cups

Baking powder, 1 tablespoon

Fine sea salt, ¼ teaspoon

Unsalted butter, 6 tablespoons

Heavy cream, 1 cup

Whipped cream (page 248)

MAKES 6 SERVINGS

In a bowl, toss the strawberries with 3 tablespoons of the sugar. Cover and refrigerate until the berries release their juices, at least 2 hours or up to 6 hours.

Preheat the oven to 400°F. Have ready an ungreased rimmed baking sheet.

In a bowl, sift together the flour, the remaining 3 tablespoons sugar, the baking powder, and the salt. Cut the butter into tablespoons and scatter over the flour mixture. Using a pastry blender or 2 knives, cut the butter into the flour mixture just until the mixture forms coarse crumbs the size of peas. Add the cream and stir just until the dough comes together.

Turn out the dough onto a lightly floured work surface and knead gently just until smooth. Using a light touch, pat out the dough into a round about ½ inch thick. Using a 3-inch round biscuit or cookie cutter, cut out as many dough rounds as possible and place them 1 inch apart on the baking sheet. Gather up the scraps, pat them out again, and cut out more dough rounds to make a total of 6 shortcakes. Add them to the baking sheet.

Bake the shortcakes until golden brown, 15–18 minutes. Let cool on the baking sheet on a wire rack until warm.

To serve, split each shortcake in half horizontally and place a shortcake bottom, cut side up, on a dessert plate. Top each shortcake bottom with a heaping spoonful of strawberries with their juices and a dollop of whipped cream. Place the shortcake top over the whipped cream and serve at once.

PUT A SPIN ON IT Blackberries, blueberries, raspberries, nectarines, and peaches (or a combination) all go great with shortcake. For a grown-up variation, substitute ¼ cup orange-flavored liqueur, such as Grand Marnier, for the sugar, then add a little sugar to taste, if you wish.

BASIC RECIPES

CHICKEN STOCK

Whole chicken with giblets, 1 (about 4 pounds)

Yellow onion, 1, coarsely chopped

Carrot, 1 large, coarsely chopped

Celery, 1 large stalk, coarsely chopped

Fresh flat-leaf parsley, 4 sprigs

Fresh thyme, 4 sprigs, or ½ teaspoon dried

Black peppercorns, ¼ teaspoon

Bay leaf, 1

MAKES ABOUT 2 QUARTS

Pull the yellow fat from the cavity of the chicken, chop it, and set aside. Using a large, sharp knife, cut the chicken into 2 wings, 2 breast halves, 2 drumsticks, 2 thighs, and the back. Reserve the heart, gizzard, kidneys, and liver for another use.

In a stockpot, heat the chopped fat over medium-low heat until it melts. Add the onion, carrot, and celery and raise the heat to medium. Cover and cook, stirring occasionally, until the vegetables soften, about 5 minutes.

Uncover and add the cut-up chicken, the giblets, and cold water to cover by 1 inch (about 3 quarts). Raise the heat to high and bring to a boil, skimming off any foam that rises to the surface. Add the parsley, thyme, peppercorns, and bay leaf, reduce the heat to low, and simmer gently, uncovered, until the chicken breasts show no sign of pink when pierced with a knife in the thickest part, about 45 minutes.

Remove the breasts from the pot, leaving the rest of the parts simmering in the stock. Remove the skin and bones from the breasts and return them to the pot. Set the breast meat aside. Continue simmering the stock until full-flavored, about 30 minutes more.

Remove the stock from the heat and strain through a colander set over a large heatproof bowl. Remove the thighs and drumsticks from the colander. Discard their skin and bones along with the solids in the colander. Add the meat from the drumsticks and thighs to the reserved breast meat. Let cool, cover, and refrigerate for use in soup or another recipe.

Let the stock stand for 5 minutes, then skim off the fat from the surface. Use at once, or let cool, cover, and refrigerate for up to 3 days or freeze for up to 3 months.

BEEF STOCK

Beef marrow bones, 2½ pounds

Meaty beef bones, such as shank, neck, or ribs, 1½ pounds

Canola oil, 1 tablespoon

Yellow onion, 1, coarsely chopped

Carrot, 1, coarsely chopped

Celery, 1 stalk with leaves, chopped

Fresh flat-leaf parsley, 8 sprigs

Fresh thyme, 6 sprigs, or ½ teaspoon dried

Black peppercorns, ¼ teaspoon

Bay leaves, 2

MAKES ABOUT 2 QUARTS

Position a rack in the upper third of the oven and preheat to 425°F. Spread all of the beef bones in a large roasting pan. Roast until the bones are nicely browned, about 40 minutes.

Just before the bones are ready, in a stockpot, heat the oil over medium-high heat. Add the onion, carrot, and celery and cook, stirring occasionally, until lightly browned, about 5 minutes. Transfer the browned bones to the stockpot. Pour out and discard the fat in the roasting pan. Place the roasting pan over high heat. Add 2 cups cold water and bring to a boil, stirring with a wooden spoon to loosen any browned bits on the pan bottom. Pour the contents of the pan into the pot. Add cold water to cover the bones by 1 inch. Bring to a boil over high heat, skimming off any foam that rises to the surface. Add the parsley, thyme, peppercorns, and bay leaves. Reduce the heat to low and simmer, uncovered, until the stock is full-flavored, at least 3 hours or up to 5 hours.

Remove and discard the bones. Strain the stock through a colander into a large bowl. Discard the solids in the colander. Let the stock stand for 5 minutes, then skim off the fat from the surface. Use immediately, or let cool, cover, and refrigerate for up to 3 days or freeze for up to 3 months.

BASIL PESTO

Garlic, 1 or 2 cloves

Pine nuts, ¼ cup

Fresh basil leaves, 2 cups packed

Extra-virgin olive oil, ½ cup

Parmesan cheese, ½ cup freshly grated

Kosher salt and freshly ground pepper

MAKES ABOUT 1 CUP

With a food processor running, drop the garlic through the feed tube and process until minced. Turn off the processor, add the pine nuts, and pulse a few times to chop. Add the basil and pulse a few times to chop coarsely. Then, with the processor running, add the oil through the feed tube in a slow, steady steam and process until a smooth, moderately thick paste forms, stopping to scrape down the bowl as needed. Transfer to a bowl and stir in the Parmesan. Season to taste with salt and pepper.

Use the pesto at once, or transfer to a storage container, top with a thin layer of oil, cover tightly, and refrigerate for up to 1 week.

MARINARA SAUCE

Plum tomatoes with purée, preferably San Marzano, 2 cans (28 ounces each)

Olive oil, 3 tablespoons

Yellow onion, 1 large finely diced

Garlic, 2–4 cloves, minced

Hearty red wine, ½ cup

Red pepper flakes, ¼ teaspoon

Bay leaf, 1

Fresh basil, ¼ cup chopped

MAKES ABOUT 6 CUPS

Pour the tomatoes and their purée into a large bowl. Using your hands, crush the tomatoes between your fingers. (Don't squeeze too hard or you'll be squirted with tomato juice.)

In a large, heavy nonreactive saucepan, heat the oil over medium heat. Add the onion and cook, stirring occasionally, until tender, about 5 minutes. Stir in the garlic and cook until fragrant, about 1 minute.

Add the wine and bring to a boil. Add the crushed tomatoes and their purée, red pepper flakes, and bay leaf. Raise the heat to medium-high and bring to a boil, stirring frequently. Reduce the heat to low and simmer, stirring occasionally to prevent scorching and adding water if the sauce thickens too quickly, until the sauce has thickened, about 1½ hours. During the last 15 minutes of simmering, stir in the basil.

Discard the bay leaf. Use the sauce at once, or let cool, cover, and refrigerate for up to 4 days or freeze for up to 3 months.

KETCHUP

Crushed plum tomatoes, 1 can (28 ounces)

Light corn syrup, ¼ cup

Cider vinegar, 3 tablespoons

Yellow onion, 2 tablespoons minced

Red bell pepper, 2 tablespoons minced

Garlic, 1 small clove, minced

Light brown sugar, 1 tablespoon firmly packed

Kosher salt, 1 teaspoon

Freshly ground pepper, ⅛ teaspoon

Ground allspice, pinch

Ground cloves, pinch

Celery seeds, pinch

Yellow mustard seeds, pinch

Bay leaf, ½

MAKES ABOUT 1½ CUPS

At least 1 day before serving, combine all of the ingredients in a heavy saucepan over medium heat. Bring to a boil, stirring frequently. Reduce the heat to medium-low and cook at a brisk simmer, stirring frequently, until the mixture thickens and has reduced by half, about 1 hour.

Rub the ingredients through a medium-mesh sieve into a heatproof bowl, discarding any solids that are left in the sieve. Let cool completely. Transfer to a covered container and refrigerate overnight to allow the flavors to blend before using. Use at once or refrigerate for up to 2 weeks.

MAYONNAISE

Large egg, 1

Fresh lemon juice, 1 tablespoon

Dijon mustard, 1 teaspoon

Fine sea salt, ¼ teaspoon

Freshly ground white pepper, ⅛ teaspoon

Olive oil, ¾ cup

Canola oil, ¾ cup

MAKES ABOUT 1½ CUPS

Place the egg in a bowl, add hot tap water to cover, and let stand for 5 minutes to take the chill off. Crack the egg into a food processor. Add the lemon juice, mustard, salt, and white pepper. Combine the olive and canola oils in a glass measuring cup. With the processor running, add the oils through the feed tube in a slow, steady steam and process until the mayonnaise is thick. Add 1 tablespoon hot water and process briefly; the texture will become noticeably creamier. Taste and adjust the seasoning. Use at once, or cover and refrigerate for up to 5 days.

RÉMOULADE

Mayonnaise (above or purchased), 1 cup

Cornichons, 1 tablespoon minced

Nonpareil capers, 1 tablespoon, rinsed

Fresh flat-leaf parsley, 1 tablespoon minced

Fresh tarragon, 2 teaspoons minced

Spicy brown mustard, preferably Creole, 1 teaspoon

Anchovy paste, ½ teaspoon

Garlic, 1 small clove, minced

MAKES ABOUT 1 CUP

In a bowl, mix together all of the ingredients until well blended. Cover and refrigerate for 1 hour before serving. Use at once or refrigerate for up to 4 days.

POACHED EGGS

Distilled white vinegar, 2 tablespoons

Large eggs

In a wide saucepan, combine 8 cups water and the vinegar and bring to a boil. Fill a bowl halfway with hot tap water and place it near the stove. Reduce the heat to medium-low to keep the water at a simmer.

Crack an egg into a small bowl or ramekin. Slip the egg from the bowl into the simmering water. Using a large metal spoon, quickly spoon the egg white back toward the center of the egg to help the egg set in an oval shape. Simmer gently until the egg white is opaque and the egg is just firm enough to hold its shape, 3–4 minutes.

Using a large slotted spoon, lift the egg out of the simmering water. Trim off any floppy bits of white and carefully transfer the egg to the bowl of hot water. Repeat to poach as many eggs as needed. With practice, you will be able to poach 2 or 3 eggs at the same time, but keep track of the order in which you add the eggs to the pan so you don't overcook any of them. The hot water will keep the eggs at serving temperature for up to 10 minutes.

NOTE The fresher the eggs, the more attractive your poached eggs will be because the whites will form a neater, rounder shape. Check the date on the carton or, better yet, buy your eggs from the farmers' market.

PIZZA DOUGH

Active dry yeast, 1 envelope (2½ teaspoons)

Warm water (105°–115°F), ¼ cup

Extra-virgin olive oil, ¼ cup

Fine sea salt, 1½ teaspoons

Sugar, 1 teaspoon

Bread flour, 3 cups, or as needed

MAKES ENOUGH DOUGH FOR TWO 12-INCH PIZZAS OR 6 CALZONE

At least 10 hours before making pizza or calzone, in a small bowl, sprinkle the yeast over the warm water and let stand until foamy, about 5 minutes. Transfer the yeast mixture to the bowl of a stand mixer fitted with the paddle attachment. Add 1 cup cold water, the ¼ cup oil, the salt, and the sugar.

With the mixer on medium-low speed, add the flour to make a soft dough that does not stick to the sides of the bowl. Stop the mixer and cover the bowl with a kitchen towel, wrapping it around the paddle attachment. Let stand for 10 minutes.

Remove the towel and the paddle attachment and fit the stand mixer with the dough hook attachment. Knead the dough on medium speed, stopping the mixer and pulling the dough off the hook if it climbs up, until the dough is smooth and supple, about 8 minutes. Transfer the dough to a lightly floured work surface and knead by hand for 1 minute. Shape the dough into a taut ball.

Lightly oil a large bowl. Add the dough, turn to coat it with the oil, and arrange smooth side up. Cover the bowl tightly with plastic wrap. Refrigerate until doubled in size, at least 8 or up to 36 hours. Remove the dough from the refrigerator 1–2 hours before rolling it out.

FLAKY PASTRY DOUGH

FOR A SINGLE-CRUST 9- OR 10-INCH
PIE OR QUICHE

All-purpose flour, 1¼ cups

Sugar, 1 tablespoon (optional; see note)

Fine sea salt, ¼ teaspoon

Unsalted butter, 5 tablespoons, chilled

Vegetable shortening, 2 tablespoons, chilled

Ice water, about ¼ cup

FOR A DOUBLE-CRUST 9- OR 10-INCH PIE

All-purpose flour, 2½ cups

Sugar, 2 tablespoons (optional; see note)

Fine sea salt, ½ teaspoon

Unsalted butter, ½ cup plus 2 tablespoons, chilled

Vegetable shortening, 3 tablespoons, chilled

Ice water, about ½ cup

In a large bowl, whisk together the flour, sugar (if using), and salt. Cut the butter and shortening into chunks and scatter over the flour mixture. Using a pastry blender or 2 knives, cut the butter and shortening into the flour mixture just until the mixture forms large, coarse crumbs the size of peas.

Drizzle the ice water over the flour mixture and toss with a fork until the dough forms moist clumps. If the dough seems too crumbly, add a little more ice water.

Form the dough into a disk (some flat flakes of butter should be visible), wrap in plastic wrap, and refrigerate for at least 30 minutes or up to 2 hours. Or, overwrap with aluminum foil and freeze for up to 1 month, then thaw in the refrigerator before using.

NOTE Add the sugar if you are using the pastry dough for a dessert recipe and omit it if you are using it for a savory dish, such as quiche.

SEMISWEET CHOCOLATE CURLS

Semisweet chocolate, about 6 ounces, in a single piece

Heat the chocolate in a microwave on medium-low (30 percent) to soften just slightly, about 15 seconds. Using a vegetable peeler, shave curls from the chocolate and let them fall onto a sheet of parchment paper. Refrigerate the curls to firm them slightly before using, about 10 minutes.

WHIPPED CREAM

Heavy cream, 1 cup

Sugar, 2 tablespoons

Pure vanilla extract, ½ teaspoon

MAKES ABOUT 2 CUPS

In a chilled bowl, combine the cream, sugar, and vanilla. Using a handheld mixer on medium-high speed, beat until soft peaks form. Use at once or cover and refrigerate for up to 2 hours before serving.

INDEX

weldon**owen**

415 Jackson Street, Suite 200, San Francisco, CA 94111

Telephone: 415 291 0100 Fax: 415 291 8841

www.weldonowen.com

A division of

BONNIER

COMFORT FOOD

Conceived and produced by Weldon Owen Inc.

415 Jackson Street, San Francisco, CA 94111

Tel: 415-291-0100 Fax: 415-291-8841

www.weldonowen.com

In Collaboration with Williams-Sonoma, Inc.

3250 Van Ness Avenue, San Francisco, CA 94109

A Weldon Owen Production

Copyright © 2009 Weldon Owen Inc.

and Williams-Sonoma, Inc.

First paperback edition printed in 2012

10 9 8 7 6 5 4 3 2 1

ISBN-13: 978-1-61628-385-8

ISBN-10: 1-61628-385-8

Printed in China by Toppan-Leefung

WELDON OWEN INC.

CEO and President Terry Newell

VP, Sales and New Business Development Amy Kaneko

Director of Finance Mark Perrigo

VP and Publisher Hannah Rahill

Creative Director Emma Boys

Executive Editor Kim Laidlaw

Senior Designer Diana Heom

Production Director Chris Hemesath

Production Manager Michelle Duggan

Photographer Ray Kachatorian

Photographer Assistant Conor Collins

Food Stylist Lillian Kang

Food Stylist Assistant Alexa Hyman

Weldon Owen gratefully acknowledges
Leslie Evans, Carol Hacker, Elizabeth Parson,
Sharon Silva, and Sharron Wood